SCHOOLIN

This is ... ways in which the sweeping
social a ... period have impacted on the
educatic ... ve research to paint a vivid
picture ... ersities were moulded by
external ... moting the modernisation
of socie

The boo

- the n
- the g
- new
- the c
- the b

Explori
argues
explain
social a

Roy Lo
Head o
his wri
years a

SCHOOLING AND SOCIAL CHANGE 1964–1990

Roy Lowe

London and New York

First published 1997
by Routledge
11 New Fetter Lane, London EC4P 4EE

Simultaneously published in the USA and Canada
by Routledge
29 West 35th Street, New York, NY 10001

© 1997 Roy Lowe

Typeset in Garamond by Routledge
Printed and bound in Great Britain by T.J. International, Padstow,
Cornwall

British Library Cataloguing in Publication Data
A catalogue record for this book is available from the British
Library

Library of Congress Cataloguing in Publication Data
Lowe, Roy.
Schooling and social change, 1964–1990 / Roy Lowe.
Includes bibliographical references and index.
1. Education–Social aspects–England. 2. Education–Social aspects–
Wales. 3. Politics and education–England. 4. Politics and
education–Wales. I. Title.
LC191.8.G72E535   1996
306.43'2'094209045–dc21 96-51714   CIP

ISBN 0 415–02397–1 (hbk)
ISBN 0 415–16689–6 (pbk)

This book is dedicated to the memory of
Paul Eades
who taught at Shenley Court Comprehensive School from 1977 to 1996.
He was teacher, counsellor and true friend to my daughters.
Those in positions of influence who bring into question the commitment
and professionalism of teachers should never forget that there are
thousands, in schools and within higher education, who give
unsparingly of their time and their energy to those in their charge.
Among them Paul Eades was one of the very finest. Those of us who had
the privilege of knowing him will not forget.

CONTENTS

ILLUSTRATIONS

FIGURES

TABLES

ACKNOWLEDGEMENTS

I am indebted to many people who have helped to make it possible for me to write this book. Numerous friends and colleagues have offered advice and comment. There is not space to mention them all, but I owe particular thanks to Ian Grosvenor, Clyde Chitty, Andy Miles, Roger Backhouse, Ruth Watts, Gary McCulloch, Sheldon Rothblatt, Rob Phillips, Gareth Elwyn Jones and Peter Cain. They have all listened to my ideas and given practical help in a number of ways. I am indebted, too, to many of my ex-students, both undergraduate and postgraduate, at the University of Birmingham, who listened patiently to what I had to say about the education system and its linkages with wider social change and who, through their comments and argument, helped me formulate my own ideas. Among them were Richard Clark, Beth Michael and Liese Perrin, all ready to take me on in discussion, and, in the process, forcing me to clarify my ideas. Several good friends and fellow professionals sharpened my thinking in ways they were not always aware of. They include Peter Weatherall, Steve Gullick, Gerry Owen, David Hardman and Keith Dennis. If this book has any virtues they are, in part, attributable to all these people.

As ever, my work has only been made possible by the library staff of two universities, both of which I thank. At Birmingham, Heather Metcalfe and the staff of the Education Library were unfailingly kind and helpful, as was Christine Penney. On my arrival at Swansea, the rounding-off of the chore was made much easier by colleagues in the Education Library at Hendrefoelan, in particular Paula Kingston and Madelaine Rogerson. Secretarial help has been unstinting from Helen Joinson, Suzanne Davies and Mair Jenkins. I am most grateful, too, for the opportunity of a term's study leave from the University of Birmingham which enabled me to work towards the completion of the manuscript.

I am grateful also for having been given the chance to present my ideas at several international conferences. In particular I thank Phil McCann and the members of the Canadian History of Education Society, Noeline Kyle and friends in Australia at the ANZHES gathering, Czeslaw Majorek, Richard Aldrich and other key figures in the International Standing Conference for the History of Education, and Donald Withrington at Aberdeen. The cross-referencing which follows from these contacts is an invaluable part of the scholarly process, and I greatly appreciate the opportunities which these people afforded me.

Finally, I thank my wife Kathy. Her teaching career has straddled the period covered by this book. She has at all times been a model professional and an inspiring and encouraging teacher to countless young people in a variety of contexts. Her advice, comment and help has been as sharp, constructive and unstinting as ever. I thank all of these people, but take full responsibility for the views expressed in this book. I have enjoyed writing it and have taken immense pleasure in the friendly exchange of ideas which is always part of the process. If those I have named here and all readers find some merit in it, I will be satisfied.

Roy Lowe
University of Wales, Swansea
October 1996

INTRODUCTION

This book is an attempt to analyse and explain some of the changes which
have taken place in education in England and Wales during what might be
described as the modern period, the years from 1964 until 1990. It is,
therefore, a sequel to my *Education in the post-war years* which took such an
analysis as far as to 1964. It is not, though, a strictly chronological or
comprehensive account of the more significant events of the period. That
task has already been undertaken by authors such as Brian Simon. Rather,
what I have tried to do is to examine the changing social, economic and
intellectual contexts within which educators and educationalists worked. I
have tried to seek out what seemed to me to be the more significant
determinants of the educational provision and to show the ways in which
they impinged on schooling, a term which I use in its widest sense to cover
both state and private schools as well as agencies of higher education. My
attempt is to get at the question of why things turned out as they did, or at
least why they might have been likely to. My approach is to identify a
number of key changes which were taking place in society and to show how
they related to the educational provision. Although these are dealt with
separately, chapter by chapter, which makes it possible to dip into the book
for insights on particular issues, I am also attempting to develop an
argument which runs through the book. This is, in brief, that it is only by
seeing the interrelatedness of these issues that we can begin to understand
the social dynamic which, in a modern society such as that under
consideration, makes the educational system itself central to the processes of
social change and one of the key arbiters of the form they take and of the
impact they have on the people.

Throughout the book, several issues are central, and I have tried to focus
on the cluster of questions which they raise. First, I outline the underlying
and persistent characteristics of our schools, colleges and universities. This
sketch of some of the most significant changes taking place in the education
system is used to illustrate the argument that there is a strange contrast
between the deep-seated changes taking place in wider society and the
relative inflexibility of school systems. This chapter seeks to explore the

1

underlying and persistent characteristics of our education system. To what extent do patterns of restricted access to elite routes through education, received views of what constitutes a good education, and a general lack of responsiveness to seemingly swift socio-economic changes explain the fact that in many respects our education system looked, in 1990, remarkably similar to that which had existed during the immediate post-war era? In brief, how far are our schools and our institutions of higher education inoculated against sweeping social changes by their own historical characteristics? And if they are, then what are the mechanisms by which this process takes place? This is the problem I have tried to tackle at the outset.

Several things follow from this analysis. First, there is a set of unresolved questions around the ways in which the transformation of the economy which took place at this time, linked to Britain's changing position in the world economic order, impinged upon the schools and universities. The second chapter tries to unravel, therefore, the question of whether attempts to reconstruct technological education were merely action-replays of earlier unsuccessful efforts to compensate for some of the worst characteristics of an education system which is caste-ridden and which continues to give pride of place to a liberal education, or whether they are more properly conceived of as responses to the emergence of a new technology which has an increasingly ubiquitous impact upon daily lives. Contained within this puzzle is the old chestnut of whether technological education should be for all, or for a selected few. Should the City Technology Colleges introduced by Margaret Thatcher's Government be seen as an echo of the post-war technical secondary schools and before them the Higher Grade Schools of the closing years of the nineteenth century, all targeted at particular social groups, or were they part of a wider initiative to ensure that the education system as a whole was linked more closely to the emerging high-tech industries? To what extent has the educational response to the economic transformations of the sixties and seventies been part of the cause of our comparative national decline in the economic league tables of the developed world? Or is the apparently increasing dysfunctionality of the education system in economic terms merely evidence for the view that formal education systems are never more than marginal to the processes of economic change? This is the second set of issues tackled.

Linked to this are the debates which raged around the construction of the curriculum more generally, and these are the subject of the third chapter. This account of the slow retreat from progressivism and child-centred education towards approaches which were more heavily didactic and teacher-centred attempts to show the parallels between what was happening in the primary schools, the secondary sector and within higher education. Related to the questions of how the curriculum was best delivered were deeply politicised issues concerning the extent to which there should be a focus on 'the basics' or on a core curriculum. Interlinked with this were contrasting perceptions of the continuing significance of 'high culture' set against growing evidence of the increasing dominance of the popular media and of new aesthetic forms. At the heart of this chapter there is the argument that many of these battles were, in essence, about who should control what went on in schools, and that this question drew its significance from the fact that schooling was patently and intimately linked with the economic transformations taking place and with the wider social changes described elsewhere in the book. It was the fact that educationalists were clearly seen to be fulfilling a variety of social functions which led to issues around the curriculum being so sensitive and so fiercely contested.

No account of the development of education during these years could neglect the impact of changing patterns of suburbanisation. There are a number of questions surrounding the growth of our towns and of transport systems which relate very closely to the development of education. New and changing residential locations resulted in new lifestyles and new preoccupations, and in the reconstruction and reformulation of social class systems. As part of this process we can discern the emergence of new demands of schooling systems and of new struggles for control of the schools. The changing clientele of schools in particular locations led inexorably to changes in the schools themselves. At its lowest level the question raised in this part of the book is that of the extent to which the emergence of a 'Thatcherite' rhetoric around education was an inevitable response to these social changes, which were themselves linked to, and part of, the economic changes underway.

The issue is more complex than this, however, and raises the deeper problem of whether the emergent structure of schooling in Britain was in some ways predetermined by these trends in the provision of housing. Implicit in my approach is the view that some understanding of the impact of suburbanisation is necessary for any proper explanation of the changing bases of social class, and that the changed demands this made of the education system are all part of our understanding of the dynamics of educational change. Within these social tensions gender remained an important element. Both the construction of gendered identities and the ascription of gendered roles were part of the functions of the education system, much as many working in the schools and colleges may have resisted such a notion. The question of how it was possible for British society to 'modernise' in any meaningful sense without the disadvantages under which the majority of women suffered being swept away remains an enduring puzzle. One of the keys to understanding it is to engage with the extent to which the education which both boys and girls received contributed to these processes of self-identification and to the persistence of 'gendered' views of society into the final years of the twentieth century. So, the fifth chapter attempts to offer an explanation of the seeming irony of an education system

3

which appears to have reinforced rather than alleviated gender distinctions and to have compounded this by deepening the rifts between women from differing social classes during this era of significant social change. I argue that one key to understanding this apparent oddity lies in the extent to which the economic changes underway depended, in part at least, on the ascription of differing gender roles and on the continuing subordination of women, both in terms of pay and conditions of employment. It fell to the education system to lubricate this process, and I have attempted to show something of the detail of this development.

The other increasingly evident seismic rift in modern British society was ethnicity. The structure of the job market, as well as patterns of suburbanisation, worked to marginalise the growing number of ethnic minority citizens during the years between 1964 and 1990. The part which the schools played in this process is considered in Chapter Six. Eugenic ideas had been used earlier in the twentieth century to legitimate social class distinctions and, in their extreme form, to support suggestions that sterilisation policies might be used to deal with the problem of what was then called 'degeneracy'. I argue here that it was the reapplication of these eugenic ideas to 'race', and their survival after the Second World War and the Holocaust, which go a long way to explain the ways in which the education system came, in practice, to bolster the position of so-called 'indigenous' white citizens. As I try to show, education was one of the agencies through which ethnicity came increasingly to be seen, during the period under review, as one of the tokens of social class.

One further important development which impinged upon schooling is identified, and this is the phenomenon of bureaucratisation. Although social theorists have built a whole research industry around the bureaucratisation of society and have argued that its effects are pervasive, being felt in almost every area of social activity, there has, as yet, been little attempt to relate it to the working of schools and colleges. In Chapter Seven I seek to apply theories of bureaucratisation to the day-to-day working of the education system and argue that the standardisation of practice and the emergence of new power hierarchies worked, if anything, to confirm and reinforce the essentially conservative social functions of that system.

My account of the emergence of a new politics of education is located, consciously, at the conclusion of this catalogue of social change. I believe that the application of 'New Right' theory to education followed almost inevitably from the wider social and economic processes which I deal with in this book. There has been much writing on the emergence of a new educational rhetoric during this period, and there are already numerous analyses of both its content and its educational impact. My emphasis is on the origins of New Rightism and on the question of whether it merely represents old Conservatism in a new form or whether there really has been an infusion of new elements into otherwise familiar popular debates. It is impossible to develop this theme without saying something about the development of the mass media in their modern form, and both this part of the book and that which precedes it on bureaucratisation depend in part on an acceptance of the historical significance of new rhetorical and communicative styles. Between 1964 and 1990, education developed its own jargon at just the same moment that it became susceptible to new forms of political jargon. The two phenomena are not entirely unrelated.

So, what I am trying to do in this book is to locate the educational developments of the period firmly within their changing socio-economic context. It has become something of a truism among historians of education that any account of schooling which neglects the society within which schools developed is badly flawed. It is worth reminding ourselves that it was as long ago as 1966, writing in Tibble's *The study of education*, that Brian Simon pointed out that

> education is a social function, and one of primary importance in every society. It should be one of the main tasks of historical study to trace the development of education in this sense, to try to assess the function it has fulfilled at different stages of social development.

In a telling passage, which rings as true for us today as when Simon wrote it, he warned against those who wrote about education with 'little explicit awareness of the social presuppositions of their thought'. I cannot resist the aside that many of those who profess strong views on educational practice and educational policy at the present time, including some charged with giving advice to their fellow professionals, fall into precisely that trap. Simon refers back to Sir Fred Clarke, whose influential book on *Education and social change*, published in 1940, was written with an insistence on

> a new function for the educational historian, that of unravelling the social and historical influences which have played so potent a part in shaping both the schools and what is taught inside them.

It is in this spirit, and with this emphasis, that the present book is written. Arguably, there has never been a greater need than at the present time for analyses which pause to reflect on the deeper significance of the sweeping changes which have taken place within our educational system during this most recent period. Certainly, many of the changes which have taken place have been justified at the time either as putting right the wrongs and shortcomings of the past, or, alternatively, as restoring values and structures which existed at one time and have since fallen into neglect. If this book helps to unravel some of the deeper realities of those recent changes, it will have done its job.

1

THE POWER OF THE PAST

Looking back from the vantage point of the mid-1990s, one of the most striking things about the English education system is how little it has changed since 1964. I have argued in an earlier book, *Education in the Post-War Years*, that the form taken by English schooling into the 1960s was already largely determined by the historical residue, by a preference for established practice and procedures which tended to inoculate education and educators against radical change. If ever one was to look for a significant restructuring of English education it would surely be during this most recent thirty years, a period which has seen both economic and social transformations. Yet it is impossible to avoid the judgement that much of the landscape of English education today would be immediately recognisable to a visitor whose most recent acquaintance with it was in 1964, and some of its key features are almost unchanged.

Broadly, what I mean by this is, first, that schooling remains structured and differentiated in modern England. Not only does the clear distinction between private and public sectors remain, with roughly similar proportions of students passing through the two sectors, but, within each, a clearly recognised hierarchy of schools and institutions persists, and seems likely to continue to do so. Further, although there have been some modifications in the 'pecking order' of schools and universities, those which were widely esteemed during the 1960s remain by and large the most sought after.

Second, educational practice remains largely unchanged, despite the expenditure of enormous energy and finance in efforts to reform curricula and to disseminate ideas on new approaches to teaching. In their internal organisation and their day-to-day working practices schools are as remarkable for what has survived during the last thirty years as for what has changed. Third, within the educational profession, the same established career hierarchies persist, modified slightly perhaps in response to increases in scale, but broadly similar in their impact, and having the effect of discriminating against women, against ethnic minorities and between social classes, albeit often unconsciously so. And this last point relates to, and is

6

part of, a broader phenomenon, which is the survival of a particular set of values and attitudes within our educational system.

In the next few pages I will look briefly at each of the sectors of our education system to try to substantiate these rather wide claims. Perhaps the best starting point is the schools themselves. A quick glance at the numbers of schools of different types at the beginning and end of the period (Tables 1.1 and 1.2)[1] shows in broad terms what changes took place. The figures for 1964 cover England and Wales: those for 1988 England only. Unfortunately, a direct comparison is made very difficult, if not impossible, by changes in the way in which the Ministry, and later the Department of Education and Science (DES), collected and codified their statistics. However, there is sufficient comparability between these two sets of figures to allow us to conclude immediately that the broad structure of the system persisted. During the late eighties, schools were still organised as primary or secondary, and the co-existence of state and private sectors continued.

In brief, primary schools remained relatively small (the average number of pupils in each school was fairly stable, falling from 189 to 187 during this twenty-year period), but secondary schools grew spectacularly, with the average number of pupils rising from 482 to 739. The reasons for this growing contrast between the two sectors are not far to find. While primary schools continued to perform a 'community' function (a role which was seen as increasingly important given the growth in scale of urban life and changes which were taking place in the structure of the family), the secondary schools

Table 1.1. Schools in 1964 (England and Wales)

Under LEA control	Boys	Girls	Mixed
Primary			
Infants	2	3	5,445
Junior/infant	8	77	12,153
Junior	307	256	4,279
All age	46	46	319
Secondary			
Modern	745	770	2,391
Grammar	418	425	455
Technical	77	33	76
Bilateral	9	13	47
Comprehensive	34	30	131
Not under LEA control			
Direct grant grammar	82	95	2
Independent			
(recognised as efficient)			
Primary	468	59	247
Secondary	138	143	18

Table 1.2. Schools in 1988 (England only)

	Boys	Girls	Mixed
Under LEA control			
Primary			
Infants	0	0	2,839
Junior/infant	1	1	10,570
Junior	10	6	2,628
Middle			
Middle schools	2	2	1,186
Secondary			
Modern	24	28	170
Grammar	56	61	36
Technical	2	1	1
Comprehensive	169	185	2,799
Sixth-form college	0	0	104
Independent			2,273

were closer to the eye of the political storm, more at the mercy of reorganisation schemes, and increasingly perceived as successful in so far as they were large enough to generate sixth forms of a reasonable size and to offer a broad range of curricular choices. It is worth remarking, too, that the large urban comprehensive schools which attracted so much comment during the seventies and eighties were in reality untypical: the vast majority of secondary school children, including those in the comprehensive sector, were in schools of less than 1,000 pupils in size. There were significantly more private schools than in 1964, but they still catered for less than 8 per cent of the population.

If we look more closely at the categories of school, a number of shifts in emphasis quickly become apparent. Within the primary sector, many separate infant schools had disappeared. By 1988 the bulk of the primary provision was through mixed junior/infant schools, a type of school which was already well established as the main provider of primary schooling by the mid-sixties, but which had become the dominant type twenty years later. All-age schools, a relic of the pre-war system which was done away with in the 1944 Education Act, disappeared completely during the 1960s, their survival until then telling us a great deal about the parsimony with which some local authorities had implemented the 1944 legislation. By 1988 there were over a thousand middle schools at work. These by-products of local authority reorganisation schemes began to appear in the late sixties: most of them have survived. Turning to those secondary schools provided by the state, we see that technical and bilateral schools had virtually disappeared during the period under review; the number of grammar schools shrank dramatically, and the comprehensive school came to dominate this sector.

Sixth-form colleges were a new feature in the educational landscape, with over a hundred in existence by 1988. The ending of direct grant status in 1976 forced the majority of the direct grant schools into the private sector, and this goes some way to explain the increase in the number of independent schools recognised by the DES. The other key factor which accounts for the swift growth of the private sector is the founding of a large number of small preparatory and junior schools whose existence was necessarily more tenuous than that of older and larger foundations, and it is the relatively small size of these institutions which explains the apparent contradiction of a significantly greater number of schools catering for a similar proportion of the population.

It must not be assumed, though, that this catalogue of change suggests a transformation of our educational system. For many schools, what occurred during this period was a change of designation and a slight but significant change of role. Most of the grammar, technical and bilateral schools which disappeared during this period reappeared as comprehensive schools in the 1988 statistics. Similarly, the 10,570 junior/infant schools at work in 1988 included many which had been listed under a different heading in 1964. I will have more to say later in this book about what this might have meant in terms of the changing social functions of these schools.

Perhaps most significantly, what does emerge clearly from these statistics is that the period saw a decisive shift in favour of mixed education. Within the state sector single-sex primary schools virtually disappeared, while at secondary level there was a similar trend. But here it was a trend with its own peculiar characteristic. Briefly, the more prestigious the school, the greater the chances of its remaining single-sex. By 1988 there were three times as many single-sex grammar schools as there were mixed. Put another way, this means that the single-sex grammar schools can be shown in retrospect to have been those which were most likely to survive into the 1980s. Meanwhile the development of other kinds of secondary schooling, particularly of comprehensives, meant an increasing reliance on mixed education. Within the private sector, which was historically far more committed to the provision of single-sex education, it is impossible to be precise about the impact of this trend into the 1980s, although it was clearly well established. Many girls' private schools remained single-sex. Comparatively few boys' schools did: one investigation has shown that, by 1981, of 211 Headmasters' Conference schools, 46 were co-educational in the full sense of the term and a further 72 were admitting girls at sixth-form level.[2] This was a stratagem which enabled these schools to gain the benefit of fees from female pupils while remaining predominantly 'male' in ethos and exclusively so in the intake of younger pupils. It is this variegated nature of the approach to co-education in the private sector which makes it so difficult to generalise about, and which probably explains the fact that the annual returns of the DES ceased to classify these schools by sex during this period.

9

Even here, though, the trend was inexorable, and inclined towards mixed schooling.

To a considerable extent, these trends were historically mediated. Carol Dyhouse,[3] June Purvis[4] and others have shown how, during the nineteenth century, an education system developed which educated boys and girls for separate spheres – boys for public life and employment, girls for the home and motherhood. It is clear, too, that for differing social classes this meant different things, with single-sex schooling being far more the preserve of the middle and upper classes, and elementary schools never departing from the model established in small rural communities where there were simply not the resources to educate boys and girls separately. As elementary schools became larger during the nineteenth century and came to cater for the new townships, this model was modified through the introduction of boys' and girls' departments in the larger schools, but it never disappeared completely. During the early twentieth century, an influential 'progressive' lobby for mixed schooling developed: Alice Woods campaigned tirelessly for mixed education between 1903 and 1931,[5] reflecting a middle-class concern for greater individual liberty and calling for experiments in co-education which could test 'what differences are inherent and unalterable, and what merely the results of a different upbringing'[6]. A small number of progressive private schools was appearing which tried to do just this. Abbotsholme was founded as early as 1889, and Bedales only four years later. Within the boys' schools there was a growing number of educators, such as the Reverend Cecil Grant, who favoured co-education because it was likely to lessen the risk of homosexuality in the public schools.[7] Equally pervasive was the argument that girls were likely to have a civilising effect on boys. Against this growing lobby for mixed education were ranged those heads of girls' secondary schools who saw the dangers of girls becoming in one way or another subordinated to boys in mixed schools. When the 1904 Regulations for secondary schools insisted on a common curriculum for boys and girls, the Headmistress of Winchester High School for Girls was one among several who wrote to the Board of Education to remind them of

> the strong desire to avoid over-pressure; and, with this end in view the number of hours instruction has been fixed at 16 ... Your Regulation makes it necessary ... Either to change entirely the character of the school ... or else to forgo entirely a grant from the Board.[8]

Doubts about co-education were shared by Maude Royden, who argued in 1919 that girls were likely to leave 'initiative and leadership to boys' if they were educated together.[9] Thus, most of the attitudes and arguments which have been rehearsed around the topic of mixed education since 1964 were already established at the start of the century.

It is hardly surprising, then, that the Newsom Report, *Half our future* (a title which referred, not to girls, but to pupils of average and below average ability of either sex), warned in 1963 that:

> In addition to their needs as individuals, our girls should be educated in terms of their main social function – which is to make for themselves, their children and their husbands a secure and suitable home and to be mothers.[10]

During the following few years the reconstruction of mixed and single-sex education took place in the absence of any large-scale public discussion and in ways which were largely predetermined by these historical precedents. As the requirement that the state should provide universal secondary schooling was increasingly implemented through comprehensive reorganisation, the tradition that state schools were predominantly mixed was unthinkingly taken up and never seriously challenged. At the same time the partial moves towards mixed education in the private sector were influenced by so called 'progressive' ideas which had been in circulation for much of the twentieth century. It is hardly surprising that all this resulted in the same arguments being reworked in the context of the late twentieth-century feminist movement. It seems likely, too, that the accident of the way in which co-education was introduced in different sectors of education between 1964 and 1988 may have led, inadvertently, to a confirmation through schooling of social class contrasts between girls. Those girls who failed the eleven-plus during the 1960s and 1970s and entered secondary moderns, or who entered the new mixed comprehensive schools, may have undergone a gendered educational experience which unconsciously echoed the preparation for housewifery and motherhood which girls received in the late nineteenth-century elementary school, except that by the 1960s it was the minor professional jobs leading to marriage into which girls were propelled by peer-group pressure and often unspoken teacher expectations. A Department of Education and Science survey in 1975 showed clearly that in the new mixed secondary schools the contrasts and stereotyping between boys and girls in curriculum choice were becoming greater,[11] and this is shown clearly in the examination performances reported later in this chapter. By contrast, those girls who passed the eleven-plus and aspired to single-sex grammar schools entered a world which shared many of the values of the girls' public schools. But it remained, of course, the larger independent schools which were most successful in winning high academic honours for their pupils, as was shown by Kathleen Ollerenshaw in 1967.[12] One of Roedean school's professed objectives in the late sixties was the production of 'good professional women'.[13] For the successful girls from these schools, the universities and established professions such as teaching, medicine and the law beckoned, but on terms which led to differentiated career routes for males and females. For the rest, a particular kind of clerical work was available. As June Purvis has summarised it:

11

The girls who have attended an elite independent school might work behind the counter at Harrods, but not at Woolworths.[14]

Another characteristic which differentiates developments in the primary sector from those taking place at secondary level during these twenty years is the size of schools. The next set of statistics show that, while primary schools remained roughly the same size during the period under review, secondary schools became significantly larger (see Table 1.3).

Table 1.3. The size of schools (numbers of pupils)

	Primary		*Secondary*		*Nursery*		*Independent*	
Year	*Schools*	*Pupils*	*Schools*	*Pupils*	*Schools*	*Pupils*	*Schools*	*Pupils*
1964	20,827	3,937,000	5,496	2,650,311	439	22,403	3,825	568,931
1988	19,319	3,618,000	4,153	3,070,172	560	11,407FT	2,273	522,949
						38,596PT		

In respect of staffing ratios, too, there were some enduring contrasts, as is shown in Table 1.4. The secondary sector continued to be far better staffed than the primary, and there was little erosion of the striking differences between staffing ratios in the state schools and private schools, the latter by and large being far more lavishly resourced. Undoubtedly, in those localities

Table 1.4. School staff–pupil ratios

1964	
Maintained sector	*Pupils:Teacher*
Infant	29.6
Junior/infant	27.6
Junior	29.8
All age	26.0
Secondary modern	20.3
Grammar	17.5
Technical	17.4
Bilateral & multilateral	18.8
Comprehensive	18.4
Direct grant grammar	17.1
Independent sector	
Nursery	11.4
Primary	12.4
Secondary	11.3
1988	
Maintained sector	
Nursery	19.4
Primary	22.0
Secondary	15.4
Independent sector	11.3

where secondary education was reorganised on comprehensive lines, the invidious disparities in staffing ratios which had existed at secondary level within the state sector in 1964 largely disappeared. But it should not be forgotten that the transfer of many direct grant grammar schools into the private sector after 1976 meant that many of the more prestigious secondary schools were exempted from this trend.

Much of this was reflected in the performance of pupils, and in this respect, too, it is possible to discern enduring patterns which are measurable in terms of examination results and staying-on levels. The continuities in examination performance at 16 years of age are striking, and are very suggestive of the ways in which the schools themselves perpetuated patterns and attitudes even during a period of extensive reorganisation. Table 1.5 makes a comparison between external examination results in 1964 and 1988. Several characteristics are immediately evident and can be seen to have been relatively constant. Although there was an increase in the numbers succeeding in sixteen-plus examinations, the total achieving 'O' level equivalent grades in 1988 remained a small minority of the age cohort and is

Table 1.5. Examination passes at 16-plus (thousands)

Subject	1964		1988	
	'O' level results England and Wales		'O' level results England only	
	Boys	Girls	Boys	Girls
English language	98.7	96.4	118.1	154.4
English literature	50.0	74.7	–	–
History	47.6	48.1	47.2	51.1
Economics	4.2	1.5	14.2	10.2
Geography	51.8	39.1	62.4	48.4
Latin	17.6	16.3	9.5	9.9
French	45.9	51.4	40.4	65.1
German	8.0	10.2	–	–
Modern languages (other than French)	–	–	16.9	27.8
Mathematics	109.6	49.9	120.4	97.4
General science	9.8	5.6	–	–
Physics	44.8	8.4	73.3	31.2
Chemistry	35.0	10.2	55.3	38.3
Biology	22.2	49.7	43.1	63.0
Art	21.8	35.1	–	–
Practical subjects	21.8	35.1	–	–
Vocational subjects (including Arts and PS above)	–	–	17.1	71.1
Religious knowledge	10.6	26.1	–	–
Religious studies	–	–	15.9	24.8

comparable with the number who succeeded in 1964. The broad balance between subjects was largely the same, too. Latin in 1988 generated less than 20,000 'passes', about half the numbers succeeding twenty years earlier. The number of students presenting in Economics had quadrupled.

Apart from these dramatic changes, both the proportions of students in different subject areas and the total numbers remained surprisingly constant. Perhaps the most striking change is that, although most subjects remained 'gendered' to some degree at the end of the period, attracting predominantly male or female students, there was clear evidence that the subjects traditionally favoured by males (mathematics, physics, chemistry and economics) had at least become accessible to females. Conversely, in biology there had been some levelling of the number of males following the subject. Elsewhere in the curriculum, in modern languages and vocational subjects, for example, the preponderance of females had increased rather than diminished during the twenty years. These figures provide clear evidence of the maintenance of gender distinctions in schools and suggest, too, that there were subtle changes taking place in the subject choices made by students of differing gender during this period. What this comparison overlooks is the large number of students who, by the late 1980s, were leaving school with some kind of nationally recognised and externally examined award. The DES returns show a total of 437,000 attempting GCSE in England during 1988 and a further 107,000 entering for CSE examinations (in 1988 both examinations were available). The method by which these figures were presented makes accurate generalisation about the less successful students (those awarded below Grade C at GCSE) very difficult. But it is clear from the figures that, in total, 377,000 students were awarded passes in one or more subjects at a level equivalent to the old 'O' level pass in 1988.

Two points emerge from Table 1.6, which shows the overall numbers passing at Advanced Level GCE in 1964 and 1988. Setting aside the notoriously contentious and emotive arguments as to whether Advanced Level became harder or easier during this period, and assuming that achievement levels remained comparable, these figures show a significant upturn in the number of students passing at 'A' level, in total 66,000 in 1964 and 99,000 in 1988. But this was only achieved through a levelling-up of the performance of girls. In 1964, 40,000 boys passed one or more 'A' level as against 27,000 girls. By 1988 the number of boys passing was 50,000 but the number of girls had risen to match this figure at 49,000. Thus, on the face of it, there was an equalisation of educational opportunities between the sexes during this period. But a glance below these global figures shows at once the persistence of gender distinctions. In 1988 girls still had a smaller chance than boys of passing four or more 'A' levels (although it has to be said that the gap had lessened since 1964, when boys were more than four times more likely than girls to pass in four or more subjects). In 1988, girls

Table 1.6. Advanced level passes (thousands)

1964										
No. of passes	0		1		2		3		4 OR MORE	
	M	F	M	F	M	F	M	F	M	F
Maintained										
Grammar school	2.37	2.08	3.89	4.15	6.05	6.04	11.24	7.35	3.84	1.06
Technical school	0.43	0.25	0.55	0.28	0.38	0.13	0.42	0.05	0.24	0.02
Comprehensive school	0.32	0.27	0.36	0.24	0.33	0.23	0.48	0.24	0.07	0.03
Direct grant school	0.33	0.32	0.55	0.60	0.76	0.87	2.06	1.44	0.93	0.37
Independent	1.11	0.59	1.33	1.03	2.08	1.03	3.26	1.18	1.10	0.22
Totals	4.56	3.51	6.68	6.30	9.60	8.30	17.46	10.26	6.18	1.70

1988										
No. of passes	0		1		2		3		4 OR MORE	
	M	F	M	F	M	F	M	F	M	F
Maintained										
Sixth-form college	7.72	7.14	0.3	0.47	1.85	2.16	5.39	5.73	3.12	2.91
11–18 comprehensive	–	–	1.76	1.82	5.62	6.89	15.03	14.9	10.7	8.51
Grammar school	2.65	2.92	0.08	0.15	0.58	0.92	3.15	3.54	2.68	1.46
Totals	10.37	10.06	2.14	2.44	8.05	9.97	23.57	24.2	16.5	12.88

were more likely than boys to pass in one or two subjects: the key change was in the numbers passing three 'A' levels, where girls outnumbered boys by 1988, a significant improvement on their chances twenty-four years earlier. What also emerges from these figures is the extent to which the comprehensive sector was responsible for this levelling of chances between the sexes: the fall-off in the number of girls passing in four or more 'A' levels remained a characteristic of the grammar schools until the late 1980s, by when it had been virtually eliminated in the comprehensive sector.

The figures for performance in individual subjects at Advanced Level (Table 1.7) show that the gender bias which was increasingly evident at sixteen-plus was intensified in those who stayed on at school during this twenty-year period. Maths, physics, chemistry, history and French all experienced an absolute decline in the number of boys passing in the subject: in French the decline was particularly sharp, with only a third as many boys passing in 1988 by comparison with 1964. This was compensated for, in all cases, by an increase in the number of girls passing in these subjects. But this was not sufficient for the sciences, in particular, to shake off their traditional preponderance of boys, while the sharp upturn in the number of girls passing

Table 1.7. Advanced level passes by subject (thousands)

Subject	1964		1988	
	M	F	M	F
Maths	30.0	5.0	27.8	13.6
Physics	23.5	3.8	20.5	5.9
Chemistry	16.3	3.9	16.2	5.9
Botany	1.3	1.5	–	–
Biology	4.1	2.9	9.0	12.5
Zoology	2.6	2.6	–	–
Geography	8.0	5.2	12.8	8.5
Economics	6.1	1.0	–	–
Economics, British constitution and economic history	–	–	16.8	10.0
English literature	9.3	13.7	10.8	23.4
History	13.9	8.7	10.7	11.5
French	6.7	8.9	3.7	9.4
German	2.2	2.2	–	–
Other modern languages	–	–	2.2	5.4
Latin	3.0	2.7	–	–
Classics	–	–	2.0	2.7
Art	3.7	4.6	–	–
Music, drama and visual arts	–	–	5.9	9.4
General studies	–	–	16.9	11.3
Vocational subjects	–	–	2.4	4.5

in English and, to a lesser extent, history resulted in those subjects becoming 'gendered' by the late eighties in a way that had certainly not been the case in the mid-sixties. There were undoubtedly a variety of factors at work here, including the changing job market and the response of young people to images of gender which were current in society at large. But one undoubted factor was the reconstruction of sexual distinctions in mixed educational settings, particularly comprehensive schools and sixth-form colleges. We do not as yet have precise figures comparing the patterns of 'A' level entry by gender in grammar and comprehensive schools, but they could well be illuminating.

We have already seen some enduring historical patterns in respect of the staffing ratios of schools, and these were indicative of deeper underlying continuities in the structure of the teaching profession (Table 1.8). Within the primary sector, female teachers continued to outnumber males, with the disparity becoming slightly more marked. In 1964 roughly a quarter of the teaching force was male in the primary sector, by 1988 it was closer to one fifth. At secondary level there was a levelling-up in a sector which had historically been dominated by males. Whereas in 1964 there were roughly two female teachers for every three males teaching in secondary schools, by 1988 the numbers were more nearly equal, with comprehensive schools in

Table 1.8. Full-time teachers in State schools (thousands)

School	1964		1988	
	M	F	M	F
Infant and junior	34.1	103.5	–	–
All age	1.3	2.1	–	–
Primary	–	–	36.5	133.1
Secondary modern	44.0	32.8	4.4	4.1
Grammar school	23.8	15.9	3.4	2.8
Technical school	3.4	1.4	0.08	0.06
Comprehensive	6.2	3.8	111.0	92.7

particular being the agency by which this equalisation was achieved. These figures offer clues to the ways in which teaching as a career reflected wider social patterns of linkage between gender and power in modern British society. Put crudely, what these figures suggest at first glance is that the prestige of institutions was in some ways reflected or reinforced by the extent to which they employed males or females: greater prestige was attached to a career in the secondary sector, and more males were to be found there while the less well-rewarded and well-regarded primary sector was increasingly dominated by women.

This generalisation is confirmed if we go on to look more closely at career hierarchies within teaching as measured by the ratio of head teachers to teaching staff in general (Table 1.9). Within the primary sector there was a

Table 1.9 Career hierarchies in schools

School		1964			1986		
		H/Ts	Others	H/Ts as per cent	H/Ts	Others	H/Ts as per cent
Infant	M	13	51	25.5	67	375	17.8
	F	5437	32039	16.9	3097	24284	12.7
Junior/Infant	M	7319	16134	45.3	7589	19997	37.6
	F	4919	45312	10.9	3563	62386	5.7
Junior	M	3873	17886	21.7	2429	9911	24.5
	F	969	25962	3.7	655	19437	3.4
Secondary Modern	M	3067	44020	7.0	202	4422	4.5
	F	839	32743	2.5	47	4155	1.1
Grammar	M	872	23766	3.6	100	3427	2.9
	F	426	15909	2.7	63	2826	2.2
Technical	M	153	3426	4.5	3	84	3.6
	F	33	1449	2.3	1	65	1.5
Comprehensive	M	163	6421	2.5	3064	110933	2.8
	F	32	3819	0.8	501	92704	0.5

small but significant erosion during this period of the chances of women aspiring to headships, even though a greater percentage of the teachers was female. This was particularly marked in junior schools, where by 1986 almost 25 per cent of the male teachers were in headships while the percentage of women in the top job had slipped from 3.7 per cent to 3.4 per cent. Yet the number of male teachers in these schools had fallen from nearly 18,000 to just below 10,000, while the total number of women had fallen far less dramatically. There were similar, if less marked contrasts in the junior/infant schools and even at infant level. What these figures also show is that, during these years, the key reorganisation in the primary sector was in the development of junior/infant schools, which in 1986 employed in total 21,000 more teachers than in 1964. This figure was matched by far smaller numbers of teachers employed in separate infant schools or in separate junior schools.

Meanwhile, at secondary level, the arrival of mixed schools and the growth in the size of schools did nothing for the career chances of women except to diminish the likelihood of their achieving headships. Within comprehensive schools, particularly, the percentage of men in headships rose, while the percentage of women fell, despite the fact that, as we have seen in Table 1.2, the vast majority of these schools were mixed. By 1986, a man in a comprehensive school was five times as likely as a woman to be in the head's chair. It is difficult to think of a more effective way for society to transmit messages about distinct gender roles to its young people than through this contrast.

It is worth pausing to reflect on the deeper processes at work here. How was it that, in an era when society became increasingly conscious of women's rights, the situation of women could deteriorate within a sector of the economy which might, on the face of it, be thought to be particularly receptive to new ideas? At this remove any answer can only be speculative, but it seems reasonable to pick out several key factors. First, undoubtedly, the historical fact of women being consigned to the role of minor players within teaching (a characteristic which extended back at least as far as to the establishment of universal elementary schooling in the late nineteenth century) meant that expectations of the role of women teachers were already deeply embedded within the teaching profession. Second, as the character of the schools changed during the twenty or so years under review, matching changes that were taking place elsewhere in the economy, it is perhaps unsurprising that new roles in developing power hierarchies and increasingly bureaucratised institutions were seen as distinctly masculine, or that various ancillary and support roles (particularly that of secretaryship) were identified as most suitable for women. A further retarding factor may have been the numbers of women for whom teaching represented a second family income alongside that of a male 'breadwinner'. This factor may have made significant numbers of female teachers more ready to acquiesce in the suppression of their own career ambitions and more prepared to countenance clearly defined career routes for males. It certainly meant, as in other sectors of the economy, that many female teachers left teaching or taught part-time during the years that their own children were young. Whatever the factors at work, it seems ironic that schooling was an arena where the 'gendering' of roles within employment, which has been shown to be a continuing characteristic of twentieth-century Britain,[15] was intensified rather than diminished.

If we turn in conclusion to post-school education, we find a similar resistance to change (Table 1.10). The sector is remarkable as much for what survived as for what was destroyed or changed radically, though it must not be overlooked that the period saw the upgrading of thirty technical colleges to polytechnic status, the designation of ten colleges of advanced technology as technological universities in the aftermath of the 1963 Robbins Report, the setting up of the Open University and the complete restructuring of the colleges of education during the 1970s. As Table 1.10 shows, these changes were bound to have some effect. There was a clearly identifiable shift in emphasis from part-time to full-time courses, and at the end of our period far more students were embarked on degree courses than had been the case in

Table 1.10. Enrolment in further and higher education

1963–4 (thousands, England and Wales) Full-time	M	F	Total
Non-advanced FE	60.4	61.9	121.5
Advanced FE: CAT	9.7	0.9	10.6
Other	21.4	6.6	28.0
Teacher training colleges	16.7	37.5	54.2
Universities	66.3	28.0	94.4
Part-time in FE			
Day	486.9	126.3	613.2
Evening: in major establishments	411.6	367.4	779.0
Evening: in evening institutes	348.5	672.0	1020.5
1987–8 (thousands, England only)			
Full-time	M	F	Total
Non-advanced FE	149.7	188.7	338.4
Advanced FE (including Polytechnics)	91.3	102.5	193.8
Teacher training in other FE establishments	3.3	29.3	32.6
Universities	140.6	95.7	236.3
Part-time in FE			
Day	444.1	382.3	826.4
Evening	272.4	417.5	689.9

1964. Yet there were still in 1988 over one and half million young adults in England alone whose only post-school education was received part-time within the further education sector. They far outnumbered the 800,000 students receiving full-time education. Admittedly, this was in contrast to the situation in 1964, when part-timers had outnumbered full-timers by something like seven to one, but it does show the power of the familiar English practice of marginalising post-school education by offering it part-time.

A closer look at these figures shows, too, that the gender distinctions which we have observed in other sectors of the education system were evident also in higher and further education, and that they persisted. Within the universities male students continued to outnumber female, although the gap had narrowed slightly. Whereas during the mid-sixties females were outnumbered by males by more than two to one, by the late eighties they made up 40 per cent of the student cohort with the total number of female students having more than trebled during the intervening years. The gap was still significant, but diminishing. Meanwhile, in the less prestigious sector of advanced full-time further education (which included the polytechnics), there was a majority of female students by the end of our period, although they had been scarcely represented twenty years earlier. By the late eighties, too, teacher training institutions were almost exclusively female (twenty-nine thousand female students and only three thousand male). This was a sector in which females had always predominated, but in which the old gender distinctions were becoming more marked. In part-time further education, arguably the least prestigious sector of the post-school provision, the steady increase in the numbers of students on day release courses was achieved through the greater participation of females. In contrast, the number of males on evening courses fell markedly, so that by the late eighties this was a sector in which there was a predominance of women. Here, too, the evidence suggests that established historical patterns proved remarkably resistant to social change. Evening classes in the further education sector are a good example of this. In 1964 those males who were involved in evening work were more likely to be found at the major establishments, the colleges of technology and colleges of advanced technology. By contrast, female students were more likely to be found in evening institutes, which generally taught to a lower level and offered more directly vocational qualifications. The continued clustering of females into this part-time sector into the 1980s suggests that successive generations were following historically established routes into employment.

Similarly, the career hierarchies in teaching, which we have commented on earlier in this chapter as being particularly favourable to males, were also being laid down at the start of young teachers' careers. In 1964, in colleges of education, there were 15,524 men and 36,476 women embarked on three-year general courses, a ratio of roughly two women to each man being trained to teach. But there were only 245 women against 702 men enrolled for the new four-year B.Ed degree courses which were being set up in some of these colleges. This is a ratio which was almost exactly the reverse of that for all students in training, yet there were at this time over 10,000 women in colleges of education who had passed at least one Advanced level GCE examination, and only 4,300 similarly-qualified men. If we look for a moment beyond the teacher training colleges at the statistics for all students training to teach in England and Wales, we find that the numbers embarked on graduate (i.e. PGCE) courses were roughly comparable: 2,221 men to 2,020 women. In contrast, there were 43,000 women on non-graduate courses and only 18,000 men! These figures offer a stark testimony to the way in which females who had the qualifications to enter more prestigious courses chose not to do so, but settled for lower qualifications over a shorter period of training: they help explain the contrasts in career outcomes which were clearly evident twenty years later. As had been the case for many years, teacher training continued to offer an outlet for able females who did not go to university. It provided a compensatory route to a career which was perceived as secure, respectable and appropriate for females.

The evidence collected in this chapter suggests that the most significant changes which occurred within the English education system during this period were gradual rather than sudden, and were to a large extent historically mediated. All of those involved in education, whether as pupils, teachers, parents, commentators or politicians, brought with them perceptions of what schooling was and what it should be which were derived in part from their own earlier experiences and in part from images and expectations of schooling which were widely shared. It is only through a set of processes such as this that, for example, the opportunities opened up to females by the general spread of co-education could be used in reality to heighten existing gender contrasts.

This example reminds us that this process of 'historical mediation', by which a society chooses to use its education system to confirm its own values and to enshrine established practice, occurs not simply because it is convenient, or least stressful for those involved, but because that system, in its workings and its structures, is performing an important social function. In England, as in other countries, schools and colleges play a vital role in determining who will and who will not be the beneficiaries of the wealth that is generated, and who will hold and exercise power. This is not to say that this system is entirely, or even largely, meritocratic, since the most powerful groups in society continue to use the divisions and distinctions within the education system (including a highly esteemed private sector) as a way of confirming their own position. This extends even to the identification of 'good' and 'bad' knowledge: Modern Greats at Oxbridge remains more prestigious than automobile engineering at a provincial college of further education. In a society in which wealth and power are unequally distributed the education system performs a vital role in maintaining and justifying those inequalities. Access to the professions, to secure employment and to a comfortable position in society is mediated in large part by the schools and through the higher education system. This is not to say that the education system offers the *only* route to secure employment and success, but that it is almost certainly the most important agent; we could hardly expect otherwise when we consider that schools are the one agency which involves the vast majority of the population throughout their formative years. This has been the case in England at least since the industrial revolution, and probably for a longer period. Equally, there is no suggestion that those involved in education are involved in some vast act of duplicity; there is no doubt that most of the agents in this process, and perhaps all of us to some degree respond unwittingly to drives and conditioning of which we are barely conscious. At the local level during the period we are considering there can be little doubt that the vast majority of schoolteachers remained committed to the goal of 'doing the best' for their pupils, seeking to widen opportunities and experiences for those in their charge as far as possible.

Yet, in sum, as we look back on the working out of competition at all levels the outcome was ultimately a reinforcement of the *status quo*. It is the fact that, historically, education legitimises the structure of society which makes it so resistant to change. It is for this reason that, ironically, we can expect schooling to be particularly unresponsive to social change in such a relatively kaleidoscopic period as the most recent thirty years has been. In England, perhaps more than in any other country, there is an important sense in which our educational past is our present. Certainly, no analysis of our recent educational history can afford to overlook the power of the past, and it is for that reason that I have chosen to deal with it first in this book. We go on now to look at some of the other key determinants of schooling in modern England.

2

EDUCATION AND THE ECONOMY

The transformation experienced by the British economy between 1964 and 1990 was enormous. It was so complete as to defy brief analysis. It posed challenges for the education system which were every bit as great as those which became evident during the first industrial revolution. But the extent to which formal education was inoculated against change by its own characteristics and cultural inheritance, as was argued in Chapter 1, meant that the educational response to the changes taking place in the economy was, at best, partial and was posited in large part on perceptions of the economic significance of schooling which were necessarily flawed. The outcome was, first, that the educational system became increasingly dysfunctional economically while, at the same time, preserving its capacity to impose and sustain social class differences. Thus, the secondary effect of these changes was that schools and colleges became, if anything, stronger arbiters of who precisely would be the beneficiaries of economic transformation while playing only a marginal role in the generation of that transformation itself. Also, as this dysfunctionality became steadily more apparent, it became easier for critics, particularly from the New Right, to emphasise the need for regeneration and reconstruction of the education system, for a closer linkage of what went on in schools with the changing demands of the workplace.

It is difficult to understate the economic sea change which occurred between 1964 and 1990. The management by the state of the economy, based largely on Keynsian principles, had meant that Britain was able to participate in and experience a fairly lengthy period of economic growth and stability from the mid-1930s until the early 1970s. The fact that this was based in part on the over-stimulation of the old manufacturing industries (made more or less inevitable by the fact of two World Wars and their demands of the economy), meant in turn that the old industrial areas and the major towns and cities associated with them would be particularly susceptible to the effects of economic recession and restructuring. By the early 1970s, it was becoming clear that this economic growth was unsustainable in its existing form.[1]

23

After the 1971 collapse of the Bretton Woods agreement, Britain suffered as much and probably more than any of the developed countries from the effects of the rise in world oil prices which began in 1973 and from the downturn in world trade which resulted. Ron Martin has identified five key components of the economic transformation which followed.[2] First, the period saw a massive shrinkage of Britain's industrial base. By the late 1980s over a third of manufacturing industry had gone and over three million jobs had been lost. Much of that loss was focused in specific regions, which suffered particularly badly. Set against this was a sudden expansion of new technologies. From the early seventies onwards, information processing and microtechnology grew fast enough to become, in themselves, key components of the economy at the same time that they transformed the administration of older businesses. Further, there was a significant growth in the service sector of the economy, with 3.5 million new jobs being created. Keynsian devices for managing the economy fell out of fashion and, although governments in reality retained a tight grip on business activity through direct regulation and fiscal policy, there was a clear shift from government pump-priming towards Social Darwinism in the marketplace. Finally, changes in the global economy meant that, in a very real sense, nothing could ever be the same again for British industry and commerce. The emergence of the Pacific Rim economies, 'structural changes in international monetary relations and institutions', Britain's greater reliance on Europe after the collapse of the Commonwealth as an economic force and the general slow-down which affected the economies of all developed countries meant, in combination, that the context of British economic activity and the external constraints upon its development were permanently altered.

All of this meant that Britain experienced real economic growth during the period. Gross domestic product continued to increase: during the late sixties it averaged over 3 per cent per annum, falling back to 1.4 per cent during the mid-seventies and rising again to nearly 2 per cent during the 1980s, despite the absolute decline which marked the start of the decade. But this economic growth has contained within it two characteristics. First, it has been achieved against a constant political backdrop of economic crisis. This sense of crisis coloured much public comment and gave urgency to this aspect of the debate on education. Second, Britain's growth was slower than that of almost all her rivals in the developed world, and this was, of course, part of the explanation of the chronic sense of crisis. By 1987 the United Kingdom was fourteenth out of twenty-four OECD member states in respect of *per capita* growth rates.

The explanations offered by economic theorists for these changes are varied, and the analysis which is adopted colours deeply the view which must be taken of the relationship between economic development and the educational system. On the one hand, some commentators suggest that what was at work here was a variant of the 'Kondratieff' effect. First popularised by Joseph Schumpeter in the late thirties, this explanation rests on the belief that it is possible to identify cycles of economic activity. According to Kondratieff, periods of relatively sudden technological development generated economic expansion which took about fifty years to work itself out before the inevitable market saturation led to recession. As Peter Hall has pointed out, the 'nagging point' about this ferociously contested theory is that, in reality, economic development has seemed to bear it out with a slump around 1930, a revival beginning a few years later and extending into the fifties and sixties, followed by a descent into depression during the 1970s and then further economic renewal and regeneration. As Hall says: 'It is small wonder that . . . a number of people are again taking Kondratieff–Schumpeter very seriously.'[3] While it might be possible to argue that formal education systems can help set the scene for technological innovation and hence economic development, in reality the transformations which have revolutionised world and national economies have taken place *outside* formal education systems. This is therefore a set of ideas which carry with them the corollary that education is necessarily (or at least very probably) marginal to economic development; that school systems may reflect economic and technical change but are unlikely to play much part in generating it.

Alternative economic explanations eschew grand theory of this kind and place greater emphasis on the multi-faceted nature of development.[4] Some accounts, for example,[5] identify the inflexibility of long-established developed economies, the deadening impact of state intervention, the failure of wage rates to respond to rising unemployment, and an over-emphasis on military rather than civil research, as key elements in the explanation of British failure. Among the factors which they would consider are the availability of an appropriately trained labour force to enable participation in economic growth. Although few practising economists would place formal education at the heart of any explanation of economic transformation, many would allow it some small place.[6]

At the other extreme, commentators such as W. D. Rubinstein place great emphasis on attitudes and expectations in their explanations, and see the school and university system as being central to attempts to regenerate British enterprise. Rubinstein has observed that:

> possibly the most commonly heard explanation for Britain's economic decline is that which we will call the 'cultural critique'. According to this argument . . . the reasons for Britain's decline lie in the effects of British culture on British entrepreneurship. . . . The chief mechanism for the inter-generational transmission of anti-business values is the British education system.[7]

This chimes with the Weiner thesis[8] and the work of Corelli Barnett,[9] both of whom have offered blistering critiques of the deadening hand of education on the development of the British economy. But even this approach implies that, while the failings of the education system may have impeded economic change and modernisation, there is little if any evidence that in reality what went on within the formal education system has promoted growth and modernisation. The rather wistful picture of what might have been has, as its central figure, an education system which is inherently conservative.

It seems, then, that whichever explanation of economic change is adopted, there must be a question mark over the claims of politicians like Harold Wilson, who, in his famous 'science and socialism' speech, anticipated that a transformed education system could help to precipitate a 'white hot technological revolution', adding that 'to train the scientists we need will mean a revolution in our attitude to education'.[10] In similar vein, James Callaghan emphasised in his Ruskin speech thirteen years later that schools should play a fuller part in preparing pupils for working life as a key to economic development: he stressed the need for 'a more technological bias in science teaching that will lead towards practical applications in industry rather than towards academic studies'.[11] Despite these statements of intent and countless attempts by successive governments to apply these ideas in practice, the reality has been that investment in education has made only marginal differences to patterns of economic change.

One has only to consider a few of the skills increasingly deployed during the period in the faster growing parts of the economy to realise that schooling played a very small part in their development. While the use of computers and word-processors became steadily more widespread, the vast majority of those who used them to earn their living had, in reality, picked up the necessary skills 'on the job' after entry to the workplace. Much the same was true of the growing realisation of the importance of good management at both micro- and macro-levels. Only at the end of our period did schools, colleges and universities respond significantly to the growing demand for management courses, largely engendered by those who had already realised the value of such skills in employment. The appointment of staff who had the ability to speak more than one language became increasingly important for the survival of firms dependent on competition in the international marketplace. But the drive to promote Modern Languages within schools and the shift from Classics was belated and never more than partial. Britain remained the 'poor relation' of Western Europe in respect of its language skills and this shortcoming was only in part redeemed by the accident that English was, year by year, becoming more widely accepted as the language of international communication. The inherent conservatism of the education system, particularly in respect of curricular matters, ensured that this was so. But, in the context of this book, the fact that many teachers and many participants in the political debate believed that the education system could and should be one of the key levers of economic regeneration, was in itself significant.

But, if there is doubt about the extent to which the development of the education system impinged on the economy, there can be no doubt that the changes taking place in wider society put schooling under tremendous stress. First, the shifts which took place in wage structure impinged directly on children as well as involving a redefinition of the labour market for which the schools were preparing them. Although, during the sixties and seventies pay differentials remained fairly static, Mrs Thatcher's arrival at Number 10 marked the start of a decade during which the gap between highest and lowest paid widened alarmingly. During the 1980s, the top 10 per cent of wage earners enjoyed income rises of almost 50 per cent in real terms, while the poorest 10 per cent experienced income improvements of less than 3 per cent. Figures released in 1990 showed that the contrast was not simply one of extremes, but that average income was increasing ten times as fast as that of the poorest 10 per cent during these years too.[12] This had the direct effect of throwing one-fifth of children into the band of those households receiving less than half the average income (one widely accepted criterion of poverty) as against only 14 per cent similarly placed a few years before. Not only were more children becoming the direct victims of poverty, and therefore less able to benefit from the schooling opportunities available to them, but this widening gap meant that many of those in employment were able to think in terms of private education or to afford the marginal expenditure to support their children's education in ways which were increasingly denied to the poor. So, a first direct effect of these economic transformations was to intensify the contrasts between differing social groups in respect of their ability to benefit from formal schooling.

Second, this economic transformation resulted in an intensification, rather than a lessening, of gender contrasts in employment. Price and Bain have shown how, between 1961 and 1981, the numbers of women in professional positions rose slightly, but that the key gains were in clerical and sales work. They conclude:

> The proportion of managerial, higher professional and supervisory jobs taken by women has been rising in recent years but still remains at levels that imply substantial under-representation of women in these occupations. In the case of managerial and supervisory jobs, women take approximately half the number that could be expected if they were represented in proportion to their overall share of the labour force; for higher professionals they take only one third. Women have always been in a majority in the lower professional...category because of the preponderance of two majority-female occupations – teaching and nursing – in this category.[13]

In 1986, a half of all females in employment were in clerical jobs. As a further corollary of this, women's wage rates continued to lag behind those of men: into the late eighties male wages remained on average about half again of those available for females. Often this was for similar work which was

27

identified differently according to the nature of the labour force. Each of these developments had an impact on the task facing the schools.

A further characteristic of these economic transformations was the decline of the 'gold watch' career. While it remained common into the 1960s for individual workers to think in terms of a defined career route which stretched out over a working lifetime, the reality, increasingly, was that of premature retirements and of mid-career transformations to meet the changing demands of the workplace. As Jacques Mazier has observed:

> the introduction of new forms of work intended to increase labour market uncertainty – temporary work, sub-contracting, part-time work – were designed to achieve greater flexibility and mobility in the management of labour.... Both governments and firms were trying to overcome labour market rigidities.[14]

These policies, which helped to transform the labour force during our period, were also intended to assist employers by taking pressure off their wage bills. One immediate result of the casualisation of labour was a reduction in wage rates. This, too, was pregnant with significance for schooling. On the one hand, those career routes which did seem to offer relative security in employment became increasingly prized: the result was that a growing number of parents was sensitised to and ready to bear the costs of supporting children through the more protracted educational routes which led towards the professions. The scramble for success in external examinations became more fierce. On the other hand, the demands for schools to prepare a more flexible and adaptable workforce also became stronger.

The pressure upon schools to generate good external examination results was also compounded by the general shift towards the tertiary sector of the economy and the drift towards accreditation in all forms of employment. As the demand for formal qualifications grew year by year, schools found themselves increasingly susceptible to a 'consumerist' view of their role which placed the generation of entrants to higher education and employment firmly at the top of their list of priorities. Between 1961 and 1981 there were significant shifts in the distribution of the occupied labour force. The percentage in non-manual employment rose from 35 to 52. Within this category, managers rose from 5.4 per cent of the total labour force to 13.7 per cent; higher professionals from 3.4 per cent to 4.8 per cent. Meanwhile, those in manual work fell from 59 per cent of the working population to 47 per cent.[15] If the first part of the twentieth century had seen a marked increase in the clerical labour force, the later years of the century saw a take-off in managerial and professional employment which more than compensated for the slow-down in the growth of clerical labour. A key part of this, of course, was the swift growth of new high-tech industries and the widespread application of technology across the economy. The general recognition that education was increasingly at the centre of political debate stemmed, in large part, from these changes.

Linked to these changes was a steady and apparently inexorable rise in the numbers of unemployed, so that by the end of our period, chronic unemployment seemed to have become one of the prerequisites for the functioning of the economy. From the end of the Second World War until the late sixties, unemployment in Britain stood at less than 2 per cent. A sudden rise during the early seventies was followed by further increases, which proved to be semi-permanent during the second half of that decade. 1981 witnessed another significant jump, so that despite the fact that several modifications were made to the way in which figures were collected, even the official returns of unemployment showed it to be running at over 13 per cent by the end of the period covered by this book.[16] This aspect of economic development had a major impact on the nature of the debate on the role of the schools as we shall see, and certainly made it easier for critics to portray the education system as failing the economy.

Another aspect of these changes was the growing contrasts between employment in the private sector of the economy and in the public sector. As Harold Perkin has shown in his monumental study of the growth of professionalism in modern Britain, it proved much simpler to impose government policy, especially on matters such as pay levels, on those working for the government, whether at local or national level, than on workers in private industry.[17] The National Plan, introduced by Wilson's Government in 1966, and a succession of pay freezes and pay and price controls, all served to sharpen the tensions between workers in the two sectors, so that by the end of the 1980s this divide had become one of the seismic rifts of modern British society. It, too, had profound implications for schooling.

Finally, there were regional shifts which also had massive implications for educators. As Peter Hall has pointed out:

> the contraction of employment in older industrial staples like textiles, deep coal mining, steel manufacture and ship-building is paralleled by an expansion of such newer industries as electronics and aerospace, as well as producer services such as finance, insurance and real estate.... These processes ... result in pronounced regional shifts: new industries tend to grow in places different from those where the old industries are contracting.... The English north east and Mersey-side are the contracting economies; East Anglia and the south west region of England are the complementary areas of growth.[18]

The implications of this have been neatly summarised by Ron Martin:

> Geographically, the result of this reorganisation has been a far-reaching restructuring of the patterns of uneven urban and regional develop-

ment, a succession of regional role reversals, and a marked widening of spatial socio-economic inequalities.... The precipitate decline of industrial activity in the older cities has left them, and especially their inner areas, economically, socially, physically and fiscally debilitated. Alongside increasing problems of inner-city unemployment, a dramatic shift of jobs into services ... has led to a pronounced dualisation of the urban labour market and to sharp spatial juxtapositions of poverty and prosperity.[19]

Thus, for educators, the implications are both regional and local to the cities and their suburbs. Vast areas of southern Britain became the venues for economic regeneration and, in the process, came to send disproportionate numbers of their young people through protracted and expensive educational routes which led to secure employment. In contrast, the old declining urban areas, each with their well-established and prestigious grammar schools, experienced shifts in their social structure which changed the demands made of the local school systems. Within the urban areas, the close proximity of poverty and plenty, which Martin pointed out, meant that neighbouring schools came to find themselves dealing with sharply contrasting clienteles. Both of these characteristics of the education system had been evident for over a century, as researchers like Bill Marsden have shown.[20] But now the social contrasts and their educational implications were heightened as a result of these economic changes.

As we turn to examine the educational responses that were made to these changed circumstances, we see at once that between 1964 and 1990 Britain experienced a re-run of an old historical phenomenon. While there had been, for over a century, those who agitated for the schools, colleges and universities to do more to prepare their students for the changing world of work, in reality, this function was only undertaken as an ancillary to the stronger imperative for the education system to 'sort the sheep from the goats'. Given the high prestige of the professions, the enduring strength of the view that the best preparation for life and for leadership in the modern world was a liberal education, and the preoccupation of the political left with seeing that the social sifting which went on within education was as fair as was possible, lobbying for technical and vocational education was constantly marginalised and forced to be done within that broader frame of reference. The result was that, whenever initiatives in technical education were made, they were quickly construed as being appropriate for only a particular band within society, and the schools and colleges which were set up all experienced 'academic drift', a process by which, despite the intentions of their founders, they soon came to imitate prestigious institutions offering a liberal education in their quest for status. So, to exemplify, the civic university colleges of the late nineteenth century were, without exception, intended to cater for the industrial and technical needs of the townships they served. Within a few years of obtaining recognition as universities in their own right they were expanding in the areas of Arts and Liberal Studies so as to resemble, as closely as possible, the existing accepted model of what constituted a 'university'. Much the same happened to the higher grade schools which were originally planned to give an extended schooling to elementary school pupils destined for local employment in trade, industry and the minor professions. As soon as they appeared to be set fair to do just that, during the 1890s, the threat they offered to the existing municipal grammar schools led to them being first hamstrung and very soon closed down. They were only permitted to survive into the twentieth century by taking on the form and curriculum of the very schools whose shortcomings had led to their foundation in the first place.

Almost identical processes occurred during the twentieth century. The central schools, higher elementary schools and (after the Second World War) technical secondary schools all found themselves taking on the appearance of pre-existing institutions in order to survive. The particular problem posed for government at the start of the period covered by this book was that the secondary technical schools were seen to have failed in their main intention. Those which survived had become municipal grammar schools in all but name. As we will see, similar evolutions took place in respect of the technical sector of higher education during the period under review.

So, the experience of our period became that of a succession of central and local government initiatives which sought to regenerate technical and vocational education. The failure of the secondary technical schools made the case all the more urgent. But efforts in this direction were clouded by the fact that there was never a clear or enduring position on whether these initiatives were intended for particular groups of students (with particular aspirations or from particular social backgrounds) or whether they should influence all schools and all pupils. Despite the growing urgency of political clamour for an education system which would link more closely with this swiftly changing economy, the reality was that initiatives either became subsumed and marginalised within the pre-existing academic hierarchy, or became 'tracked', catering for small groups of students from a relatively narrow social band and thus contributing to the process by which the education system confirmed social hierarchies and sustained a socially segmented society.

The position has been neatly summarised by Michael Sanderson. Writing of this recent period, he observes that 'the technical schools have been stifled by a set of English cultural attitudes'.[21] It is worth reminding ourselves that this reverence stifled not just the technical schools, but the whole attempt to relate schooling to the economy. The second factor he identifies is the tension between the production of specialists and generalists. The 'new universities' movement of the fifties and sixties was posited on the need to challenge

31

over-specialisation within higher education. In the process, the narrowness of technical and vocational curricula was brought into question. On the one hand, as Sanderson shows, this 'reinforced suspicions of the technical school as something too narrow, specialised and vocational'.[22] But, on the other, the debate on the widening of curricula was put on the back boiler during the seventies and eighties, and this helps explain the ways in which the New Right lobbied for technical education without the perceived need for its recipients to be trained in both the necessary skills and the wider human considerations attaching to their specialisms. In this way, the debate on technical education was narrowed during our period. Finally, Sanderson stresses Edward Boyle's recollection that:

> There were two traditions in the Department of Education: the social justice tradition, wanting to widen opportunity... And the technical college tradition – education for investment, education for efficiency. They were described in the early 1960s as the dialectic within the Department.[23]

It is this tension which helps explain why, when new initiatives such as comprehensive education were being pursued, the regeneration of vocational education was not made central to its functions. The debate on social equity and on the contribution these new schools might make towards equalising opportunities overlooked the ways in which a refurbishment of vocational education might have done this, for the very reason that vocationalism was seen, historically, as inferior and therefore to be avoided.

As Sanderson concludes:

> The movement to create a thriving secondary technical sector... was stifled in the post-war years. This failure had implications far beyond the 1950s and 1960s and the secondary technical sector itself. It lay near the heart of England's educational defects and declining economic performance in the post-war years.[24]

We will now examine the form those implications took.

From the outset, the enthusiasm of politicians and of the Ministry of Education in particular to do something to galvanise technical education was clear for all to see. At the end of 1963 the Robbins Report had set out the template for a major expansion of higher education, with the ten Colleges of Advanced Technology (CATs) being upgraded to Technological Universities and six Advanced Institutes of Science and Technology being recommended. For almost a decade the National Council for Technological Awards had been offering diplomas to students completing advanced courses. Now technological courses were to have full recognition at degree level and the Council upgraded to become the Council for National Academic Awards (CNAA). It was soon to overtake the University of London as the biggest degree-awarding institution in the country. This was all of a piece with government policy over several years. Successive White Papers on Technical Education had appeared in 1956 and 1961, and an extremely upbeat Report on the progress of the technical colleges was published in 1963. The University Grants Committee (UGC) had reported over 45,000 students on courses in science and technology in 1962 and looked forward confidently to a doubling of that number by the end of the decade.

The drive to expand provision at higher education level was matched by efforts to promote business studies and technology in Colleges of Further Education. In 1960 National Certificates in Commerce replaced the old national awards in Business Studies. A Certificate in Office Studies was introduced in 1963. It covered English, general studies, business and clerical duties. Ordinary and Higher National Certificates and Diplomas in Business Studies were set up in an effort to give academic respectability to what had previously been very low-prestige areas of study. In March 1964, the Crick Committee, reporting on *Higher awards in business studies*,[25] recommended more new courses in this area based on four or five years of sandwich study, 'designed to prepare young men and women with good academic qualifications... for careers in business'. It was foreseen that the newly constituted CNAA would give these courses honours degree recognition. But the optimistic tone of the Department of Education's Report on these developments could not disguise what was happening on the ground in reality:

> Nearly all area and local colleges... provide courses, mostly day and evening, for secretaries. In general, the courses are taken by girls of fifteen to eighteen.... For young women with 'O' and 'A' level passes some of the larger colleges offer full-time secretarial courses of up to two years duration, often with an emphasis on one or more foreign languages.[26]

Almost inexorably, one immediate consequence of this upgrading of Further Education courses was that they became more clearly gendered than ever before.

Nonetheless, these courses continued to receive DES backing. In November 1965 the Department reported that the numbers of students on these Diploma and Certificate courses was steadily growing: 71,000 on ONC courses, 53,000 on HNC. The Diplomas remained more exclusive, with only 9,300 on Ordinary courses and 8,200 on Higher. More than half of the Certificate students were enrolled on Engineering courses: this subject was the most popular at Diploma level too, although Business Studies was another quickly growing field of study at this level. In a triumphalist summary of what was on offer, the DES Report concluded that:

> Technical education stands on the threshold of great advance. The

National Certificate and Diplomas have set standards which are respected throughout the educational, industrial and commercial worlds and the new pattern of courses is designed to ensure that they continue to meet the needs of our modern industrial society.[27]

This expansion of the formal provision at post-school level was to sound the death knell of the apprenticeship system which was at its peak in the mid-sixties, accounting for over a third of all male school leavers but only 5 per cent of girls. During the following two decades, the decline in manufacturing industry was to be matched by a decline in the number of apprentices associated with it. From a peak of 240,000 apprentices in 1965, the number fell to 140,000 in 1974 and 54,000 in 1989.[28] The shift towards preparation for employment in institutions of further and higher education was, in the event, to be mediated in part by the new Industrial Training Boards set up under the terms of the 1964 Industrial Training Act. This was to lead, in 1973, to the establishment of the Manpower Services Commission which eventually was to be the agent of a new phase of government policy. But during the 1960s there can be no doubt that the shift towards more formal routes into employment in industry and commerce and towards the accreditation of courses stemmed in large part from government initiative.

This frantic activity at post-school level disguised the fact that there was no coherent policy to promote vocational work within the schools themselves. The 1963 Newsom Report had emphasised the importance of vocational and technical subjects at secondary level, but had few clear ideas on how exactly they might be fostered, and there was little practical response to this aspect of its proposals. Gary McCulloch has shown how the 1959 Crowther Report advocated an 'alternative road' to the teaching of technology, but that, in reality little was achieved.[29] Crowther's ideal was that practical activities might be used to foster a broad scientific curiosity. In 1965 the Institution of Mechanical Engineers gave its blessing to this approach to the teaching of applied sciences in schools, publishing a report on *Engineering among the schools*. At about the same time, the Schools Council turned its attention to the subject, publishing the proposals of an HMI who had been seconded to work at Manchester University under the title of *A school approach to technology*. It suggested a closer linkage of existing subjects such as science and mathematics with workshop theory. McCulloch has described it as 'an explicit attempt to build upon the ideas put forward by Crowther'. The Schools Council went on to publish its own working paper on *Technology and the schools* and, in September 1967, funded a full-scale curriculum project to the tune of £180,000. Yet, in reality, there was little noticeable impact on the established secondary school curriculum and, by the early seventies, the Project had foundered, partly as a result of the pressure brought to bear on it by the Association for Science Education.

There can be little doubt that one key reason for the failure to redefine technical education in the schools at this time lay with the extent to which the success of the Nuffield Foundation Science Project diverted attention and discussion towards the pure sciences. This project, first set up in 1962, gained backing from the Schools Council and devised programmes of teaching for both primary and secondary schools. Perhaps the main reason for its success lay in the fact that it resulted in the preparation of materials for teaching, first to 'O' level and, from 1964 onwards, to 'A' level. Conferences to promote this work involved representatives of higher and further education as well as industry, so it is hardly surprising that this came to be seen as the way in which the schools were putting their house in order in respect of technical education.[30] A further factor which focused attention on the teaching of pure science was the fact, pointed out by the 1968 Dainton Committee, that the number of students embarking on specialist science courses was starting to fall after two decades of increasing popularity for science at fifth- and sixth-form level.

Some schools experimented with programmed learning, which was also being advocated by the DES during the late sixties, but in the main, debates on schooling did not focus on curriculum reform. This was partly because of the inevitable fact that, if the new comprehensive schools were to gain general acceptance, they had to convince the public that they could deliver the curriculum of the more prestigious schools they sought to replace. Another reason lay in the public preoccupation with access to secondary education and the contest between supporters of comprehensivisation and the grammar school lobby. So, in the event, the reorganisation of secondary schooling had the effect of damping down discussion of curriculum reform rather than promoting it.

If we seek to summarise the impact of policy on technical education during the mid-sixties, we are forced to the view that, lacking a clear vision of how best to galvanise the schools into reform on the question of vocational training, policymakers looked to the restructuring of further and higher education to provide the new avenues into employment which seemed so badly needed. But this policy failed to take account of the continuing prestige and attractiveness of the established elite routes through schools into what were seen as the better universities. Those social groups which made best use of this 'fast track' into the major professions saw no need to redirect their children through the quickly developing courses in colleges of further education and newly promoted technical colleges. It was entirely natural, therefore, that these routes became the province of the respectable working classes, first generation owner-occupiers and first generation sedentary workers. The changes taking place in the economy and in the social structure were being silently matched by the education system, and even promoted through official policy. And, in the process, the 'tracking' element in modern British education, by which particular individuals were born into particular locations and social strata, and found their life chances confirmed rather than modified by the education system, was reinforced rather than overthrown. This was probably the greatest single result of a set of policies towards technical education which were, from the outset, ill thought-out and far from comprehensive in their scope.

But this was far from clear to policymakers at the time, and the Government continued to press ahead with exhortations and statements of intent. In September 1965, the National Plan was published, setting out the Labour Government's proposals for all aspects of the country's economic development. Education was to play a key part. As the Plan emphasised:

Education is both an important service and an investment for the future. It helps to satisfy the needs of the economy for skilled manpower of all kinds . . . and the demands of individuals for education as a means both to improved economic prospects and to a richer and more constructive life.[31]

The sum of £1,459 million which was annually devoted to education represented 13.5 per cent of overall public expenditure. It was planned to increase that to £1,923 million, or 14.5 per cent, by the end of the decade. But, although a vast increase in the resources allocated to schools was foreseen, the Plan avoided the question of what that might mean in terms of curricular restructuring. Instead, the familiar themes of school building, teacher supply and school running costs were rehearsed. Only when the National Plan came to further education did it refer to the relationship between what was actually taught and industrial output. As the DES Report on the National Plan commented:

The long run increase in productivity in Britain must depend heavily on the greater skill and technical proficiency of the labour force, and a great effort is being made to develop courses for technologists, technicians and other trainees. The importance of further education is apparent at all levels.[32]

To achieve this, the Robbins proposal for an expansion of the technical and further education sectors to 50,000 students by 1973/4 was hurriedly revised upwards to 70,000 by 1969/70. It was foreseen, too, that the number of teachers in the education system as a whole would rise by over 100,000 before 1970. It was stressed that 'the planned increase of 32% over five years in the level of expenditure devoted to education reflects the degree of social priority placed by the Government upon this sector of the public services'.[33] Education was to assume a more significant position within public spending as a whole, thus guaranteeing that it would become more central to political debate; but there was little on how exactly that money might be most precisely targeted to ensure the economic growth which was so urgently needed.

It is probably this failure to identify coherent policies for the reform of curricula at school level which explains the drift during the 1970s towards stop-gap measures by which successive governments sought to alleviate the growing problem of youth unemployment. As the number of registered unemployed school leavers rocketed from 10,000 in July 1974 to 240,000 three years later, the government was forced into reactive policies and into using new agencies to implement these policies. The most important of these was the Manpower Services Commission. Set up as a defensive response to rising unemployment, it was to become, during the 1980s, one of the main levers used by the Thatcher Government to gain direct influence over the working of schools and to redirect their activities. But its role during the 1970s was far more one of plugging the gaps and compensating for the failure of the secondary technical sector during the whole post-war era.

Under pressure from the Labour Party to do something about unemployment, the Conservative Secretary of State for Employment, Maurice Macmillan, introduced in 1973 the Employment and Training Act, which he claimed to be:

> a new initiative in tackling some of the major economic and social problems faced by the country... the Bill will anticipate, and as far as possible eliminate, shortages of skilled manpower which hold up economic progress.[34]

The Act established the Manpower Services Commission, which began work in January 1974. Within a few months the Commission was working through its Training Services Agency to counteract the problem of youth employment. The Training Opportunities Scheme, which had started in 1972, was taken over by the new TSA. It immediately set about the provision of specialist training for school leavers; this was quickly followed by the Job Creation Programme in October 1975 and the Recruitment Subsidy for School Leavers a few months later. This desperate effort by government to reduce unemployment moved the MSC to the centre of debate. In an attempt to bring order to what was in reality a series of near-panic responses, the MSC set up the Holland Committee to take a broad look at the provision available for the young unemployed. Its report, published in May 1977 on *Young people and work*, made suggestions on the coordination of these efforts. The direct result was an expansion of the MSC and an increase in its powers. A Youth Opportunities Programme was started in the following year to provide work experience for school leavers, but it succeeded only in generating a cheap pool of labour for employers and was soon seen as unsuccessful, since the majority of the 630,000 young people who embarked on YOP programmes ended up on college courses anyway. This meant that, by the early eighties, the MSC was desperate for new initiatives. The events of the 1970s had shifted the debate on schooling and the economy away from what went on in school towards what happened to school leavers, while the sudden upturn in unemployment after Thatcher's coming to power made the

37

problem seem ever more pressing. A succession of initiatives had proved ineffective. Thatcher's Government, with its greater readiness for proactive policy formulation, now turned the MSC into a device to control the schools more closely.

The agent of this transformation was Lord Young. At the same time as seeking to improve the career guidance and work preparation available in schools, he replaced the Youth Opportunities Programme by the Youth Training Scheme, which set out 'to provide some form of education and training to all those under eighteen'.[35] This funded one year of training and had some impact on the provision at further education level. Beyond this, the emphasis on what went on in the schools was re-affirmed through the Technical and Vocational Education Initiative (TVEI), introduced in November 1982. Now the MSC, which came under the Department of Employment, was to become a major source of funding for what went on in schools alongside the DES. Although part of the justification for TVEI was that it would suffuse a new approach of technology throughout the secondary schools, in reality it soon became possible to identify what McCulloch has called a 'TVEI enclave', a relatively narrow band of pupils who found their way into the scheme. This was partly because there was no serious attempt to build a set of external examinations which would rival the existing sixteen-plus and eighteen-plus examinations in status. A number of Labour-controlled local authorities boycotted the scheme, suspicious of its real intentions and fearing, as *The Times* put it, that TVEI and YTS schemes were 'no more than anti-riot devices keeping sixteen year olds off the unemployment register and off the streets'.[36] But the scheme continued to expand, being fully national in the summer of 1987 and funded to the tune of £900 million over ten years.

Indeed, under Keith Joseph at the Department of Education and Science, it became increasingly clear that the perception of technical education as best suited for particular pupils was once again coming to the fore. When forced to back down on the issue of reintroducing grammar schools in certain areas, he offered the now famous observation that 'if selection between schools is largely out, then I emphasise that there must be differentiation within schools'.[37] This policy was pursued in 1986, first through the establishment of the National Council for Vocational Qualifications, set up to coordinate efforts to rationalise awards in this area. But still there was no serious attempt to match the established examination boards, so that, as Brian Simon has pointed out, what was in prospect was a re-establishment of the tripartite system by the back door, the academic track to be examined by the GCE boards, NCVQs for the middle band, and the Lower Achieving Pupils Project for the 'bottom forty percent'.[38] The outcome in practice was certainly that these new awards did not distract significant numbers from the familiar route for high achievers, but they did confirm the role of technical education as being intended for the runners-up in the academic rat race.

In the autumn of 1986 a further twist was given to these separatist policies by Kenneth Baker's announcement of City Technology Colleges. These were to have a strong emphasis on 'technological, scientific and practical work' and were not simply a reworking of the ideal of the secondary technical school, but were intended expressly to weaken the position of the local authorities whose schools they would compete with. Funding was intended to come from industrial and commercial sources, although within a few years the bulk of their support came from central government. Both Michael Sanderson and Gary McCulloch have reviewed their early development, and have emphasised the extent to which the reality differed from the aspiration.[39] Most significantly, in our context, Geoffrey Walford researched the intake to the Solihull CTC and found that half of the pupils came from skilled manual class backgrounds, while only 1 per cent had parents in professional or managerial occupations.[40] Once again, what was billed as academic differentiation proved to be no more and no less than social stratification in disguise.

Similarly, in respect of further and higher education, the intention to upgrade technological education soon ran into difficulties. The policy of what seemed at the time to be almost limitless expansion of the university sector was being costed within the newly designated Department of Education and Science. Civil servants such as Toby Weaver, aware of the fact that university places placed a far heavier demand on the public purse than places in further education, sought to put limits on the planned Robbins expansion which had promised a place to every qualified student. In February 1965 it was announced that there would be no more new universities designated during the next decade. Two months later, Antony Crosland's Woolwich speech pointed out the 'twin traditions' of higher and further education in Britain:

> on the one hand we have what has come to be called the autonomous sector, represented by the universities, in whose ranks, of course, I now include the colleges of advanced technology. On the other hand, we have the public sector, represented by the leading technical colleges and the colleges of education.[41]

This acceptance by Harold Wilson's Government of 'the binary principle', as devised by influential civil servants, was to be of enormous significance for the development of technological education at post-school level. On the one hand, by limiting costs it made possible the achievement, in part at least, of the Robbins Committee's aspiration for a mass system of higher education. By the end of the 1980s, the total number of students embarked on degree courses had tripled. On the other hand, the nature of degree-level teaching was inexorably transformed, as it proved increasingly difficult to afford the individual supervision and small-group teaching which had for almost a century been a key feature of university work in Britain. Equally significantly, the pressure on the newer institutions to respond to market forces meant an 'academic drift' of the kind which had been experienced historically within the higher-grade schools and technical schools, so that within a relatively few years even the so-called technological universities were becoming distinct in name only.

Given the failure of the schools to develop courses in technology which attracted the most able students and the lack of a qualification route which the universities could recognise immediately, it is hardly surprising that what became known as 'the Dainton swing' away from the sciences and technology intensified during the late sixties. The growing number of young people proceeding to Advanced level examinations did not mean proliferation of courses; rather, the new comprehensives were keen to demonstrate that they could compete in the established high-prestige areas of the curriculum. As Derek Aldcroft has shown, there was a significant upturn in the popularity of Economics at Advanced level, but no serious threat to the basic structure of the examination pattern and 'strong resistance' to any attempts to devise separate technical and vocational courses alongside existing subjects.[42] The resulting situation was neatly summarised in the first ever edition of *The Times Higher Education Supplement* in September 1971. For the 1,968 vacancies in Engineering courses at universities that year there had been a total of only 1,240 applications. Pure Science was little better off: 3,571 vacancies and 2,700 applications. Meanwhile, for the 2,000 places available in Arts subjects there were over 10,000 applicants and in the Social Sciences 6,000 applicants for only 900 places.

The newly-designated technological universities were committed to growth in technology. Their representatives (admittedly while they were still designated as Colleges of Advanced Technology) had promised the Robbins Committee that their expansion would involve over 60 per cent of places going to students in technological subjects. Not only were these places more expensive to provide but, as can be seen from the figures above, the schools were simply not generating the students to fill them. By the mid-seventies, almost a third of the student cohort in these technological universities were on Arts or Social Science courses. One of the causes of this was the policy of the UGC itself, which in November 1967 announced that the planned expansion of the university sector as a whole would be based largely on an increase in the number of Arts students. This reflects the failure of the UGC to move beyond a familiar view of university work, despite strong lobbying at that time for a greater emphasis on technology. Academic drift, coupled to the realities of the marketplace, was forcing them to conform to the pre-existing image of a university.

Yet despite this trend, which was already establishing itself in the mid-sixties, the government pressed ahead with the implementation of its binary policy. A 1966 White Paper, *A plan for Polytechnics and other colleges*, promised the redesignation of the remaining Colleges of Technology as Polytechnics by 1970. In the following year, Crosland emphasised that:

> in terms of type of degree and the balance between teaching and research, as well as the comprehensive character of the student intake, we see the Polys as fulfilling a distinctive role from the universities.[43]

This steady evolution towards full university status, which was to be finally realised in 1992, also involved a steady drift away from technological subjects. In retrospect it seems obvious that this was what was about to happen: at the time it was far from clear. As Sanderson has shown, in the mid-sixties 43 per cent of students in these institutions were on Engineering and Technology courses: by 1974, by when thirty of the Colleges had been designated as Polytechnics, the number had fallen to 20 per cent.[44] The attempt, in the years following the Robbins report, to plan and oversee the development of the system as a whole resulted, not just in its expansion, but in its transmutation into something different. In that process the study of technological subjects was further marginalised.

The last gasp of this expansionism proved to be the 1972 White Paper, *Education, a framework for expansion*. Ironically, in several areas, its publication marked the moment historically when contraction set in. But this is not to deny the sincerity of the attempt by Heath's Government to continue to pursue growth. Introducing this White Paper, Margaret Thatcher, the then Secretary of State for Education, stressed that:

> opportunities for higher education are not ... to be determined primarily by reference to the country's future needs for highly qualified people; although attempts to relate supply to likely demand in certain specialised professions ... will be no less important than before. The Government consider higher education valuable for its contribution to the personal development of those who pursue it; at the same time they value its expansion as an investment in the nation's human talent in a time of rapid social change and technological development.[45]

One account has described this as 'one of the latest in a long line of liberal Conservative measures designed to increase opportunity for young people in higher education'.[46] But, once again, the commitment to growth omitted any detailed oversight of the structure of the system: the details of the extent to which higher education related to economic development were left at the mercy of the market.

This was broadly true of each of the succeeding policy initiatives towards higher education. Labour's *Higher education into the nineties* (*the Oakes Paper*), published in 1978, ran several models of the growth required, but had little to say about the implications this would have for the curriculum, apart from pointing out that different growth rates would generate differing levels of demand for sandwich courses and part-time work. Even more ironic was the administration of the economies announced in the 1981 Expenditure White Paper. Following hard on the heels of a £411 million cut in educational expenditure shortly after Thatcher became Prime Minister, this round was to be administered by the UGC. Although efforts were made to protect Engineering, Medicine, Mathematics, Computer Science and Business Studies from the worst effects of these cuts, some of the technological universities were among those hardest hit. Salford's support was cut by 44 per cent, and that of Bradford and Aston by a third. Sir Edward Parkes, who chaired the UGC at this time, was forced to defend himself and his committee in *The Times* from the charge of an anti-technological bias.[47] As the closer planning and control of the system came to involve value judgements, it is significant that some technological universities, such as Loughborough and Bath, emerged from this episode with their popular reputations enhanced.

Under increasing financial pressure during the 1980s, and with tight prescriptions of the pattern of growth required, it might have been expected that, at last, technological education would come into its own, particularly in view of the aspirations of Thatcher's Government for economic renewal. But, given the continuing reluctance of sixth-formers to embark on science courses and routes into technology, it is hardly surprising that many technological courses remained among the least prestigious at the end of the decade. The first formal assessments of research activity made by the Universities Funding Council in 1989 claimed that, in eight technological universities, only one excellent department could be found, although 14 were rated as poor in quality. Sanderson has noted that this placed them below the new universities as well as the big civics in public esteem.[48] This is a sad testimony to successive attempts by government to galvanise technological education at the highest levels, and it reflects the enduring prestige of the Humanities and Pure Sciences in modern Britain. There was only one significant exception to this trend. Derek Aldcroft has pointed out that, as career opportunities closed down in other areas, the independent schools began to steer a growing number of their alumni towards Engineering courses at University level.[49] As the route towards the boardroom changed, with a growing expectation that Business Management or Applied Science at undergraduate level would lead to the upper echelons of the engineering industry, it was the public schools which responded. By 1977, one survey showed, Engineering was the preferred career route of the majority of independent school leavers. In this way the established pattern of 'tracked' routes from the most prestigious schools via particular university departments to the upper niches of the professional sector was subtly reworked during the period under review.

Meanwhile, the further education sector continued to play its part in the establishment of separate routes into distinct modes and levels of employment. The tendency for the larger and better known providers of further education to drift into the higher education sector continued. In the same way that the CATs became technological universities during the 1960s, and a few years later the remaining thirty technical colleges became Polytechnics, in 1988 the Education Reform Act shifted more advanced FE colleges from local authority control and towards full recognition as part of the higher education system. But this still left over 400 further education colleges in England and Wales, which, because they were still answerable to the local education authorities, meant that they were generally perceived as meeting local needs and were often quite entrepreneurial in their approach.

So the fall in the number of day release students in the FE colleges during the late seventies, which was never reversed, was matched by around 30,000 students on YTS schemes. The colleges began to do a brisk trade in 'O' and 'A' level courses, offering either resits for school leavers or a range of subjects not readily available in schools. RSA awards, City and Guilds qualifications as well as the newer BTEC courses were all on offer within these colleges. In a situation in which the government was increasingly ready to construe preparation for employment in industry and commerce as 'training', the FE colleges were ideally placed to respond, although as Jack Mansell has pointed out, this meant that, for those working within the FE colleges, it proved 'increasingly difficult to maintain any kind of educational ideology in the face of a more instrumental approach from employers and trainers'. [50] This trend was confirmed in 1990 through the introduction of Training and Enterprise Councils, which became responsible for over £3 billion worth of funding into this sector.

So, although by the late eighties the FE sector continued to educate over three million students, the numbers on part-time courses had declined to an all-time low and the contribution of the colleges to access courses for both adults and those aged 16 to 19 was impressive, the overall situation of further education remained problematic. As Jack Mansell has summarised the situation:

> Our post-16 educational culture is class ridden and this is exploited by those who wish it to remain divisive. In general, the middle-class financially support their children in 16–18 education and prefer the school-based examination route. The working class generally require income support for their 16-plus school leavers, and immediate employment is the preferred option.... Full-time post-16 education is too often regarded as an emergency alternative to employment. [51]

This may be an over-generalisation, but it captures neatly the nature of the trap in which the further education colleges found themselves by the late eighties. The challenges posed by a quickly changing employment situation allied to a new politics of education did not result in their emergence as fully accepted partners in the post-school provision. Rather, their function as a bridge between school and work for a particular segment of the population was confirmed: they, as much as any other element in the system, played their part in the segmentation of society.

So, in summary, the picture which emerges from this account of the responses made within education to the transformation of the economy is gloomy. The stresses imposed by economic change were considerable. They made many of the workings of the education system appear outmoded and dysfunctional. It was inevitable that the sweeping changes which took place in employment and in the structure of the economy as a whole would generate a political agenda. Education came to be seen by many observers, especially those on the Right, as both the scapegoat for slow economic growth and the key to modernisation, although, as I have argued above, the realities of the case were very different. Among the causes of economic decline, education was never more than a small contributory factor at most. There is little evidence that its restructuring could have done much to modify trends which were global in scale and very deep-seated in their nature. At best, it seems, schools, colleges and universities might have helped to lubricate the economic changes which were taking place by a rather quicker and slightly different set of responses geared towards the generation of different attitudes and skills among those about to enter the labour force.

But to enter upon this speculation is to begin reflecting on what some have called 'the ifs of history'. The reality was that the education system remained historically so deeply committed to a different end, the establishment and preservation of social difference, that it was barely conceivable that such a transformation might have occurred. Preparation for entry to the professions and to the more powerful positions within society was construed, historically, within a belief system, a set of widely held assumptions, that those who aspired to them were in various ways distancing themselves from other employments and were distinguished by the acquisition of more than simply the skills needed to do the job. Within these widely recognised social hierarchies, employment in trade and industry remained relatively low in prestige, and it is notable that, for most of the twentieth century, as several commentators have pointed out, the management and control of these activities often fell to those with a liberal arts education in one or other of the high-prestige institutions. In this historical context, it was impossible to expect a transformation of the education system which could resuscitate the status of applied science and vocational education, particularly in a time period as brief as that covered by this book, however traumatic the wider changes taking place in society. It was inevitable that whatever changes did occur would involve the location of those studying and working in these areas of the economy within a social hierarchy, at the same time as determining their employment potential.

What happened in the event was that, at first, during the sixties and early seventies, successive governments sought to bring about economic transformation by investment in education without challenging accepted assumptions about established patterns of educational provision. Increasingly, as unemployment inexorably rose and even social order itself seemed at moments to be threatened, there was a shift towards more precisely targeted expenditure, and new agencies were set up to administer that expenditure. The increasing readiness to plan the patterns of educational expenditure soon became, especially under Margaret Thatcher, a determination to use financial controls to restructure and modernise. Not only did the bureaucracies supervising the education system become larger and more powerful, as will be argued in greater detail later in the book, but the 'moral panic' which they generated over he apparent failure of educators to bring about economic success became more pervasive and more widely accepted.

But, try as they might, the concerted efforts of politicians and administrators could not have prevented the continued segmentation of the education system, even if that had been their intention, and there is precious little evidence of any such collective will. Hardly surprisingly, just as the secondary technical schools had come to occupy a particular social niche, somewhere below the grammar schools in prestige but clearly preferable, for most parents, to the secondary-moderns, new initiatives in vocational education all fell into similar social hierarchies. With the coming of comprehensive schools, generally larger than the schools they replaced, this segmentation was often achieved through pupils from differing social backgrounds making their way, by and large, through differing curricular choices towards different forms of post-school education and employment. When new kinds of institutions were established, such as technological universities or city technology colleges, they, too, soon found themselves in a clearly identified position within an educational and social hierarchy. The historically mediated function of the education system of confirming difference became as important, if not more important, than the content of the curricula to be conveyed. Even more damaging for those who enthused over the possibilities for vocational education, the distinctiveness of the curriculum in these schools and colleges came to be seen as one of the badges of their social role. In brief, it proved impossible, in such a short time scale, to break down long-established prejudices within Britain on the status and role of technical education. The developments described in this chapter worked, if anything, to confirm those prejudices. Whether this particular variant of the 'British disease' did much damage to the nation's economic prospects is at best questionable, as I have argued. Between 1964 and 1990,

45

significant new forms of technical and vocational education began to emerge. It is doubtful whether they did anything to rescue the low status of employment in trade, commerce or industry in modern Britain; they certainly strengthened the power of the education system to sustain a segmented and socially divided people.

3

CONTESTED PEDAGOGIES
THE STRUGGLE FOR CONTROL OF THE CURRICULUM

Whether we are considering the primary sector, the secondary schools or the universities and higher and further education, no issue engendered more interest and controversy during the period under review than the struggle for control of the curriculum. It was a struggle which took on slightly different forms in each sector, but in which the central controversy was remarkably similar. Across the education system, it was the power of the professionals to define their own working practices which came under increasing attack and was steadily eroded. This chapter is an attempt to describe that contest and to show its significance in the context of the central argument of this book.

PRIMARY EDUCATION

For those working in primary education, the question of curriculum reform had two inter-linked parts: on the one hand, there was a lively debate over the structures within which teachers operated, particularly over the issue of streaming, and following from this was the question of precisely what should be taught, and how. The mid-sixties saw an intensification of the debate in each of these areas of policy.

Streaming had been under attack since it became an established element in the post-war educational settlement. Brian Jackson's 1964 survey, *Streaming: an education system in miniature*[1] showed that it was widespread, with something like 94 per cent of all primary schools using it as a device to arrange their pupils. Even more damaging was his demonstration that this was linked, in almost all cases, to an unwitting social stratification of pupils, with the majority of those allocated to upper streams being drawn from professional and managerial family backgrounds, while the children of parents in unskilled or semi-skilled manual occupations were far more likely to be found in the lower streams. Perhaps more surprising was his discovery that, by and large, the teachers in primary schools were markedly hostile to suggestions that streaming should be abandoned. Yet, in a situation in which the primary schools were feeders to different types of secondary school, and in which the 11-plus examination was still widely used, this attachment to early streaming and the unwillingness of the teaching profession to countenance change in this area is more comprehensible, especially in view of the educational routes which most teachers had themselves followed.

But a number of developments were beginning to make streaming appear increasingly anachronistic. Edward Boyle wrote in his 1962 Report as Minister of Education of the 'vigorous discussion' which was taking place on streaming, and publications such as J. W. B. Douglas's *The home and the school*, which appeared in 1964, stressed the harmful effects of streaming at primary level. By this time the thinking of educational psychologists such as Cyril Burt, whose writings had played a great part in legitimising selection at every level, was becoming increasingly unfashionable. The steady growth in the number of comprehensive schools during the sixties and seventies enabled more LEAs to abandon compulsory intelligence testing at eleven. The call for de-streaming, particularly at primary level, was becoming widespread.

This was of enormous importance for curriculum development, since the connections between de-streaming and 'child-centred' or progressive education were widely recognised. The two issues were inextricably linked, so it is hardly surprising that the mid-sixties was also a period when calls for curriculum reform at primary level were also loudly heard. In Philip Taylor's words:

> after the Second World War, 'free activity', the play way and readiness were to become bywords in primary education culminating in the root metaphor of the 1952 *Handbook of suggestions*: 'First the blade and then the ear, then the full corn shall appear'. Primary education came to be seen as cultivation.[2]

Several factors worked together to ensure that the 1960s was the decade during which these ideas reached their zenith in England. The 1964 Education Act enabled some local authorities to abandon transfer at 11-plus by introducing middle schools. This freed the schools in these areas from the tyranny of intelligence tests while at the same time undermining the respect in which these tests were held generally; this enabled child-centred approaches to be more widely deployed. The establishment of the Schools Council led immediately to the widespread dissemination of new approaches to primary school teaching. The Council's Curriculum Bulletin No. 1 in 1965 dealt with *Mathematics in primary schools* and was widely circulated. The availability of this and later Schools Council publications strengthened the self-confidence of teachers to modernise the curriculum and was undoubtedly a factor in reinforcing a sense of professional expertise at this time.

Also, the demographic factor was significant. The continuing high birth rate of the early sixties, together with the fall-out from primary school teaching of married women to have children, necessitated a sharp upturn in recruitment and, following the Robbins Report, a swift expansion of the teacher training colleges now redesignated Colleges of Education. This had several results. First, the introduction of three- and then four-year courses of teacher training and of the B.Ed degree gave an academic respectability to initial teacher training which it had previously lacked, and meant that the new entrants to primary school teaching might have been expected to have greater self-confidence in terms of curriculum definition and teaching method. The growing army of college tutors fed these students on a diet of Piagetian psychology and background work in the educational disciplines, all intended to enhance professional self-awareness and autonomy. Brian Simon has taken a gloomy view of the impact of all this, commenting that

> the result was that, just at the moment when a penetrating pedagogic guidance was required by trainee teachers, both in the primary and to some extent in the new type secondary schools, it was scarcely forthcoming. . . . The actual practice of teaching was not illuminated by theoretical insights.[3]

It is difficult to map precisely the impact of these innovations on classroom practice, but they cannot be ignored in any explanation of changes in pedagogy.

Most observers are agreed so far that it is possible to identify a small number of local authorities in which ideas on new approaches to pedagogy were widely disseminated. Peter Cunningham has described Oxfordshire as 'one of a handful of authorities which gained a reputation for the progressivism of their primary schools'.[4] Here the key figure was Edith Moorhouse, an ex-teacher who, as Assistant Education Officer, had built a team of advisers who actively encouraged curriculum innovation in rural primary schools. Similarly in Leicestershire, Stewart Mason's appointment of L. G. W. Sealey as Adviser for Primary Education in 1957 resulted in the adoption of practical approaches to the teaching of both science and mathematics in that county.[5] Three other authorities, the West Riding of Yorkshire, Bristol and London, have been identified as leaders in the primary school teaching revolution. In Yorkshire the active encouragement of Alec Clegg, the CEO, was vital; in Bristol, E. M. Parry, a local inspector who became a member of the Plowden Committee, was a key figure; and in London, Christian Schiller, a retired HMI based at the University Institute of Education, played an important role. Schiller's courses, which ran from 1957 until 1963, were made available to a small number of experienced teachers who were seconded for one year. They were to prove the nucleus of a diaspora which became widely influential during the late sixties and early seventies, several of them going on to work as advisers committed to the cause of curriculum reform in the primary schools.[6]

The Nuffield Foundation also became an important focus for primary school curriculum reform at this time. It sponsored a major project on the teaching of mathematics from September 1964 which had the effect of widely disseminating a knowledge of the theoretical work of Z. P. Dienes, who, according to Brian Simon, 'profoundly influenced the scope and character of mathematics learning.'[7] The Foundation also ran projects on the teaching of science and modern languages at primary level. As Simon summarises it:

> primary education was now beginning to be seen as perhaps the major stage...within the whole educational cycle. Participation in one or other of these projects...implied involvement at the edge of knowledge, in terms of a breakthrough in the understanding of children's learning, concept development and intellectual growth generally. The fact that a major government enquiry, known to be sympathetic to such developments, was sitting only added to the general sense that things were on the move.[8]

The Government enquiry in question was that of the Plowden Committee (working alongside the often forgotten Gittins Committee for Wales). The 1967 Plowden Report marked the high-water mark of progressivism in English primary education.[9] It may also have been, as Cunningham suggests, the last great educational policy statement by 'an anti-democratic consensus among the elite of educational policy makers',[10] a view which throws into doubt the extent of the attachment of the profession as a whole to progressivism. But there can be no doubt that, both in terms of its tone and its reception, the Report trumpeted the acceptability of curriculum reform at primary level. Its central aims were to ensure that primary schooling became child centred in the best sense of the term, that the educational process should focus more on the individual pupil, and that there should be a general shift away from streaming. It advocated a far greater emphasis on the early years of schooling as well as a much closer linkage of home and school. Further, it declared that increase should involve 'positive discrimination' by which those pupils and schools with the greatest identifiable need should be given most help. To make all this possible, a massive increase in the funding available to the primary sector was called for.

A fairly rosy picture of the impact of Plowden and of the extent of progressivism during the following few years has been provided by Robert Dearden. He commented on the freeing of the curriculum which followed the publication of the Report, adding that

> this put strong pressure on a move towards some form of group work, simply because the teacher could not simultaneously cope with a teacher-demanding activity being engaged in by a wide diversity of pupils all at once.... Classrooms became much more colourful places as more time was found for creative work. Topic work flourished, though sometimes for no better reason than that it kept children engrossed while the teacher attended to something else.... The contribution of

educational publishers to making possible some of these changes deserves note. Teacher–pupil relationships became more relaxed and friendly, though not merely permissive, and parents became more welcome in schools. Plowden's ideal may have proved practical only for a few. . . . But something of the spirit of Plowden has found a permanent place.[11]

While this may be true, it must remain doubtful to what extent a set of aspirations and attitudes which became effectively the spirit of the age was borne out in reality in the teaching strategies adopted in the majority of classrooms during the seventies and eighties. A Report published by the NFER in 1970 showed that there had indeed been a major shift away from streaming in the primary schools.[12] Another development which suggests the importance of the Plowden philosophy was the introduction of open plan primary classrooms, particularly in those progressive local authorities already identified. In Oxfordshire, Robin Tanner and Edith Moorhouse worked not only to ensure that new school buildings were in this idiom, but also that the adaptations being made to older buildings allowed for a more informal structuring of learning. Peter Cunningham has shown how this was linked to particular approaches to arts and crafts, to nature study and to movement within the school and the classroom.[13] Visitors to these open-plan schools generated a rash of enthusiastic accounts which popularised progressivism on both sides of the Atlantic and almost certainly gave the impression that the new primary education was far more widespread than was, in fact, the case.

What can be seen in retrospect as a more significant and more pervasive set of influences was the growing backlash which identified progressivism and child-centred approaches in the primary schools with falling standards. This first emerged in the 1969 *Black Papers*. Although the first of these contained only one contribution on primary education, the second, appearing in October, had five. These essays made direct links between practices in schools and what Eysenck called 'the rise of a new mediocracy'. This echo of early twentieth-century eugenic theory involved the claim, made by Cyril Burt in the second *Black Paper*, that standards in schools were falling. One of the causes, the authors claimed, was the abandonment of tried and familiar pedagogic practices. C. W. J. Crawford, a junior school Head, offered his summary of contemporary trends:

> More and more the emphasis in primary education is on 'modern methods': 'New Mathematics', 'Creative English', 'Projects', 'Learning to Learn', 'Discovery Techniques' . . . high sounding but rather vague terms. . . . Spelling, handwriting, punctuation and comprehension have had far too much attention in stereotyped formal English teaching, and tables are 'out'. Freedom is replacing sergeant major authoritarianism and didacticism in the classroom. Timetables are an anachronism. That

51

is, I think, a fair summary of present day educational trends.... But how many primary schools have, in recent years, been conducted in a rigid, repressive way?... To have strict silence and rigid discipline with much mindless learning by repetition is unnecessary and undesirable, but to go to the other extreme is, if anything, rather worse.... It would seem to be a negation of commonsense if one were to deny the right of a cultivated adult to pass on his knowledge in anything like a didactic way.[14]

It was arguments such as these which did much to construct the debate about primary school curricula during the next two decades.

The other key element in the *Black Paper* critique was the demand for a greater focus on the core curriculum at primary level, and this, too, quickly became a central issue whenever the primary school curriculum was under consideration. As one of the contributors to the second *Black Paper* put it:

It is the task, and duty of the primary schools to ensure that basic skills, or the three Rs, should be learned as soon as possible.[15]

The view that the key role of the primary schools was to establish the basics of literacy and numeracy attracted wide support. The result was a growing contrast during the early seventies between what was actually going on in the schools and what a large section of the popular press claimed to be the case. One 1972 HMI Report commented favourably on the work being done in a large sample of open-plan schools, even though these were still but a small minority of the overall total. Similarly, the 1975 Bullock Report failed to substantiate claims in the press that standards were falling in the primary sector. This was also the moment, historically, when a number of schools experimented with the Initial Teaching Alphabet. This attempt to accelerate the acquisition of reading skills was to prove a gift to traditionalists, and soon petered out.

It was probably in 1976 when, for the foreseeable future at least, the freedom of the professionals to pursue their own private debate about the nature and content of primary school curricula was decisively blunted. The two developments which did most to bring this about were, first, the appearance of the Auld Report on the William Tyndale School, and second, the publication of the Bennett Report. At the William Tyndale School, an attempt by the teaching staff to develop a 'child-centred' curriculum was, after a lengthy and acrimonious dispute, forestalled by the Inner London Education Authority: the Auld enquiry was initiated to adjudicate. As Brian Simon has pointed out, what mattered most was the public impact of the Report rather than its contents:

Teaching had been brought into disrepute.... Immense damage had been done to the teaching profession as a whole. Teachers' traditional control of the curriculum – their autonomy – was called into question.

52

Teachers, schools, even local authorities as a whole, must be made 'accountable'. It was only after the Tyndale affair that the whole 'accountability' movement swept the schools and their teachers.[16]

The Bennett Report, resulting from a major research project conducted at the University of Lancaster, was widely reported as being critical of child-centred approaches to primary school teaching. The gloss which was put on it by the educational press was that children benefited most from 'traditional' teaching methods and from teaching situations which were carefully structured and teacher dominated. This report, coming at the same moment that Prime Minister James Callaghan initiated the 'Great Debate' on education, kept primary schooling in the public eye and further weakened those who spoke up in favour of experimentation.

Although the retreat from progressivism was gradual, it became steady and inexorable from this time onwards, as the government first gave itself stronger means to influence the primary school curriculum and then began to use them to increasing effect. The establishment of the Assessment of Performance Unit in 1975 to monitor what was going on in schools, and the setting-up of the Taylor Committee in the same year, were early portents. A direct result of the Great Debate was the Government's Green Paper, *Education in schools*, which spelt out the growing determination to take the lead in educational reform. Within a few months Circular 14/77 required all local authorities to report on the curricula followed in their schools. There followed, as Jayne Woodhouse has put it:

a flood of central guidelines from the DES and HMI...aimed towards establishing a common area of the curriculum together with agreed aims and objectives for all stages of compulsory schooling.[17]

Perhaps the most significant of these documents was the HMI survey, *Primary education in England*, published in 1978, which, on the basis of widespread research, debunked the myth of falling standards and showed how little the primary schools had in reality progressed beyond the heavily didactic methods and restricted curriculum of the elementary schools.

The Oracle research project undertaken at Leicester University between 1975 and 1980 also threw doubt on the extent of the classroom revolution which had taken place in the primary schools. In a summary of this research, Brian Simon concluded that:

teaching was found to be largely didactic in character. The promotion of enquiry or discovery based learning appeared almost non-existent....As regards the content of education, a major emphasis on 'the basics' was also found...There was little evidence of any fundamental shift, either in the content of education or in the procedures of teaching and learning.[18]

Despite this, the years after Thatcher's assumption of power as Prime Minister saw a steadily increasing determination by the DES to control the curriculum, both at primary and secondary level. The Department's *Framework for the school curriculum*, published in 1980, stressed the need for traditional approaches and emphasised the core curriculum. Opposition to this document came directly from the NUT, and by implication from the Inspectorate, whose *View of the curriculum*, published at almost exactly the same time, saw education as far more than the utilitarian acquisition of information. There can be little doubt that this rift between the administrators, working on behalf of the politicians, and the educational professionals helps explain the marginalisation of the Inspectorate (and eventually its complete restructuring) during the 1980s. Increasingly, it was to be DES policy statements and ultimately legislation which were used to impose the governmental view.

This was precisely what happened in the event in respect of the primary school curriculum. *The school curriculum*, published in 1981, was far more assertive in tone. Mark Carlisle emphasised that this document represented 'our own firm views. We want education authorities and schools to be guided by them.'[19] Three years later at the North of England Education Conference, Keith Joseph was spelling out the need to specify far clearer objectives for every stage of the school curriculum. The *TES* commented that the government was planning 'a more direct assault on the primary school curriculum than anything so far attempted'.[20] Shortly afterwards, the appearance of *The organisation and content of the 5–16 curriculum* marked a toughening of the DES line. But this itself was to be overtaken when, two years later, the House of Commons Education, Science and Arts Committee produced *Achievement in primary schools*, taking the direct oversight of the primary school curriculum away from the DES and placing it under Parliamentary scrutiny. This called on the Secretary of State, as part of his or her role, to draw up curricular guidelines which should be followed by local authorities and schools.

In this context, the enactment of the 1988 Education Reform Act was little more than an increment in a lengthy process. By introducing a National Curriculum, the Act made clear that, in the last resort, power lay with the Secretary of State. Working through the Schools Examination and Assessment Council and the National Curriculum Council, the Secretary of State was given the power to reject or modify any proposal and, in effect, to completely disregard the representations of either professional bodies or the teachers themselves. Primary education was now redefined as Key Stages One and Two, both to be the subject of Standard Attainment Tasks so that children would be tested at every stage of the educational process. Working under the supervision of the Secretary of State, the Task Group on Education and Testing (TGAT) ensured that primary school teachers had little direct control over the curriculum they were to teach. This measure threatened to transform the atmosphere of the primary schools, and it was only because it was to prove extremely difficult to implement that the teachers retained any significant influence. If the power of the professionals to specify the primary school curriculum was destroyed in 1988, their continuing ability to interpret it in practice was to ensure that their complete marginalisation was, in the long run, impossible. But the details of that process must await an account of more recent developments. In the context of this book, we must limit ourselves to the observation that, at primary level, by 1990 the pendulum had swung clearly in favour of governmental influence in curriculum matters. That emphasis ensured that the move towards child-centred approaches to teaching, which had been most marked during the late sixties, but which had never had the widespread influence its opponents claimed, was for the time being, at least, a thing of the past.

SECONDARY EDUCATION

At secondary level, the period 1964 to 1990 was no less traumatic, and the overall outcomes were to prove remarkably similar. For those working within the secondary sector (the author was a young schoolteacher at that time) the sixties and early seventies seemed to be a period of ferment in which more or less every aspect of the curriculum was undergoing significant change.

Although much of the innovation and impetus to reform took place within specific subject boundaries, there was a wider context which needs to be borne in mind. First, the attack on streaming was as well-established at secondary level as at primary. Most of the comprehensives already at work had been obliged to stream fairly rigorously so as to reassure parents that the needs of 'the grammar school child' were not being lost sight of. The appearance, in 1970, of *Half way there* probably marks the high point of the de-streaming movement at secondary level.[21] During the following few years many secondary schools, particularly the new comprehensives, experimented with new modes of arranging children, following the suggestion by Benn and Simon of various ways in which the comprehensive schools might move away from strict streaming arrangements. They reported that there were:

a significant number of schools definitely moving over to non-streaming. It seems clear that this movement is still gaining pace.[22]

Although many of these arrangements stopped well short of complete de-streaming, involving variants of 'setting' and 'banding', these strategies did reflect widespread reservations, at management level at least, about the continuation of a system of secondary education which systematically separated one child from another.

A second factor which had widespread implications was the drive to ensure that the transmission of information and the whole process of learning was made more efficient in schools. The shock administered by Russian entry to the 'space race' reverberated throughout the English-speaking world. This, together with the growing awareness that schools would need to be in touch with economic changes which were themselves accelerating quickly, meant that educationalists were particularly susceptible to new ideas on pedagogy. It is no coincidence, then, that Jerome Bruner's view that the key function of the teacher was to give pupils an understanding of the central structure of the problems inherent in topics being taught reached a wide audience.[23] Bruner's work had first received attention in the late fifties, but the appearance of his *Towards a theory of instruction* in 1966[24] ensured that he was to be a leading figure during the following period. Ideas such as these became the staple diet of tutors in the expanding Colleges of Education. No less significant was the thinking of Krathwohl and Bloom, whose attempt to identify *A taxonomy of educational objectives* (in other words, to strip each item of learning down to its basic components) had an impact on pedagogic debate in every area of the secondary school curriculum.[25]

Another issue which impinged generally on curriculum reform was the fact that discrete subject boundaries were themselves under criticism from some educationalists. Although hardly anyone was advocating a complete abandonment of subject distinctions, one spin-off from some of the courses being advertised at the new universities, and also from North American theorists, was that the pressure to think in terms of grouping particular subject areas became powerful during the late sixties. One particularly influential thinker in this respect was E. Fenton, whose work on the teaching of social studies advocated what he identified as an 'inductive approach' on the part of teachers.[26] The outcome was that a small but significant number of schools experimented with new subject groupings within the social sciences; the post-war civics movement gave way to the drive for a new approach to the teaching of Social Science, by which attempts were made to reflect the new directions in academic sociology, politics and economics within the schools. Similarly, History, Geography and Religious Education became likely targets for amalgamation of one sort or another. In some schools experiments were tried in the teaching of integrated sciences, and this initiative was to culminate in the balanced science courses which were widely adopted for external examination purposes during the 1980s. The precise nature and extent of these shifts is a subject for much closer study in its own right, but in this context, it is important not to overlook the fact that cross-curricular links were becoming important considerations for secondary school teachers.

Also, it is important to bear in mind the changing context within which teachers worked at this time. The expansion of teacher training, and the drive towards an all-graduate profession, coincided with a new determination on the part of young teachers to set about the implementation of these new ideas in practice. Local authority teachers' centres, together with a plethora of in-service courses, many of them concerned directly with pedagogic issues, meant that familiarity with these new ideas became one of the criteria by which teaching competence came to be judged. The Schools Council Working Paper No. 10, published in 1967, had advocated the establishment of stronger teachers' groups to plan curriculum development and, in response, a number of local authorities set up teachers' centres: by 1968 there were over two hundred such centres at work. During the late seventies and into the eighties, the emphasis of much in-service work shifted inexorably away from classroom practice and towards management issues. But, for a short while at least, the widespread availability of ideas on pedagogy made the implementation of this new thinking appear to be more than a pipe dream.

All of these ideas and initiatives might have been expected to impinge on pupils across the whole range of secondary education, and seemed particularly pertinent for the technologists and engineers of the future and for those who would hold positions of responsibility. But a coincidence of events conspired to ensure that the group of pupils who were most affected in practice were those in what were thought of as the middle and lower ability bands. First, the 1963 Newsom Report, *Half our future*, focused discussion on the needs of this group, and the general acceptance that the school-leaving age was to be raised in the early seventies to sixteen (this was, in the event, implemented in 1972) led to much of the effort on curriculum reform being focused in this area. At the same time, attempts to broaden external examinations for both sixteen and eighteen-year-olds sharpened the focus on the needs of this same group. The introduction of CSE examinations in 1965 meant that there was now an examination route available for the 'Newsom child', and much effort was spent on seeking to make it as 'user friendly' as possible. Similarly, calls to broaden the existing 'A' level examinations led to proposals for qualifying examinations at the end of the lower sixth year (Q levels) and a smaller number of further examinations (F levels) at age eighteen. Although this plan, which emerged from collaboration between the Standing Conference on University Entrance and the Schools Council, was quickly shelved, the discussions which led to it involved a focus on the needs of the student of middle ability, or 'the new sixth-former', as some commentators called the members of this group. The result was that most of the impact of the curriculum reform movement at secondary level was felt in the new comprehensive schools and by a particular group of pupils. For those within the selective sector, the battle to defend the *status quo* meant, by and large, a rejection of novel approaches which could be castigated as a dilution of standards. Thus the gap between the 'haves' and the 'have-nots' was ironically widened rather than diminished by the curriculum reform movement during the sixties and seventies.

This emphasis was certainly reflected in a number of research projects and reports during the late sixties and early seventies which grappled with the problem of how best to cope with those pupils who would be staying on for an extra year and would not have done so but for the raising of the school-leaving age. The second Schools Council Working Paper, *Raising the school leaving age*, published in 1965, called for a major restructuring of school programmes and a closer linkage between schools and the employment market. Its view of the implications of ROSLA was unequivocal:

> More of the same will not bring success. It is not the 'extra year' that makes the difference.... What is at issue is the bringing of the best traditional view of what constitutes a liberal education within the grasp of ordinary people.... How can all be brought to have some kind of hold on their personal lives and on their place in, and contribution to, the various communities ... in which they play a part.... The view of the curriculum put forward in this paper is therefore holistic.... It should possess organic unity.[27]

This was followed by *Society and the young school leaver* in 1967, which advocated a 'total curriculum' involving a range of established school subjects. Similarly, from 1967, the Schools Council's Humanities Curriculum Project, which was to have a wide impact, devised a set of strategies which involved both the scrapping of existing subject boundaries and a new approach to teaching by which the students themselves took responsibility for structuring their own learning. A more conservative approach was adopted by the Keele Project on Integrated Studies in the Humanities. This sought to preserve existing subject boundaries but to achieve integration through what was, in effect, closer collaboration between school departments.

Perhaps the key agent of this 'golden age' of teacher autonomy in terms of curriculum definition at secondary level was the Schools Council. Even the circumstances of its establishment showed the extent to which teacher involvement in curriculum reform was thought to be paramount. Having referred in the Commons in 1960 to 'the secret garden of the curriculum', David Eccles set up the Curriculum Study Group in 1962 as a 'relatively small, commando-like unit making raids into the curriculum'.[28] It was to comprise HMIs, administrators and outside advisers. In the political climate of the time, this arrangement proved virtually impossible to implement. The chorus of protest from teachers' unions and other professional lobbies was so loud that Edward Boyle was forced to transmute the Group into the Schools Council in 1964 and to guarantee that teachers were made central to its working. The resulting commitment of the Council to teacher involvement in curriculum reform was shown by one of its own pronouncements a few years later:

> We believe the surest hope for the improvement of the secondary school curriculum lies in the continuing professional growth of the

teacher, which in turn, implies that teachers take even greater responsibility for the development of schools' curriculum policies.[29]

If we turn to look briefly at the issues raised in respect of individual subjects at secondary level, there can be little doubt that the struggle for control of the English curriculum has been among the most fiercely contested and the most politicised. The tradition which had emerged in the expanded grammar schools of the post-Second World War era, and which has remained deeply influential, was that which saw the teaching of English as involving an apprenticeship in the craft of writing (involving much teaching of sentence structure and of grammar generally) and an introduction to great literature. By the mid-sixties, with the growth in the number of comprehensive schools and a concern for the needs of 'the average child', a third element became more prominent, and this was the need to promote personal growth through the teaching of English. Leslie Stratta was a key figure, collaborating in the widely used *Reflections* textbooks and working behind the scenes to develop a National Association for the Teaching of English. The result was that a growing number of teachers came to place emphasis on creativity, on the pupil's personal development and on the wider social implications of language use. This trend became one of the early targets of the *Black Paper* authors. As Peter Gordon and Dennis Lawton have shown, 'English teaching was often singled out for special abuse' by the New Right in an attempt to re-establish more traditional approaches.[30]

It was probably the fact that the 1975 Bullock Report, *A language for life*, generated a furore in the popular press, with suggestions that standards of literacy were falling, that led to the emphasis on the teaching of English in the *Yellow Book* a year later. This document, reflecting on the fact that schools were becoming 'too easy going', called for the refurbishment of better basic standards in the teaching of English. At the same time, many teachers of English were beginning to find room for work on dialect and the vernacular, giving greater credence to the pupils' own language in an increasingly plural society. Consequently, the growing emphasis in English teaching on a wide range of skills, including oral communication and listening, took place within a context which demanded a strong element of formal work. This tension was reflected in the 1988 Kingman Report on the teaching of English and in the new National Curriculum itself, which identified speaking and listening, reading, writing, spelling, handwriting and presentation as all being necessary attainments in English.

In respect of the teaching of Mathematics, too, the period saw a retreat from the progressivism which, during the 1960s, threatened to revolutionise the teaching of the subject. Under the influence of Jean Piaget, whose work on *The child's conception of number*[31] was widely influential, teachers of mathematics set about the modernisation of their subject with a will. During the 1960s several important projects were at work, among the most notable being the School Mathematics Project, the Mathematics for the Majority Project sponsored by the Schools Council, and the Nuffield Mathematics Project. Their emphases were slightly different: while the SMP focused on approaches to the teaching of number, the other projects were, by and large, more concerned with the logical structure of mathematical problems. The Mathematics for the Majority Project sought to relate mathematical operations more closely to the day-to-day concerns of the pupils and their immediate environment. But all had the effect of eroding the attachment to formal operations, to Algebra and to Euclidean Geometry, which had become the staple diet of the grammar schools during the twentieth century and was threatening to transfer itself to the new comprehensive sector. It is worth remembering that a significant number of the departmental heads in the pioneer comprehensives, especially in what were seen as key subject areas such as Mathematics, had themselves begun teaching in grammar schools and were all too likely to fall back on tried approaches in their new schools when confronted by parental concern that there should be no lowering of standards.

All of this made the Mathematics teachers as soft a target for the New Right as the teachers of English. In *Black Paper Two*, Rhodes Boyson commented scathingly that

> discovery methods though useful in stimulating the mind are dangerous if people grow up thinking that they can in their life time discover what it has taken 10,000 years of human history to achieve.... People must learn the theorems of Euclid and the grammar of a foreign language. Traditional methods of study are generally short cuts to knowledge.... The attempt to achieve understanding by all pupils of the rules behind Mathematics and other subjects can often fail because most pupils rightly see education as a tool and not as an end in itself and want to use logarithms for their future work without worrying as to why they give the right result.... It is good that pupils should understand the reasons for long division, but not if it means getting their sums wrong.... Learning needs discipline, not the atmosphere of a Butlin's holiday camp.[32]

The 1976 *Yellow Book* stressed the complaints of employers that school leavers often had no proper grasp of mathematical skills and emphasised too the problems of teacher recruitment in this area of the curriculum. This difficulty, which persisted throughout the 1980s, meant that it became inevitable that the promise of curriculum reform was blighted by the attentions of the New Right. Accordingly, in the run-up to the 1988 Act, Kenneth Baker's demand of 'bench mark' mass testing in Mathematics steamrollered the TGAT suggestion of problem-solving approaches to secondary school Mathematics. As Brian Simon pointed out, Mathematics was only one of three 'core' subject areas (the other two were Science and

English) in which the Secretary of State intervened immediately after the passage of the 1988 legislation to ensure that the details of the National Curriculum were in line with government thinking.[33]

The pattern was similar in respect of the teaching of secondary Science. Here, the strong influence for reform was the Association for Science Education, a body which was particularly sensitive to trends in university-level teaching and to the chronic problem of recruitment to the sciences, first within schools and consequently on to university courses. The ASE had the backing of and worked with the Nuffield Foundation, which, since the early sixties, had been funding projects on the teaching of Science at secondary level. Much of its work was subsequently taken over by the Schools Council. There were several elements to this work. First, it was designed to make Science teaching less didactic and more pupil-centred by focusing on the process of discovery rather than the transmission of facts. This was also thought to be a likely way of enabling school Science to keep in touch with what was fast becoming a bewildering rate of acceleration in scientific research. Much effort was thrown into examination reform, and Science became one of the pioneering areas for multiple choice questions in external examinations. Yet, in this there was a strange irony. Although numerous enlightened university tutors gave their support to the new Nuffield 'A' level syllabuses in Science subjects, which appeared during the 1960s, it soon became clear that the more prestigious university Science departments often discriminated against potential students who were following the more innovative syllabuses. As in other subject areas, the inherent conservatism of many university dons worked as an impediment to curriculum reform at school level: the perceived needs of the most able continued to dictate the teaching received by the majority. Yet, when Ministerial attention was turned to the teaching of Science in the 1980s, this subject area proved to be as susceptible as any other to interventionism. In 1983 Keith Joseph overruled the ASE which was at that time attempting to broaden the Physics syllabus at 16-plus. He specified that the courses on offer must not extend to any consideration of the social or economic implications of Science. This precipitated a furious response from the ASE, which claimed that the ban stemmed from governmental fear of the peace movement.[34] Be that as it may, it was certainly clear evidence of the government's growing determination to control what was going on in the secondary schools in every area of the curriculum.

For teachers of History, the late sixties was a time when little short of a revolution in secondary school teaching seemed to be under way. The use of historical documents through archive teaching units offered a way of introducing pupils to the study of History, and there was a vigorous debate on the History curriculum which seemed likely to replace tried 'Eurocentric' and nationalistic syllabuses with course content which reflected the dramatic changes taking place in the study of History at university level. The

Historical Association was one strong agent for change, with John Fines being a key figure, encouraging the establishment of local teachers' groups. Increasingly influential from the mid-seventies onwards was David Sylvester, seconded from the University of Leeds to head the Schools Council History 13–16 Project. Its materials were widely adopted in schools and had a significant impact on both syllabus content and teaching method.

But it was unthinkable that a subject as politically sensitive as History would escape the attention of an increasingly interventionist government. By the mid-eighties, Keith Joseph was telling the History teachers that it was their responsibility to teach the shared values which were a distinctive feature of British society. Pluralism was to be met by a teaching profession which, in respect of History teaching, should 'foster pride in Britain' and teach past national achievements. In the event, the National Curriculum for History confirmed that the role of History teachers was to involve little more than national propaganda.[35] Although it proved impossible to put the clock back completely, and much of the pedagogic practice enshrined in the new History curriculum reflected the significant advances achieved by teachers of the subject over the previous three decades, the reality once again was that governmental intervention had put the brakes on a process of renewal which was well-established but which was seen by some on the Right as threatening the assumptions which underlay their hegemony.

The teaching of Geography was also an area of controversy during this period. By the 1960s the old 'capes and bays' approach to the subject in secondary schools had been largely supplanted by the teaching of regional geography, but it was the dramatic shift in Geography teaching within the Universities which was to be the stimulus for reform in this area of the curriculum. The trend towards more scientific and quantitative modes of study was communicated to teachers by enthusiasts such as Peter Haggart and Richard Chorley, organisers of the Madingly Conferences, at which teachers were brought into contact with developments in higher education. This trend was confirmed by three Schools Council Projects, all modelled to some degree on the North American High School Geography Project. These were Geography for the Young School Leaver, the Geography 14–18 Project and the Geography 16–19 Project. By the early eighties, materials produced by each of these three project teams were being widely used in schools. Geography for the Young School Leaver was taken up by over 60 per cent of all secondary schools, and the examination introduced at 'A' level by the University of London to examine the 16–18 Project quickly became the most popular paper at 18-plus in this subject. Keith Joseph addressed the Geographical Association in 1985, spelling out the seven key components of the Geography syllabus; this was met by a response from the Association in 1987, *A case for Geography*. It was very probably this dialogue between the professionals and the politicians which secured the place of Geography as a Foundation Discipline in the National Curriculum. But the extent to which this obscured a deep divide in the ways in which Geography was perceived as a school subject emerged clearly in the implementation of the 1988 legislation. In September 1991 a *Times* leader commented gloomily:

> The government's long campaign against Geography continued yesterday. The Education Secretary... was unrepentant in refusing to make it compulsory in secondary schools up to 16... Mr Clarke had added insult to injury by criticising the techniques of physical and social geography teaching.... Rooted in scientific empiricism, Geography is less vulnerable to the charge of subjectivity thrown at some Modern History teaching. Its relevance to the experience of pupils has been increased by project-based teaching methods.... It is, as it always was, the ideal foundation for all the Sciences.... Mr Clarke, parroting the cries of his backwoodsmen, calls for more knowledge of world place-names. Of course, such rudimentary fact-packing is a part of learning, but when did Mr Clarke last attend a Geography lesson? The essence of Geography lies not in reeling off the rivers of South America. It lies in understanding the nature of the earth and the occupation of it.[36]

In this instance, the skill of the professionals in engaging the government in a dialogue which secured the future of their subject could not obscure the fact that, at its heart, as with every other area of the secondary curriculum, the debate on what should be taught and how was deeply politicised.

There were parallels in other subject areas, too. During the 1960s teachers of Modern Languages were beginning to move away from heavily didactic methods focused on the teaching of grammar, with 'direct method' teaching seeming to offer a panacea. The introduction during the 1970s by local authorities of graded tests in Modern Language subjects, on the model of the graded tests available to music students, took the pressure off teachers to ensure that all pupils worked at the same pace. More individualised methods became possible. Under the influence of the growing army of TEFL courses, the other key trend of the 1970s was towards an emphasis on communicative language skills rather than grammatical accuracy. This was backed by an HMI Report in 1977. Yet, during the 1980s, the emphasis by the New Right of the links between language skills and national economic survival led to a renewed emphasis on grammatical competence which the selective schools, in particular, had throughout been loth to abandon.

In respect of Physical Education, the situation of the mid-sixties was neatly encapsulated in the depiction of a Games lesson in the film *Kes*, in which bored, wet and miserable adolescents were bullied into a soccer match which only a few of them relished. Several factors generated the major changes which took place in this area of the curriculum. First, there was a growing realisation that skill levels were as important as team spirit, and this was reflected in new approaches to the teaching of team games. Second, the growing evidence from the health authorities that inactivity was a

63

contributory factor to many illnesses led to an emphasis on exercise physiology and health-related fitness during the seventies and eighties. Further, one consequence of affluence was the availability of a far wider range of adult leisure pursuits, and the schools found themselves under pressure to introduce pupils to a similar range of activities. The popularity of gymnastics, largely derived from Sweden, posed an issue for teachers of Physical Education by threatening to reinforce gender distinctions, since this was far more popular with girls than with boys. But, by the late eighties, the contest for the curriculum was taking on a familiar pattern. While the professionals who devised the details of the National Curriculum identified six activity areas (athletics, dance, games, gymnastics, swimming and outdoor pursuits), the government was falling back on the importance of success in team games and the need for traditional sports such as cricket, rugby and soccer not to be lost sight of in secondary schools. It was governmental pressure, too, which led to the abandonment of the idea that pupils should take responsibility for the planning and evolution of their own involvement in Physical Education. This was an important recommendation of advisers in this subject during the 1980s, but was lost sight of in 1988.

Religious Education had, for over a century, been the 'hot potato' in political contest around schooling, and in many ways remained so during the period under review, although it did not eventually emerge as a Foundation Subject in the National Curriculum – a strange irony in view of its being the only compulsory curriculum area in 1944. In the post-war era it was usual to refer to Religious Instruction, and this designation was a fair reflection of the approach to teaching. During the 1960s the research of Ronald Goldman, deeply influenced by Piaget, threw doubt on the validity of a Biblical emphasis in RE, suggesting that approaches which built on the pupils' own experience were more likely to be meaningful. Goldman's *Readiness for religion* reconciled a child-centred approach with an introduction to Christian faith. In similar vein, Harold Loukes (a Quaker educator) argued for a 'problem-centred curriculum' which took students from the study of specific issues towards an understanding of their religious significance. All this was summarised in Matthews's influential book *The RE revolution*. By the early seventies, the influence of thinkers such as Peters and Paul Hirst was forcing further reconsideration, leading to RE being seen as a 'form of knowledge' in its own right. One implication of their work was that progressive approaches to the subject in schools were neglecting its autonomy as a discipline. The outcome was that, through the seventies and eighties, the contest continued between those who wished to emphasise the introduction to a discipline and those who sought to broaden the pupils' insight through a child-centred approach.

Hardly surprisingly, confronted by a society which was increasingly plural in religions as well as social terms, Margaret Thatcher's successive Governments fell back on an emphasis on Christianity. As early as 1975, the Birmingham Local Education Authority had been one of the first to allow the study of both Marxism and Humanism, considered as 'world religions' in their schools within their agreed RE syllabus.[37] In the run-up to the 1988 Act, Kenneth Baker was keen not to re-awaken controversy over the RE issue, and sought to marginalise it in the debate. RE was not identified as a component in the National Curriculum. The Act instructed schools to 'recognise that the principal religion of Great Britain is Christianity', but it also allowed for 'the study of other religions'. However, it proved impossible to avoid protracted debate on the religious implications of the Act, in the House of Lords particularly. The government deftly extricated itself from this impasse by identifying a 'basic curriculum' of which RE was not a part, but by insisting that 'RE and the subjects of the National Curriculum' would be obligatory in schools. In contrast to other subject areas, it was to be left to the local authorities to superintend the details of RE teaching in their schools in the light of local needs.[38]

Two further points are worth making. First, it is ironic but perhaps not entirely surprising that the subject which was most under threat in the secondary sector, Classics, was that which experienced some of the most innovative curricular reform. The Cambridge Schools Classics Project, masterminded by Clarence Greig, shifted the teaching of Greek and Latin away from language and literature towards the study of the Classical world as a whole. There can be little doubt that this enterprising initiative did much to slow down the decline of Classics in schools. Second, it must be emphasised that the debate over vocationalism has to be seen as a part of this general picture, but since it has already been extensively covered in Chapter two, it is consciously omitted from this brief survey.

These separate but interrelated battles over curriculum content at secondary level were part of a deeper, more general set of transformations. Their significance can be analysed in several ways. First, underlying the debate on syllabus and content in each of these subject areas was a divide which, at its base, had to do with views on the extent to which the whole process of teaching could and should be democratised. At the risk of crude over-simplification, it is possible to identify two sets of justifications, two underlying rationales, which each had quite different implications. On the one hand, the thinking of Piaget, which impinged on the debate in each subject area, may at the time have appeared to be essentially child-centred in that it rested on and deployed thinking on the nature of the child's own intellectual development. But, just as the ideas of Piaget, when applied to the primary sector, led to concepts such as 'reading readiness', which by implication meant that children required different and separate treatment in the acquisition of language, so at the secondary level, they engendered a vast body of research, much of it pursued during the sixties and early seventies, which threw into doubt the ability of all pupils to benefit equally from teaching. Studies of cognition were undertaken in most subject areas as researchers struggled to identify the specific demands of discrete subjects and the extent to which pupils could master them. In studies of adolescence, what preoccupied these researchers was the acquisition of formal thought, especially in subject areas which were perceived to involve abstract thinking. In History, the work of W. A. De Silva and R. N. Hallam on styles of thinking carried with it the suggestion that there was a process of natural maturation in abstract thinking which took place at different rates in differing adolescents and which meant that some aspects of the subject were unsuitable for younger pupils.[39] At one extreme this set of ideas could be extended to the point at which some pupils were seen as never developing to the point at which they could fully comprehend the issues under review, could never aspire to fully autonomous 'formal operation' in respect of abstract subjects. Goldman's work on RE had similar implications,[40] as did that of researchers such as C. Board and D. J. Satterly in the field of Geographical understanding.[41] Viewed in this light, it becomes easy to see how a body of research which had the study of the child's development at its heart could be used to vindicate separate tracks at secondary level and even the preservation of separate types of school.

On the other hand, the work of Jerome Bruner was, at its heart, profoundly democratic, posited on an essentially optimistic view of human potential and stressing the ability of pupils at any stage of development to grasp the essential elements of any set of ideas, providing they were properly structured and the central issues under consideration were laid bare. Thus, it must be borne in mind that the debate about 'child-centred' approaches to schooling, which impinged on both the primary and secondary sectors, is not a debate which can automatically be construed as undermining established and hierarchical structures and traditional approaches to teaching. It was possible, in the late sixties and early seventies, for teachers to be in touch with much of the latest research on the teaching of their subject without necessarily being committed to root and branch reform in questions of pedagogy or of the structure of the secondary school system as a whole. In this sense there was an ambiguity at the heart of the debate on secondary pedagogy which belies attempts to construe contributions to the discussion as being politically to the right or to the left; it was perfectly possible, for much of the period, to argue that, in the best interests of the child, separatism was appropriate, or conversely, to find evidence which supported the opposite view. In brief, the research which addressed these issues was itself, from the start, politicised, and this consideration must influence the view we take of it in retrospect.

Second, it needs to be emphasised that the full weight of curriculum innovation was felt, either in the 'middle ability' bands, or else in schools located in particular types of suburb. The commitment of the elite sector (the independent grammar schools) to academic excellence as they construed it meant that these were unlikely locations for extensive curriculum reform.

While teachers in these schools rightly prided themselves on being in touch with current thinking, they were, by and large, unwilling to jeopardise their students' futures by experimenting with pedagogy. When the National Curriculum was introduced in 1988, the independent sector remained aloof, as might have been expected in view of the developments that had taken place over the preceding thirty years. In so far as the external examinations themselves underwent change, these schools responded, but there remained throughout the period a tacit alliance between the universities, the examination boards and teachers in high-prestige schools, which had the effect of damping down examination reform and thereby of retarding curricular change generally. In this respect, the contest for the curriculum became a significant element in preserving and even extending the 'tracking' element in education.

Underpinning the contest over the curriculum was the deeper issue of exactly which pupils would be the recipients of particular styles of teaching and particular subject content. In the light of issues raised elsewhere in this book, it seems probable that, unwittingly, what was being moulded in the debate on the school curriculum was a situation in which it became increasingly likely for students from differing backgrounds (females, or children in working class areas or ethnic minority pupils) to each receive their own education, different in kind and degree from that on offer elsewhere within the system. The extent to which it is possible to identify sub-groups which, either through social or geographical location, underwent their own version of secondary schooling is worthy of much closer study and is an issue which necessarily follows from a historical account of curriculum reform of this kind.

If this was, indeed, the dynamic of the contest for the curriculum during the period, it goes at least some way towards an explanation of the ongoing fight over who, precisely, should be the arbiters. During the sixties and seventies the debate on the school curriculum was conducted largely among the professionals themselves. Teachers, local authority advisers who were recruited in large part from the teaching force, HMIs who had by definition begun their own careers in the classroom, and educationalists, teacher-trainers and researchers in the University Education departments: these were the key participants in discussions of what should be taught and in what ways. In so far as government was directly involved, it depended on professional advice, sometimes given through agencies such as the Schools Council, sometimes drawn from research which focused on pedagogy. The role of parents was largely to be the passive recipients of what was on offer to their children in the schools: the stance of the press and the media in general was, if not deferential, at least respectful towards the professionalism of teachers.

The growing interventionism of government, which was evident in both the primary and the secondary sectors, followed naturally from social trends which were deep seated and appear in retrospect to have been irreversible and even inevitable. Increasing affluence gave power and confidence to parents as the consumers of educational services, marked by a steadily increasing preparedness to question what was going on in schools. This changing stance was mediated by the press, reflecting the social trends which caused it and insidiously accelerating and promoting it. By the late eighties, the increasingly critical stance of the popular press towards state schooling had put teachers semi-permanently on the defensive. It is worth remarking, though, that it was a particular grouping within the parental body (in the State sector at least) which was best placed to benefit from this new power. The growing middle classes involved themselves more than ever before in support and ancillary activities around their own children's schooling. This involvement became increasingly one of the tokens of membership of the new middle class, so that a lack of interest in one's own children's' schooling became, if not a stigma, at least socially problematic.

It is hardly surprising that this situation generated new directions in curricular reform and resulted in a greater rather than less contrast between the styles of schooling available to differing social classes. A whole nexus of fringe curricular activities became the domain of this group. The Council for Education in World Citizenship, the Combined Cadet Force (particularly strong in the better-known selective schools and in some public schools), Scouting, Outward Bound activities, music groups and school orchestras, organised inter-school games competitions, skiing trips; these were among the range of increasingly popular school activities. There were, admittedly, vigorous efforts to ensure that they were made available to pupils from disadvantaged backgrounds, but in reality they became the stamping-ground of the new middle classes. Even in those large comprehensive schools which fought to ensure that pupils from as wide a social range as possible were given access to activities such as these, the reality was that they quickly became dominated by the children of the new middle class. It may be naive to think that it might ever have been otherwise, but from the historical point of view, these fringe activities have to be seen as another key element in the differentiation of curricula.

Increasingly, it became accepted that it was the responsibility of government to control these processes more directly. The underlying dynamic was that those social groups which benefited most from change were looking to governments to confirm their position, and those governments were increasingly loth to alienate potential support. Thus, the growing impact of the New Right on school curricula has to be seen, in retrospect, not as some kind of historical aberration but as an appropriate and hardly surprising response to the changes that were taking place in the deep structure of society. The drift of Labour, under Prime Minister Callaghan, away from the established party rhetoric on educational issues (which has been elegantly chronicled by Clyde Chitty[42]), and the shifts in Conservative policy during the Thatcher years, which Richard Johnson and other have identified,[43] were all responses to social change as much as symbols of the re-emergence of entrenched right-wing hostility to popular education. The further drift of Labour policy under Tony Blair is a continuation of the same process.

Given this, it was to be expected that the professionals, whose commitment to the needs of children vied with and usually marginalised a commitment to differentiation between them, would find themselves under increasing pressure to relinquish their grip on curriculum reform. The changing role of the Inspectorate, the steady oppression of the local authorities and the growing call that the teachers must be answerable to their publics, were all elements in the shift in power which, by the late eighties, saw government (largely driven by a popular rhetoric drawn from press representations of classroom practice) as the controlling force in matters to do with teaching style and subject content. The curriculum had 'gone public', but the particular public which exercised most influence in the debate was, whether it realised it or not, imperceptibly moulding schooling to its own children's' needs. Just as the post-war educational settlement had in the event confirmed the position of the middle class, so the emergent structures of the late twentieth century were ensuring that the education system remained the key agent for the intergenerational transmission of social advantage. By the later years of the century, to be middle class meant, among other things, to have been a successful user of the transformed education system. Curricula, both formal and informal, had become as never before the passports to secure employment and full acceptance among the enlarged professions. It is this key social function which explains the nature of the changes which took place in school curricula between 1964 and 1990.

HIGHER EDUCATION

In 1964 there were 126,000 students in British universities. By 1980 there were over 300,000. During this period, the proportion of female students rose from just over a quarter of all students to almost a half. In the process the age participation ratio rose from 7 per cent to 17 per cent. These are the raw statistics of the growth of British universities and they emphasise the almost kaleidoscopic nature of the structural changes which were the context for the debate over the curriculum. They were matched by similarly significant developments in the non-university sector, with the CNAA becoming a new, and extremely influential, validating agency for degree-level courses, and with, from 1970, the new polytechnic sector confirming the binary nature of the provision of higher education. During the mid- and late eighties, the growing overlap between the work of the universities and the polytechnics became increasingly evident (although significant distinctions were also apparent), as the template for a doubling of the size of the university sector by 1992 was laid down. The extent of the democratisation of higher education which these developments involved is clear from the statistic that, by 1990, almost one third of eighteen-year-olds went on from school to one or other full-time course of study. In sum, these changes were far more pervasive than those occurring within the schools, and no account of curricular change can ignore them.

The catalyst of this transformation was the 1963 Robbins Report, the first attempt by government to survey the whole post-school provision of formal education. Its publication marked a high point in respect of the planning of higher education in post-war Britain, and it spelt out the main issues and the major lines of development which were to preoccupy those in the universities and the colleges of technology for the following decade. Its significance lay in large part in the fact that, in the event, there was a major attempt to implement its main proposals, particularly during the late sixties while Labour remained in office. The spelling out of the 'Robbins principle', by which places were to be made available for all appropriately qualified students who wished to proceed into higher education, meant a doubling of numbers in less than ten years. The Report led to the immediate recognition of six new universities and the upgrading of the colleges of advanced technology which now became technological universities. It should perhaps be added that the financial implications of this expansion were soon pointed out to Harold Wilson's Government by civil servants such as Toby Weaver. Arguing that 'a substantial part of higher education should be "under social control" and "directly responsive to social needs" ' because it was answerable to local rather than national government, Anthony Crosland announced the launch of thirty polytechnics in 1965 (they were to begin work in 1970) and so ensured that the implementation of Robbins would be through a 'binary' system. Within a few years the CNAA overtook the University of London as the British institution awarding the greatest number of degrees: after 1970 it went on to become the key agent for the expansion and redefinition of these polytechnics. The recognition of teacher training institutions as Colleges of Education offering three- and four-year degree courses largely determined the form which the sudden expansion of teacher training in the late sixties was to take, and left the colleges in shape to participate fully in the spate of mergers and restructuring which was one key development of the early seventies. Equally, the Robbins recommendation that the University Grants Committee should now come under DES rather than Treasury control was one development which made possible greater governmental direction of the whole system of higher education during the seventies and eighties.

But, although the context of the debate on the curriculum was in these respects rather different from that of the primary and secondary schools, the main elements in the contest were remarkably similar. Three key issues can be discerned. First, by the mid-sixties, there were already well-established contrasting views on the degree of specialisation which was appropriate on higher education courses. This continued to be a major concern throughout the period under review, although by the mid-eighties the question had become far more one of academic departments seeking to defend their positions in a situation in which, increasingly, the prescribed 'core content' of the specialist honours degrees specified by most universities was being lessened and students were showing a greater willingness than ever before to exercise their right to choose popular courses. Second, the debate over the extent to which curricula in higher education should be geared to vocational ends mirrored that which took place at secondary school level. As with the schools, it was the most prestigious courses in the best-known colleges and universities which proved to be most resistant to the claims of vocationalism. Third, the growing susceptibility of educationalists to the demands of central and local government was as evident in higher education as elsewhere. The seventies and eighties saw a gradual erosion of the independence of those making key decisions on the nature of the curriculum in all sectors of higher education.

Over-specialisation was the central issue for the planners of the new universities. By 1964 the process of identifying appropriate courses for the new universities was well under way. The avoidance of that over-specialisation which was thought to be a major characteristic of existing courses was the main aim, and the planning process posed a major threat to established practice by raising what were seen increasingly to be issues of principle impinging on curricula across the whole range of higher education. The curriculum of the University of Keele (which took its first students in 1950), with its insistence on a year of general study prefacing courses in which all students followed elements of the humanities, the social sciences and the pure sciences, posed a challenge for the planners of the new universities. Academic Planning Boards were set up to take responsibility for the academic affairs of these new universities. They represented a range of interests, both local and national, and were to be one key instrument in the attack on 'departmentalism'. Noel Annan, the Provost of King's College, Cambridge, was involved in the planning of the curriculum for the new University of East Anglia, and became one of the most vocal and influential critics of established practice, arguing that the universities were ripe for change. In his view, it was the departmentalism of universities which had led to the over-specialisation of many honours degree courses. This over-specialisation had resulted in students having difficulty relating what was learned at university to the world at large, and also had the effect of reinforcing narrow subject boundaries and specialised courses within the schools. In common with many critics of existing practice, Annan did not see the widespread introduction of general courses as offering a panacea, but did anticipate a greater variety in degree courses. Another contemporary critic was Asa Briggs, then Professor of Modern History at the University of Leeds,

71

who argued for a complete reconsideration of the 'map of learning' since science and the humanities had come to inhabit separate continents. As the call for curriculum reform became more widespread, the National Union of Students told the Robbins Committee of its reservations about single-subject honours degree courses, and the Incorporated Association of Assistant Masters reflected in its evidence that

> there seems to be a good case for providing honours degree courses with less narrow specialisation covering a related group of subjects. These more general honours degrees would give wider opportunities to those seeking higher education and be able to fill some of the demands of industry, secondary education and other professions.

The planners of the new universities set about providing this diversity with a will. At Sussex, where the curriculum had been formalised during the early sixties, it is hardly surprising that elements of the Keele experiment were incorporated, since the first Vice-Chancellor, J. S. Fulton, had himself been closely involved in planning the Keele programme. Deeply influenced by two of the first appointees, Asa Briggs and David Daiches, Fulton and his Planning Board devised a curriculum which also drew on the Oxford School of Modern Greats (Fulton once described Sussex University as 'Balliol by the sea'). The outcome was the adoption for each student of a 'core' of specialised work which was to be contextualised within Schools of Study. Schools of European Studies and of English and American Studies ensured that Modern Greats was reinterpreted at Sussex in forms which were seen to relate the new university to contemporary issues. A similar, if more muted, attack on over-specialisation was mounted at the University of York. Here Lord James, the first Vice-Chancellor, enshrined his view that the attack on over-specialisation was best made from within the subject boundaries. The outcome was that, while York imposed more stringent demands for subsidiary courses than most pre-exiting universities, single-subject degree courses were available in several areas of the curriculum. However, the organisation of social science courses at York was closely modelled on Sussex. As the University's Development Plan spelt out, the intention was to 'avoid both the narrowing effect of extreme specialisation and the lack of purpose in extreme generality' by 'a due spread of integrated subsidiary subjects, grouped around a major subject'.

At Norwich, the University of East Anglia, which admitted its first students in October 1964, was also deeply influenced by the Sussex plan. Schools of Study became the device for broadening the curriculum, with the School of European Studies prominent. Perhaps the greatest element of novelty at East Anglia was the award of classified honours degrees based in part on course work and seminar performance. One commentator observed drily that 'course credits had swum the Atlantic'. The accreditation of course work was another element which threatened to transform existing curricula and had implications also for the modes of teaching adopted. At East Anglia, too, an attempt was made to lessen the stranglehold which the universities had on the development of Advanced level studies in the secondary schools. The first Dean of the School of English Studies, Ian Watt, persuaded his colleagues that a pass in the relevant Advanced level subject need not be a prerequisite for entry to all undergraduate courses. This stratagem enabled the development of teaching in Russian and German, neither of which was popular in the schools.

At Essex, which also admitted its first students in 1964, academic schools were to be the device which enabled increasing specialisation in succeeding years of the undergraduate course. Albert Sloman, the first Vice-Chancellor, stressed in his Reith Lectures that the universities still had a responsibility for study in depth. At Essex, progressive specialisation enabled 'students to make choice of subject on the basis of university experience in a number of subjects. Yet the range of ... related subjects will be sufficiently restricted for the student to gain some knowledge of each in depth'.

A year after East Anglia and Essex opened their doors, the first students were admitted to the University of Kent at Canterbury. Here, too, the key figure was the first Vice-Chancellor, Geoffrey Templeman, and his vision was far more that of a reworking of the Cambridge tripos. He called for the establishment of specialist departments in which the development of critical understanding would take precedence over the mere accumulation of knowledge, and echoed the immediate post-war debate on higher education by stressing that he thought it

> no longer tolerable that many scientists should continue to maintain an attitude of indifference ... to the larger consequences of what they do. It is no longer good enough for them to say that their business is with science ... and that what others make of what they discover is no business of theirs.

At Kent, too, progressive specialisation was to be the watchword of the undergraduate course. For Charles Carter at Lancaster, the objective was to establish courses which brought different disciplines together. This was to be achieved through the identification of major and minor elements in degree programmes, and Boards of Study, rather than traditional Faculties, were to be the arbiters of what was and was not acceptable within each degree programme. Lancaster, probably more than any other new university, was seen to be drawing on the conventions of the American liberal arts college, and Carter's efforts to establish marketing studies at Lancaster from the outset were further evidence of the debt to North America.

Only one of the new universities, Warwick, made any significant attempt to link more closely with industrial and commercial developments. Although the group of academics who hammered out the details of the Warwick curriculum was deeply influenced by the Sussex scheme,

Vice-Chancellor John Butterworth returned from a visit to the United States in 1963 determined to establish a School of Business Management, and, under his guidance, Warwick became the one new university to make determined attempts to enlist funding from local industries. Within a few years the extent to which these ties were eroding the academic autonomy of the institution led to a vitriolic outburst by E. P. Thompson, who resigned his teaching post at Warwick in protest. But there is little doubt that this emphasis helps explain why Warwick was able to ride the discomforts of the 1980s more readily than several of its rivals.

All of this curricular innovation reverberated around pre-existing institutions. It was not simply that university teachers who were in one way or another disaffected with practice in established universities made a conscious choice to work within these new universities where novel academic traditions were being established. Within a few years the movement of staff was in both directions, and university teachers who had experience of the delivery of these new curricula began to find their way into older institutions. This, together with the established practice of external examining, which had the effect of standardising teaching and curricula across the whole university sector, ensured that the civic universities, and even to some extent Oxbridge, made at least some response to the criticisms of over-specialisation. Although it would have been unrealistic to expect wholesale transformation of institutions which were well-established and generally respected, no university was exempt from pressure for a broadening of courses at this time. In most of the big civic universities the response was the establishment of complementary study courses or series of broad background lectures which forced all students to consider a range of issues beyond those covered by specialist honours courses. In 1960 the University of Birmingham launched a programme of interfaculty studies, which within a few years had been broadened to become a complementary studies course made obligatory for all first-year students. Encouraged by an enthusiastic Professor of Electrical Engineering, Jack Allanson, the University sustained this scheme throughout the seventies. Staff who were committed to a liberalisation of undergraduate curricula were encouraged to participate, and the present author was only one among many contributors to these courses. This model was widely imitated, as most universities at least doffed their caps in the direction of a broad, liberal education, while making little effective change to established specialist honours degree programmes. Similarly, at Oxford in January 1964, professor W. C. Neale was appointed to chair an interdepartmental committee to review the whole structure of the first and second public examinations. Although the modifications which emerged were marginal, this review emphasises that no institution was exempt from these pressures.

In his book *The Crisis of the University*, Peter Scott has argued that the values of the liberal university have been challenged in recent years by the emergence of the modern university, committed to a different set of ends. If this is the case, it may well be that these attempts at curricular reform during the sixties and seventies are best seen, historically, as an attempt (possibly the last one) to reassert the values of the liberal university in a form which gave them viability into the late twentieth century. The distinguishing characteristics of this liberal university were its commitment to the education of an elite who were encouraged during their university years towards a world-view which involved a critique of scientific and technological practice. There can be no doubt that those who were involved in this debate on university curricula, whatever their slant, shared the assumption that the universities were key elements in a modern democracy, enshrining values and a cultural inheritance which were essential to the continuation of democracy itself. It is interesting to observe that those who fought against the erosion of single-subject specialist honours degrees during this period often based their defence on the argument that, in a situation in which knowledge itself was undergoing rapid, even kaleidoscopic, transformations, and research was accelerating at an unprecedented pace, the only way for universities to remain central to this process was to allow those within them to devote themselves to specialist study in established departments, simply to enable them to keep abreast of and participate in the changes taking place.

It is interesting to note, too, that among the technical colleges it was those which had the strongest aspirations to be recognised as universities themselves that this drive to ensure that all students were exposed to courses which had this liberalising aim was most strongly felt. Malcolm Campbell has shown how Birmingham's College of Technology, as soon as it received recognition as a CAT in 1956, initiated a search for an appropriate general studies element for all students which was still under way when the institution became the Aston University of Technology in 1965.[44] Courses on the links between technology, science and social life, and on the social problems of industrialised societies, as well as aesthetic and humane studies, were made obligatory for all students. Similarly, at Salford, the Royal Technical College had insisted that all students, whether on full-time or sandwich courses, must follow a minimum two-hours-a-week programme of social studies. This, too, became an integral part of the curriculum when the college became recognised as a technological university.

Just as one of the prime movers for general education at Essex had been Jean Blondel, who had begun his teaching career at Keele, so at Bradford the key figure was Paul Coles, who had worked alongside Blondel in the Keele Politics Department during the late fifties and early sixties. Coles's contribution to the debate at Bradford was to infuse courses in industrial administration alongside general studies in an attempt to equip Bradford graduates with the appropriate qualities to assume positions of leadership in quickly-transforming industries. There were similar initiatives at the Brunel

College, at the Battersea College of Technology (soon to become the University of Surrey), at Chelsea College of Science and Technology, at Bath, and at Loughborough. Loughborough's Principal, H. L. Haslegrave, emphasised that liberal studies was to be the key to 'the development of the complete man, including his character and mind'. Within the Colleges of Advanced Technology, the debate was almost always conducted in gendered language of this kind and made assumptions about the leadership roles which their alumni would assume. It seems that this process and this rhetoric were almost a necessary part of the transformation which resulted finally in recognition as a university institution.

If the degree of specialisation which was appropriate was one key theme in the debate on curricula within higher education, another was the extent of vocationalism. As was argued in Chapter two, attempts to establish courses linked more directly to employment were widespread during the sixties and seventies and had profound implications, both in terms of an understanding of what constituted a university and in respect of the 'tracking' functions of English education, the process by which children were born to particular social locations and followed largely predictable educational routes which steered them towards particular forms of employment and lifestyle.

Two further points need to be made here. First, the rate of change in the economy at large forced universities to respond to the information revolution and to changing patterns of recruitment by establishing courses in Information Technology and Business Studies, and obliged them also to offer new components within existing courses. Changes in the mass media, generating new employment opportunities, resulted in Media Studies becoming an increasingly popular degree alternative. By the end of the 1980s, such courses were well-established in most universities and offered a large range of choice to undergraduates. Second, the demand from employers for recruits who would be flexible and adaptable had a direct spin-off within higher education by inducing students to adopt a more 'consumerist' approach to their studies. Steadily, over the period covered by this book, the prescribed specialist degree course gave way to a more modularised syllabus, within which students were given much greater opportunity to exercise choice. This erosion of pre-existing curricular patterns began in the new universities, but was soon evident across the university system. A third outcome of all this was that, given the growing sense of insecurity about employment which impinged upon all students as the spectre of mass unemployment became a semi-permanent reality during the 1980s, students came to take a more instrumental view of their studies. This had the effect of eroding the perceived significance of the curriculum debate which had been so prominent a feature of the sixties and seventies. By the late eighties, the discussion of a liberal education and how it might best be implemented had been completely marginalised; the focus in public debate was far more on how to ensure that university courses enhanced the employability of students, and this was often construed within narrow limits. A final outcome was that competition for those courses which seemed to offer good chances of prestigious and relatively secure employment became, if anything, greater. Law, medicine, some departments of business studies and a few elite schools of engineering were able to call for the highest grades in Advanced level examinations. Meanwhile, the relatively sudden shift towards a mass system of higher education left the less prestigious universities, and many of the departments in polytechnics, struggling to fill their places or to find sufficient students who had qualified through established examination routes. One positive outcome of this situation was the development of access courses, but the fact that, by and large, they steered disadvantaged and mature students towards the less prestigious institutions and departments meant that a further twist was given to the social selectivity of the system of higher education.

All of this took place in the absence of any meaningful debate upon the mode of delivery of university courses, or indeed of courses in higher education generally. During the 1970s most universities appointed one or two staff whose brief was to advise on teaching methods, but in the main their role was confined to setting up introductory courses for newly-appointed lecturers. Student counselling units became fashionable, often modelled on the pioneering work of Jan Wankowski at the University of Birmingham, but, as often as not, their brief was the alleviation of stress rather than any initiatives which led to a reform of teaching methods. By the end of the 1980s many institutions were beginning to monitor the quality of taught courses, although all too often this involved another increment in the bureaucratisation of the system rather than any significant reform of teaching.

The one initiative which did promise a major step in terms of teaching method was the Open University, masterminded by Jenny Lee, a close colleague of Harold Wilson with wide experience in the Workers' Educational Association and the Labour movement. Her 'university of the air' carried with it the promise that 'distinguished lectures' could now be broadcast to millions of listeners. There were to be correspondence courses 'of a quality unsurpassed anywhere in the world... reinforced by residential courses and tutorials.' What was envisaged became, as some commentators called it, 'the university of the second chance', with recruitment being exclusively from among the adult population. After some initial inter-Party sparring over whether this was the best way to use public money for what was, in reality, a safety valve to enable quicker realisation of the Robbins targets, the Open University took its first 25,000 students in January 1971, and quickly became a recognised element within the higher education sector. Although in reality it did not offer the opportunity of a version of university education to large numbers of adult working-class students, as was originally planned, the OU did help precipitate further reconsideration of acceptable teaching methods in higher education. During the following two decades, many institutions experimented with distance learning; the Open University was an important model for them.

Overshadowing these debates on curricula within higher education was the deeper issue of who precisely should control and supervise its growth. It was clear to all contemporaries that the Robbins revolution, as it was becoming known, involved closer planning and supervision of higher education by the State. One outcome was a right-wing backlash, which ironically was soon to appear to be in complete contradiction to the New Right policies of the 1980s which involved much tighter control by government of the higher education system. In the late sixties, the opposite was the case: Harry Ferns at Birmingham, Sydney Caine, Director of the LSE, and Max Beloff of All Souls, Oxford, became the leading advocates of an independent university which would be completely free of State interference. They argued, in a petition drawn up in December 1968, that

> the machinery for relating the State and State finance to the universities has become clumsy and wasteful and leads to increasingly resented measures of detailed control which handicap experiment and innovation. . . . We consider that a new approach to syllabus and ' teaching methods would enable an independent university to develop its own forms of excellence which could rival the best in the existing system.

After protracted and unsuccessful negotiations to find a body which would accredit the awards of the new institution (both the CNAA and the University of London became involved in negotiations but, in the last resort, baulked at the prospect), the Independent University of Buckingham opened its doors to 68 students in February 1975, prepared to awards its own 'licences'. In the event the degree of curricular innovation involved was minimal, but the challenge to a planned system of higher education was patent for all to see.

It was perhaps the difficulties faced by Buckingham in its early years (it was eventually awarded a Privy Council Charter at Margaret Thatcher's behest in 1984) which led to it being the solitary example of an independent university founded during this period. It soon became clear that the trend towards tighter governmental control which had been heralded by Robbins was accelerating, and that all institutions of higher education (whether they were in the university sector or not) were becoming increasingly subject to public policy. In an attempt to put a bridle on the runaway costs of an expanding system of higher education, the UGC was brought under much closer control by successive governments. In 1965 it was placed under the aegis of the DES, and was later used by both the Labour Government of the late seventies and Thatcher's subsequent Conservative Government to implement economy programmes which made the achievement of the

Robbins proposals an impossibility at the same time that politicians were proclaiming their continuing commitment to expansion. The autonomy of the UGC had already been eroded by the abandonment of quinquennial planning in favour of annual financial targets: by the late seventies it was becoming impossible for it to continue to act as a buffer between government and academia. It fell to the UGC, however, to implement the swingeing financial cuts imposed in 1981, and its preparedness to give a shape to the economies which largely disregarded Thatcher's rhetoric may well have sounded its own death knell. By 1984 the Jarratt Committee had been set up to advise on the efficient administration of the universities and it placed a question mark over the continuance of the UGC. In July 1985 the Croham Committee was constituted in order to review the position of the UGC. In April 1987 a White Paper confirmed that, in line with the proposals of the Croham Committee, a new Universities Funding Council was to begin work and the UGC would be done away with. At the same time, the National Advisory Board for Public Sector Higher Education would be replaced by a Polytechnics and Colleges Funding Council. The imposition of a financial stranglehold had completely marginalised debates on the curriculum. Whereas during the late sixties and early seventies academics had the autonomy and self-confidence to engage in protracted debates about appropriate curricula, and a variety of new institutions and modified practices emerged, by the 1980s what was becoming an increasingly undignified struggle for survival, both individually and collectively within institutions, meant that this looked more and more to be a thing of the past. Like schoolteachers, whether they liked it or not, academics were becoming the deliverers of curricula which in some cases (such as the 1984 regulations on the content of teacher training courses) were precisely specified by their political masters and in others were forced through the imposition of market and financial considerations. In the arena of higher education, financial and political constraints conspired together to impose a particular form on discussion of the curriculum. By the late eighties, the sense of ferment and innovation which had characterised the two previous decades had given way to a spirit of hard-nosed entrepreneurialism. The passage of time may show gains from these changes, but for those who have lived through them it is hard not to conclude that something precious has been lost.

4

SUBURBS AND SCHOOLS

One key determinant of the education system as it has developed since 1964 has been the continuing suburbanisation of English society. This period has seen the extension and rounding-off of processes which were under way as long ago as the late nineteenth century, and these have impacted directly on the schools themselves. The steady march of the towns into the surrounding countryside is something which has been going on since the coming of industrialisation. Liverpool extended its boundaries seven times between 1895 and 1952, and other cities did likewise, so what is under review in this chapter can hardly be seen as a novel phenomenon. What is important in the context of this book is the linkage between the rise of a salariat, the coming of new forms of commuting (in particular the rise of the motor car) and the patterns of owner occupation and council provision which have given a particular shape and significance to the development of housing stock in England since 1964.

At the start of the twentieth century most people in England lived in rented accommodation. The provision of housing by local authorities was insignificant and, as recently as 1914, only 10 per cent of the housing stock was owner-occupied. At the end of the First World War the Addison Act marked the start of the effort to build homes fit for heroes in the form of a significant number of council houses. It was the larger towns and cities which committed themselves to the development of large overspill council estates on what was then the fringe of the residential zone. By 1939 these estates were transforming the periphery of most of the larger towns. In cities such as London, Liverpool, Leeds, Manchester and Birmingham, similar strategies were employed to relocate significant numbers of the respectable working classes who could afford the relatively high rents on the outer edge of the conurbation. The fact that it was the larger cities which took most advantage of the governmental subsidies available before 1939 meant that they were to have a rather untypical distribution of types of council housing stock once the post-Second World War expansion of the public sector had taken place.[1] This was the first factor to impinge directly on schools in recent years; different cities with differing kinds of council house accommodation and contrasting council estates.

At the same time, during the inter-war years, there was a steady growth of private housing, much of it by way of ribbon development along the arterial roads, with the result that these new homes were the first beneficiaries of electrification and the supply of commodities which have become taken for granted since the Second World War. These new owner-occupied homes of the inter-war period helped to establish once and for all the desirability of a home of one's own in modern Britain. They also served the unwitting purpose of marking out the more desirable suburbs as the scramble to build new homes developed after the Second World War. To the south of Manchester, Altringham and Alderley Edge; to the north of Newcastle, Gosforth; on either side of Birmingham, Sutton Coldfield and Solihull; near Leeds, Alwoodley and Roundhey, all became likely targets of the post-Second World War boom in owner occupation.

Thus, much of the pattern of the immediate post-war expansion in the housing stock was given shape by earlier developments. The governmental commitment to owner occupation during the 1950s, together with the continuing availability of governmental grants to support the building of council houses by local authorities, led to an extension of these patterns into the mid-sixties; more overspill council property on the periphery of the cities and a growing number of first generation owner occupiers in new, semi-rural locations, as the cities and towns spread ever deeper into the countryside.

With the town planning movement at its height, supported by the post-war consensus that it was possible for government (both national and local) to take advantage of the best advice available to devise a better environment in which their citizens could live more comfortable lives, New Towns and Green Belt areas were designated during the 1950s to pre-empt the worst effects of uncontrolled growth. The majority of the New Towns designated during the immediate post-war period were situated around London to soak up the metropolitan overspill, and it was London in 1938 which had been the first city to be given its own Green Belt; a planning model which was widely imitated by other cities and conurbations in the years following the Second World War.

All of this meant that, by the start of the period covered by this book, the contest for urban living space, which Harold Perkin has called a 'visible gradation into discrete social layers', was already well established and was in several ways predetermining the working of schools in differing suburbs and in different parts of the country. Perkin has emphasised the way in which

the suburbs . . . each catered for the class that could afford that price of house and no more, or that level of rent on a housing estate. The classes and sub-classes sorted themselves out more neatly than ever before into single-class enclaves which did not know or speak to each other.[2]

He has pointed out, too, that one of the ways in which the new lower middle class which had appeared in twentieth-century England sought to distance itself from the working class was by seizing every educational opportunity, whether formal or informal, even those intended for the working class. So it was that Sunday schools, youth clubs, the Boy Scout and Girl Guide Movements and the Workers' Educational Association, as well as the schools themselves, became tokens of the search for respectability; an intrinsic element in the process by which social classes sifted themselves out and became mutually recognisable.[3]

The development of housing policy after 1964 served only to intensify this process. First, the mid-sixties saw the first full harvest of the high rise movement, which had been gathering pace since the 1950s. Confronted by a growing realisation of the need to do something about slum clearance in the old inner-city areas, a concern about the indiscriminate use of space on the edge of the cities, and the current fashion among architects for high rise solutions, town planners turned increasingly to the tower block to transform the old inner-city areas. In 1963 Salford, advised by Sir Robert Matthew, decided to use 22-storey tower blocks to meet its housing crisis. A year later, Southampton, confronted by the determination of the County of Hampshire to preserve a green belt around the town, also determined to seek the high rise solution. By 1966 over a quarter of all new starts in the provision of council property were high rise. It was a policy which quickly proved catastrophic; its death knell sounded when an old lady left the gas on at Ronan Point, in London's Newham, on 16 May 1968.[4]

But although brief, this high rise movement was critical for the development of schooling in modern England. It happened to occur at a moment when local authorities were looking to newly built comprehensive schools to solve the nation's educational problems, and when a particular kind of school design, influenced by the open-plan movement, was also briefly fashionable. The outcome was that the educational face of this redevelopment of the inner cities was the building of a significant number of new comprehensive and primary schools in a particular architectural style which was to date very quickly, and which were located, for the most part, in the least affluent suburbs. The extent to which this was to be disastrous, in the long run, for those in favour of comprehensive education was exacerbated by the fact that it was these very suburbs which housed the highest proportions of the 'visible minorities', first and second generation ethnic minority groups drawn from the British Commonwealth. As a final overlay, these were the very areas of the cities which were to feel the worst effects of unemployment in the economic rollercoaster which developed during the seventies and eighties.

The other face of this deepening social divide, which was to become fully apparent in the social realities and in the educational policies of the later Thatcher years, was the steady expansion of the housing market in the years following 1964. Between 1961 and 1986, the number of owner-occupied dwellings doubled from just under seven million to over fourteen million, while the total number of dwellings rose by a third to over twenty-two million. During the early sixties over 30 per cent of all households were still in privately rented accommodation. By the late eighties, this figure had fallen to less than 10 per cent. What was taking place was a filtering out into the starker social divide of those who owned their own properties (an unprecedented 63 per cent by the late eighties), and those living in council property. Council tenants comprised a quarter of all households in 1961, but a third by 1981. Thereafter there was a slight fall as the effects of the 1980 Housing Act saw the sale of over 600,000 council properties by 1984. Hardly surprisingly, it was in the main the more desirable council houses which were bought by their occupants.

All of this went on against a governmental backcloth of continuing support for the private housing market. Although the question of tax relief on mortgage repayments was occasionally mentioned as an issue by left-wingers within the Labour Party, it never really emerged as a political issue, so that, as Frank Berry points out, what happened in reality was a massive governmental shove in favour of owner occupation: 'the fact remains that at least twice as much of the taxpayer's money is devoted to subsidising owner occupation as is spent on subsidies to public sector housing.'[5]

Leasehold reform in the late sixties ended a large risk factor in owner occupation. The 1968 Town Planning Act confirmed a policy of designating conservation areas, thus helping to guarantee the desirability of some suburban areas, and the 1969 Housing Act gave further help to home owners with the introduction of improvement grants for the rehabilitation of existing housing stock. In brief, it was a golden age for the home owner, reflected in soaring house prices.

The extent to which these trends became increasingly regional is emphasised by a glance at the development of the New Towns movement. The Governmental Commission on the New Towns, chaired by Lord Reith, which reported in 1946, was deeply influenced by ideas of community, seeing units of no more than 10,000 people as the building blocks from which a township of 50,000 might be built. Its Report spoke of the need for balanced communities and emphasised the 'neighbourhood principle' as one which had underpinned its thinking. In part this strategy was based on ideas of what might make for a realistic provision of schools: while these small townships of 50,000 might, it was foreseen, generate one grammar school, each of the smaller units would need one neighbourhood secondary school. But by the time this movement was into its second phase, at the start of the 1960s, much larger urban units were foreseen at Skelmersdale,

Redditch, Runcorn and Washington. Two of the largest, Telford and Milton Keynes, were now given target populations of 250,000 each, well beyond the scope of the original concept. As the pressure of numbers forced the government to think increasingly in terms of expanding existing townships during the late sixties, new targets began to appear. Development Corporations were set up for Peterborough, Northampton, Warrington and Ipswich, and, as a final twist to the movement, the designation of the Central Lancashire New Town in 1970 foresaw the doubling of the population of Preston, Chorley and Leyland to 500,000 within a decade. The age of regional development had arrived and it was no longer possible to consider the provision of social services such as schooling in any township without looking at the distribution of population in the region in which it was situated.

It is important in this context to emphasise, too, that, although this period saw a net gain in housing stock of roughly 250,000 new properties per annum, the growth was far from continuous or steady. The building boom of the late sixties peaked with 425,000 new completions in 1968, but by the early eighties the figure was as low as 181,000, not passing the 200,000 figure again until the end of the decade.

Another element in this transformation of modern England is the extent to which it has differed between regions. The building boom of the late sixties had its greatest impact in the Midlands and the South, particularly the home counties. Equally, the upturn of the 1980s was focused particularly on East Anglia, on the quickly growing residential areas to the West of London (the M4 corridor) and, to a lesser extent, in the Midlands. This meant increasing contrasts between North and South, between the old industrial areas and those dependent on newer technology, and between the old townships and the rural and semi-rural areas around them. The 1980s saw an acceleration of the depopulation of central city areas as the drift into the countryside and into the new, more distant, overspill suburbs grew in pace.

This was all of fundamental importance for schooling, as the shape of the conurbations was inexorably changed, as lifestyles changed within them and as society used this housing market to sort itself out into discrete social groupings which were physically separate from each other as they had never been, and which had differing perceptions of schooling, differing aspirations for their children and made different demands of their schools.

So, any view of the developing social functions of the schools during the most recent thirty years must, of necessity, see suburbs and townships, not in isolation, but increasingly as part of larger conurbations and their hinterland. The accident of birth, a key determinant of location (the area in which a young person was to grow up), of lifestyle and of schooling became, among all these changes in patterns of living, of greater rather than less importance. To establish this more clearly, it is necessary to refer more closely to the development of a particular part of the country. The area chosen is the West Midlands conurbation, the region best known to the author, and particularly appropriate because it brings together elements of 'north' and 'south', old and new industry, in a way that is not always the case elsewhere in the country. It may, therefore, stand as a useful exemplar of broader trends.

Birmingham had been fairly typical of the pattern for the major townships. By 1935 there were already 31 new council estates on the edge of the city. These were not well served with social centres, shops and churches, but most had either elementary or senior elementary schools which became either primary or secondary modern schools after the war.[6] For a further twenty years the City continued to expand its housing provision on the edge of the city, so that newer council estates, or, in some cases, extensions of the old council estates, appeared. Meanwhile, the full impact of Harold Macmillan's and Anthony Eden's drive during the early fifties towards a 'property owning democracy' (as Eden called it shortly after becoming Prime Minister) was felt in other parts of the conurbation. It was in Sutton Coldfield and Solihull (both then beyond the limits of the city) and in the already established lower-middle-class residential areas such as Moseley, Kings Heath, Great Barr, Northfield, Harborne and Selly Oak, that the first post-war boom in private house building was most evident. The city, and the region, were already beginning to splinter into discrete social areas.

This left an important educational legacy for the period covered by this volume, and that is why it is important to look back a little in time in considering the nature of this suburbanisation. It is interesting, for example, that most of Birmingham's grammar schools are situated in these older, well established 'lower-middle-class' enclaves. This is illustrated in Fig. 4.2, which is referred to in greater detail later in this chapter. The existence of some of the more prestigious schools within an area is one of the symbols which work to preserve its status.

What developed in Birmingham is not quite a 'doughnut' of housing areas, as has been suggested by some of the proponents of the Chicago school of urban sociology as a model for town development,[7] but it is sufficiently close to the concept to be worth referring to. Thus, by the mid-sixties, Birmingham comprised an urban centre, with central shopping and business areas, and an old inner ring area, already feeling the impact of planning blight and having within it a disproportionate number of old properties which were, in the main, rented rather than owner-occupied. Further away again from the city centre were the newer suburbs of the twentieth century, whose existence was only made possible by the improving transport system and which were dependent, in the first instance, on commuter trains and more recently on trams, buses and the motor car. It is important to point out, too, that there was a growing 'regionality' about this pattern, with most of the old industrial areas being located on the north side of the city and much of the newer industrial and commercial development being to the south and east of the city centre. So, by the mid-sixties, contrasting characters to different sides of the city were already apparent.

During the 1960s the boom in car ownership, the continuing 'professionalisation' of society, with a growing proportion of the labour force engaged in the tertiary sector, and an unprecedented preparedness, particularly among the salariat, to travel longer distances to work, saw the rise of the satellite townships around the city. Not only was Redditch designated as a New Town in 1964, but during that decade there were significant increases in the private housing stock in Kidderminster, Stourbridge, Bromsgrove, Droitwich, Lichfield, Tamworth and other outlying small towns (see Fig. 4.1). This had the effect of siphoning off what was in effect a new commuter middle class, with home ownership increasingly part of its agenda. For these social groups, commuting became increasingly fashionable. One of its attractions to young owner occupiers, soon to become parents, was the existence of schools in these townships which seemed at least to be apart from the major reorganisation schemes which were leading to split-site comprehensives being opened in the older suburbs of Birmingham itself. Equally important, the economic realities of home ownership meant that children in these schools were likely to be surrounded, in the main, by other young people drawn from not dissimilar social and economic backgrounds. It was a coincidence which made it possible for many parents who had adopted a commuting lifestyle to send their children to 'comprehensive' schools without their having to experience the full impact of that social mixing which some advocates of comprehensives were demanding.

By now the 'desirable' suburban areas had been clearly delineated by this growing new middle class of owner occupiers. By the early sixties it was becoming clear to researchers that the clustering of immigrant communities in the inner city was directly related to housing policy and the patterns of home ownership. The pattern which emerged in Birmingham was similar to that found in London and other cities with growing ethnic minority communities. While a third of the indigenous white community was in council property, only one in twenty of the black immigrant families was similarly housed. This had to do with the system by which the cities assessed families for eligibility for council house occupancy, one important criterion being length of residence. Once forced into inexpensive rented accommodation, or else into owner occupation in the cheapest parts of the city, it was often difficult for black families to re-establish themselves on council housing lists. In many cases those who had been forced into purchasing run-down property were forced into multiple sub-letting to make ends meet. It was a situation which fuelled prejudice on one side and a sense of injustice on the other.

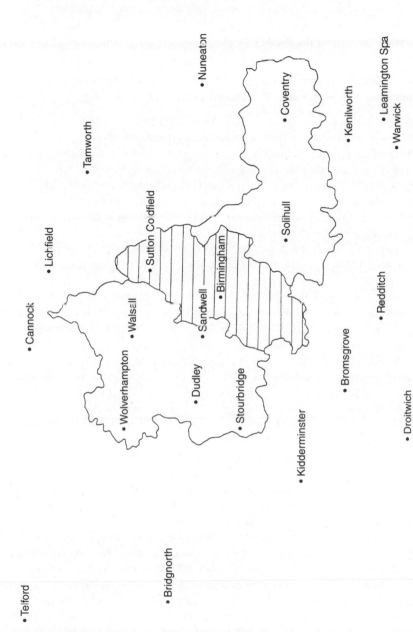

Figure 4.1. The West Midlands Region

The educational difficulties which this clustering of immigrant communities in the old urban areas engendered were summarised by Robson in 1975:

> The difficulty is heightened in the educational sphere, since, given the young age structure of coloured populations, schools in immigrant areas tend to have proportions of coloured children which are much higher than the proportion of coloured households in the area.[8]

The dangers of this situation are clear. All the ingredients existed by the late sixties for a popular association of black settlement, urban decay and the perception of an educational crisis.

This was compounded by the way that the city responded to what was nothing short of a crisis in the supply of council properties during the 1960s. The need to redevelop the old inner ring areas was pressing. This was accomplished in part by the building of high-rise council flats in a ring around the city centre. Newtown, Duddeston, Lea Bank, Ladywood and Small Heath took on a new appearance as tower blocks began to punctuate the landscape. These were the very parts of the city with the greatest density of first and second generation members of ethnic minority groups, forced by income and housing policy in the first instance into the cheapest rented accommodation in the old, decaying inner city areas. Although during the early seventies Birmingham City Council, like many others, did attempt a policy of dispersal of its visible ethnic minorities into the older council estates on the edge of the city, it proved difficult to persuade either the indigenous white community or the relocated black population that this was desirable.[9]

The result was that these new high rise blocks around the city centre became the key location for black occupancy of council property, as the vast majority of those made homeless by this redevelopment were given the chance to move into council property. Inadvertently, the city became 'ghettoised'. The redevelopment of the inner ring area meant that what had begun as a historical accident was now perpetuated by Birmingham's housing policy.

Figure 4.2, which shows the location of some of Birmingham's schools in relation to housing stock during the 1970s, offers a graphic illustration of the educational implications of this suburbanisation.[10] As can be seen, Birmingham's earliest council housing areas (all on the edge of the city) were added to during the immediate post-war period by new overspill estates. The first three comprehensive schools opened in Birmingham, all planned during the late fifties, were located on the edge of the city where these new estates had generated a demand for secondary places. They were at Great Barr to the north, Sheldon Heath to the east and Shenley Court to the south-west. They are indicated by triangles in Figure 4.2. They were schools of a particular type; as one contemporary report summarised it,

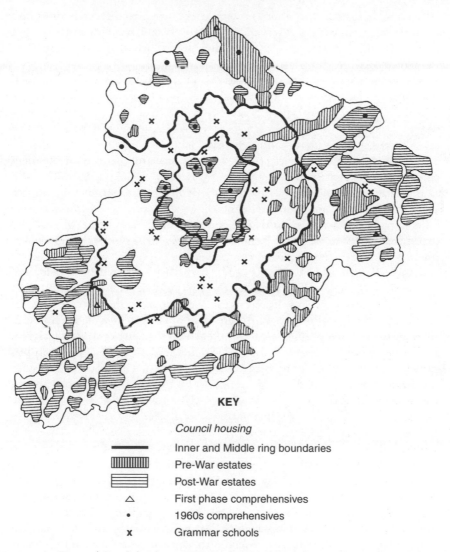

KEY

Council housing

━━━━━━ Inner and Middle ring boundaries

▓▓▓▓▓ Pre-War estates

▤▤▤▤▤ Post-War estates

△ First phase comprehensives

• 1960s comprehensives

x Grammar schools

Figure 4.2. School provision in Birmingham during the 1960s

The earliest comprehensive schools reflect little appreciation of the problem of size in their large monolithic classroom blocks with long corridors, the massed gymnasia, extended lavatories and cloakrooms. The general impression is one of anonymity overawing in its vast architectural scale.[11]

The other council house estates on the edge of the city all either had within their limits, or were adjacent to, secondary modern schools built either just before or just after the war. These were readily converted into comprehensive schools at the end of the 1960s and brought with them a particular social cachet and a reputation as recently-converted secondary modern schools.

Thus, the overspill suburban areas where much of the stock of council housing was located were given, inadvertently, either new comprehensive schools of a particular type, or schools which had existed previously as secondary moderns, bringing with them a vestigial reputation which helped to delineate their future as comprehensive schools.

Within a few years, a series of new schools was being planned for the inner ring areas as part of their redevelopment. Mount Pleasant, in Balsall Heath, Lea Mason and Ladywood, Holyhead, Holte, St George's, Broadway, Duddeston Manor and Small Heath: these were the new comprehensive schools of the late sixties, intended for the children of these rejuvenated urban areas. They are shown by circles in Fig. 4.2, this symbol being used to identify all of the 'second phase' comprehensives designed and built as such and opened during the decade. As can be seen, the vast majority were located in the inner ring areas. The fact that these schools all reflected the building idioms and the design conventions of the 1960s marked them out from other secondary schools in the city. But there were other factors which resulted in their being seen very quickly as comprehensive schools of a very different kind to those on the edge of the city. From the start their population was predominantly black, either Afro-Caribbean or Asian by origin. Within a few years, there was hardly a white face to be seen in these schools, among the student body at any rate. Inadvertently, in a fit of absence of mind, Birmingham had given itself a form of educational apartheid. It was a process which took on a similar form in other cities.

Meanwhile, if we identify all of the grammar schools operating in Birmingham during these same years (indicated in Figure 4.2 by the use of crosses), we can immediately see a very different spatial distribution. These schools were, without exception, located in areas of owner occupation, and, just as the new comprehensive schools helped to define the social class orientation of the districts in which they were situated, so did the grammar schools work, by their very presence, to confirm the lower-middle-class nature of these suburbs.

This fissure within the social class structure of Birmingham was deepened by the fact that, at about the same time, new overspill housing estates were planned on the edge of and beyond the limits of the existing conurbation. Chelmsley Wood, to the north of Solihull, Castle Vale, also to the east of Birmingham and within the city boundary, and at a greater distance Telford, in sum represented a major increment in the provision of council housing, but from the start had a much lower percentage of ethnic minority tenants. What was being created in these areas were new social units, remarkably homogenous in class affiliation and income level. Many of the young inhabitants of these estates were to be among those hit hardest by the economic downturns of the seventies and early nineties. These areas, too, were given new schools, built in the idiom of the day and usually matching architecturally the housing estates in which they were sited. At secondary level they were all comprehensive, but their intake was far from mixed, being drawn almost exclusively from the new housing areas in which they were set.

So, by the end of the 1970s, a conurbation such as that around Birmingham had given itself a stratified schooling system within which schools might be identified as comprehensive, and might be administered from the same local authority office, but found themselves dealing with such contrasting clienteles, in social class, income level and educational aspiration, that it is hardly reasonable, in retrospect, to label them in the same way. The gradations of society were reflected in gradations of attitude to school and to school work. Those who had bought into the 'better' suburban areas did so in the secure knowledge that their children would be surrounded at school by pupils drawn from similar backgrounds, supportive of the school, willing to do homework, reliable in attendance, keen to participate in extra-curricular activities, able to afford the expense of school trips, and more likely to aspire to higher education. For the predominantly white working classes trapped in the outer suburbs, and for the black communities in the inner ring, the experience was otherwise; the fact that these areas were the first to feel the effects of unemployment meant that a far larger proportion of pupils were sceptical about what the schools had to offer them. Aspirations were lower (or, to avoid imposing a social class judgement, different), non-attendance more likely, and the teachers attuned to dealing with what they perceived as 'social problems'.

It is important, too, to see the experience of one part of the country within the broader context. In many senses, what happened in Birmingham was typical of the country at large, and it is certainly true that elements at least of the picture built up for the West Midlands were echoed elsewhere. But in Birmingham, the educational aspect of this structural transformation of society was given particular colour by the decision of the local authority to continue to support several of the King Edward grammar schools at the same time that it determined (at the end of the 1960s) to reorganise all its other schools on comprehensive lines. This local decision gave a sharper edge to the contrasts outlined here in the following years than may have been the case in other parts of the country.

But what is important at national level is the way in which there were significant and growing contrasts between regions in their social composition. Although, by the mid-seventies, almost a third of the country's population was in council housing, the proportions differed widely from place to place. In Bournemouth, at one extreme, there were only 34 council houses per thousand head of population in 1975: in Sunderland, at the other extreme, there were 141.[12] Further, the exact nature of these council estates, and of the schools which served them, was partly determined by when they were built. So, for example, by the mid-seventies in the bigger cities such as Birmingham, Manchester and Liverpool, roughly half of the council houses were pre-war, the other half post-war. In smaller towns, such as Sunderland, Portsmouth and Bournemouth, where council housing had only been turned to by the local councils after the war, the vast majority of council properties were relatively new; in all of these towns, by 1975, roughly 80 per cent of council properties were post-war.

This, in turn, meant that these suburbs were more likely to be 'age related'. The older council estates had not only older schools but, by and large, older populations, with an age distribution contrasting with the newer council estates. So different localities placed different strains on their local schooling systems at different historical moments. Put simply, what this means is that a school was more likely to draw its pupils from its immediate locality during its early years of working, particularly on the council estates, but would be equally likely to extend its catchment as the pressure of numbers was alleviated. Recent research by Michael Bradford[13] has shown that, with the freeing of school catchment areas in recent years, it is hardly surprising that those schools which are situated in the better suburban areas are most likely to expand their catchment. Those in older and working-class suburbs are more likely to find difficulty in attracting pupils from greater distances, and so, in the more fiercely competitive world of the 1990s, they are among those which are most likely to suffer extreme difficulties. This process might take a significant period to work through for individual schools, but undoubtedly it was an important factor in determining the social class allegiance of particular schools for much of the period covered by this book.

Above and beyond this there were significant regional variations in the distribution of the social classes which must not be overlooked in this account. Research by Moser and Scott showed that, by the early 1950s, Dagenham (an old, planned suburb of London dating from the inter-war years) at one extreme had a population of which only 7 per cent were identified as being in the Registrar General's social classes one and two, while at the same time Coulsdon and Purley, on the other side of London, had 45 per cent.[14] Hardly surprisingly, this correlated with other phenomena. In predominantly working-class areas, pupils were more likely to leave school at the minimum leaving age; in Stoke on Trent, for example, 86 per cent of the school population left at the first opportunity. Yet in Beckenham, a predominantly middle-class area to the south of London, only a third of school pupils left at the minimum leaving age. Overcrowding within homes was more marked in working-class areas. As an index of this, it is worth pointing out that only 3 per cent of households in Dagenham were made up of one person, while the figure for a retirement area such as Hove was 20 per cent. In Hove, only 15 per cent of the population was aged fifteen and under: in stark contrast, in Huyton, a Liverpool overspill area, the figure was 31 per cent. Seventeen per cent of Huyton's population lived in homes containing six or more people. In Southgate, in London, the figure was only 4 per cent.[15] These random but pertinent examples establish a further point in the context of this book. It is clear that these contrasting urban and suburban areas were making radically different demands of their school systems. In the middle-class areas, where staying-on rates were higher, the emphasis was far more likely to be on external examination work. The less wealthy urban areas were exactly those which made greater demands of the ancillary services, of the school welfare officers, of special needs teachers and of the growing support systems for ethnic minority pupils.

Some research has suggested that, during the period we are considering, parents were participating consciously in this process of social sifting. Certainly, these trends had their impact on the social composition of schools in different suburbs. Obviously, much of the most well-known research carried out during the early sixties relates to these trends, perhaps most notably that of Jackson and Marsden on Huddersfield.[16] Flan Campbell, working with D. V. Glass in the 1950s, had already shown that one effect of suburbanisation in the south-east was to alter the social class composition of the London grammar schools, with schools in central locations taking more working-class pupils and those in the outer suburbs recruiting a growing proportion of middle-class pupils as their catchment areas changed in their social composition.[17] Robson's research on Sunderland in the 1960s led him to conclude that:

> the area of residence had a strong association with a person's attitudes to education even when occupational status held constant. In other words, it appeared that the milieu of the urban social area had an independent effect on the individual's social outlook.[18]

Research carried out at the University of Birmingham by Steve Guratsky on suburbanisation and schooling in Walsall pointed to the same conclusions.[19] He showed that, by the late seventies, access to comprehensive schools in Walsall was price-rationed through the housing market. He argued, too, that what was happening in Walsall seemed to be a fairly universal phenomenon across the country:

> The basic principle is that each school draws its pupils from its immediate neighbourhood...a principle applied by 51 per cent of LEAs in 1977....Catchment area allocation does not involve any *direct* price-rationing of school places...However, it seems clear that *indirect* price-rationing may occur through the operation of private housing markets.[20]

Guratsky showed that, at the time he was doing his research, Sneyd High

School was seen by parents to be the most prestigious comprehensive in Walsall, and he found clear evidence of a significant number of potential parents buying into the housing estate, thus guaranteeing a place at the school. One other finding relates to the argument of this chapter. Guratsky found that one criterion which made a school seem attractive to parents was its newness, and the fact that it reflected the best recent educational ideas in its design. As one parent put it: 'We've got a brand new school with the best facilities in Walsall'.[21] It goes without saying that the new schools were, by and large, most likely to be found on the new housing estates, thus confirming the linkages between a school and the status of its suburb.

Seen in this light, the campaign of Solihull residents to preserve their best comprehensive school when it was threatened by a return to grammar school status in 1981 was not, as Brian Simon has argued,[22] a triumph for the comprehensive principle but, rather, a middle-class community defending a privileged position which would be threatened by the reintroduction of the competitive criterion of merit alongside that of the ability to pay for housing in the neighbourhood of the school.

CONCLUSION

What does all this evidence add up to when considering the development of education in England since 1964? It does not mean, as may have been inferred from the drift of the argument at times during the chapter, that schools are completely at the mercy of the geographical location in which they find themselves and of trends in suburbanisation and house purchase. Obviously, the reputation, working and status of individual schools depends on far more than that, and it would be wrong to suggest that location has been the key determinant during the most recent forty years. But it has been one vital influence on the development of schooling, and heretofore it has gone largely unnoticed by historians of recent education.

The contrasts in lifestyle and outlook between social classes, which have in some senses deepened in recent times, originate in part in a physical separation which has been reflected in ongoing patterns of suburbanisation. Schools have been obliged to work within this social framework, and in many ways have reinforced it. Differential patterns of access to higher education and to the professions have, in turn, been the result of the school system working within a society which was already stratified through suburbanisation. Although the physical environments in which people live have themselves changed enormously during the period since 1964, in many cases beyond recognition, what we are actually considering is nothing short of a historical process, linking domestic environment, the social class structure and the schools themselves. All are constantly changing; but the nature of the changes which each undergoes is constrained by and in part predetermined by what is taking place in the other two fields. It is,

94

therefore, impossible to understand fully the nature of the changes which have taken place in our education system since 1964 without some awareness of the importance of suburbanisation and its links with the changing class structure.

Equally important is the way in which this interrelationship between schools and their communities has helped to determine the political agenda for education during the period. It is usual for historians to point out how educational legislation and the politics of education are largely conditioned by what is taking place 'on the ground'. Such analyses have been made of the 1902 Education Act and of the 1944 legislation. Yet much of the comment so far on the 1988 Education Reform Act and on the 1986 Education Act Part Two has focused on the extent to which they were influenced by a Thatcherite rhetoric of education, itself reflecting the power of the Radical Right and the sea-changes which had taken place in popular perceptions of schooling. In its extreme form, this approach sees the events of the 1990s as some kind of historical aberration, and it certainly focuses heavily on the debates about education at the cost of a longer look. Yet the 'longer look' which is suggested in this chapter suggests a very different interpretation. The susceptibility of large sections of society to media campaigns which have suggested that the State system of education is, at best, in crisis and, at worst, failing, and the growing readiness to countenance a more competitive education system at the cost of the familiar egalitarian ethic, are also in part reflections of the differing perceptions of schooling which grow up within a society which is itself stratified in the ways outlined in this chapter. Is it possible, and indeed likely, that many of those who have been involved on a day-to-day basis within the education service (and the present author counts himself among them) have been slow to sense the deeper realities of the changes taking place because of their own absorption in a peculiarly English egalitarian ethic, redolent of post-war Labourism and of much of the sociological research of that period which focused on the maldistribution of educational opportunity?

Is it possible that the 1988 Education Reform Act may come to be seen, not simply as an affront to the English educational tradition, but also as a measure which was, sooner or later, inevitable given the ways in which schooling had come to reflect the new social divisions of post-war English society? And is it possible, too, that this glance at the urban context within which the introduction of comprehensive schooling took place forces us to conclude that a movement which set out to promote social harmony and a fairer society was, in reality, doomed from the start because of the changing nature of the society which it sought to serve? Was the promotion of community comprehensive schools itself as likely to divide this newly suburbanised society as to reunite it? These are the gloomy speculations to which this survey of schooling and suburbanisation in modern England draws me.

5

BRIDGING THE GENDER GAP?

Education has been of an uncertain value to women. On the one hand, it has offered opportunities equal to those of males. On the other, it has guided women towards domesticity as effectively as if it had dumped them on a number eight bus to Tesco's.[1]

This quotation captures perfectly the rich irony of the expansion of educational opportunities for females during the period since 1964. There has been a real opening-up of opportunities to participate in a growing number of areas which were previously male preserves, and the legislative framework within which women operate has been significantly changed. But the net effect has been a general reinforcement of gender divisions within society as a whole. If the rhetoric has from time to time suggested that the education system was participating in a major social restructuring, the day-to-day experience of the majority of females has been otherwise. Why was this so?

To answer this question it is necessary to look first at the overall social situation of women in post-war England. By the mid-sixties the 'pronatalist' movement, which emphasised the role of woman as homemaker, was at is height. In retrospect, as several historians have shown, the involvement of women in the war effort can be seen as deadly for the women's movement. Women were idealised as war workers just because they were seen to be doing something which took them beyond their familiar and 'normal' role. Yet, at the same time, the 1942 Beveridge Report emphasised that:

In the next thirty years housewives, as mothers, have vital work to do in ensuring the adequate continuance of the British race....The attitude of the housewife to gainful employment outside the home is not and should not be the same as that of the single woman. She has other duties.[2]

This was to be the ideology which came to predominate in the post-war years, partly because of the widespread fear of a declining population (a fear which Beveridge himself shared). By the late fifties, there had been a reversion to something which was more like the pre-war situation, with two-thirds of all waged workers being male (13.8 million men and 7.2 million women). The well-established pattern of women's work being less secure and less financially rewarding than that of men had been reverted to soon after the war. The circulation of women's magazines, which disseminated a particular view of the mother as homemaker, reached an unprecedented level. As Evelyn Home counselled in the pages of *Woman*: 'It is safe to say that most women, once they have a family, are more contented and doing better work in the home than they could find outside it.'[3]

During the late fifties and early sixties, the 'Miss World' contest enjoyed a peak of popularity, its implications of sexual stereotyping as yet not publicly questioned; it serves as a reminder of the way in which the sexes reverted to established roles and stereotypes in the post-war era.

A further impetus to this pronatalist movement was given by the reaction to wartime evacuation, which was widely viewed as involving undesirable disruption for most of the children involved. One outcome was a fashionable new 'expert' advocacy which emphasised the importance of intimate and continuous child–mother relationships. The publication of John Bowlby's *Child care and the growth of love* in 1953[4] did much to re-establish the view that one key determinant of a child's future was the quality of mothering it received. It was an argument, drawn from the experience of evacuee children, which also inadvertently deepened the sense of guilt felt by career mothers during the fifties and sixties.

The years following 1964 did see a steady upturn in the employment of women; by 1988 they constituted 45 per cent of the labour force. It became increasingly common for married women to work, especially since the woman's contribution to the family wage packet placed more consumable goods and more of the luxuries associated with the coming of affluence within the reach of many families. During the late fifties only a quarter of all married women were in some form of employment; by the late eighties more than half were. The key factors which led to this change all impinged on and were related to schooling. The changes in fertility rates meant that most women experienced a shorter time with very young children in the household: at the same time the formal educational qualifications of women were greater than ever before. Schooling had helped to give to young females the expectation that part, at least, of their lives would be passed in employment. In 1950 the average time which young mothers spent out of employment was over seven years: by 1980 this had fallen to three.

But this steady advance of women into the labour market was on terms which did not threaten the ascendancy of males. During the seventies and eighties, the number of women employed full-time remained steady at 5.5 million. It was the significant increase in the numbers of those in part-time work from 2.8 million to 4.4 million which enabled more women to participate in the workplace. The reasons are not hard to find. The generally accepted expectation that it would be the mother who took the major

97

responsibility for child-rearing and home-making led to the establishment of a typical employment pattern for women, full-time during the early adult years, dropping out to bear children, and returning (often to part-time work) as they grew older. It is worth pointing out a likely linkage between the suburbanisation dealt with in the previous chapter and this phenomenon. It seems to be, at the lowest estimate, probable that as men began to commute greater distances to work their wives experienced a greater pressure to remain within the home or close to it, and thus more likely to seek part-time work.

These trends, in turn, meant that the period after 1964 saw a greater 'gendering' of employment than had ever previously been the case. The characteristic pattern of men and women distributing themselves into different sectors of the economy was intensified rather than lessened. By the mid-eighties more than half of the male labour force found itself in situations which were predominantly (i.e. over 90 per cent) male; a half of all female workers were in situations where the labour force was at least 70 per cent female. Women clustered increasingly in particular kinds of employment, most notably clerical jobs, which by 1986 accounted for half of all females in employment. The minor and caring professions, in particular nursing, primary school teaching and welfare work, all became safe havens for full-time female workers. The part-timers were to be found mostly in catering, cleaning, hairdressing and other personal service occupations. As Pennington and Westover have shown, in their exhaustive study of home working (a type of employment in which females also predominated), there were by 1975 a total of nine million women workers in England, but only one third of these were to be found in the manufacturing industries:

> the rest were concentrated in the service sector. The major employers of women since the Second World War were distribution (shops), the professional and scientific sector (nursing and teaching), and the miscellaneous service industries (catering, laundries and so on). Woman's labour outside the home therefore continued to mirror her work in the home: the majority of female employment involved the servicing of people's immediate needs.[5]

It became increasingly easy for employers to construe new low-prestige jobs (such as the steadily growing army of supermarket checkout workers) as being more suitable for females. And all of this meant, in turn, that there was little erosion of the lower rates of pay historically associated with women's work and little serious threat to the male domination of the major professions. Rosemary Crompton has described this process in some detail, and has argued, too, that, as work became more 'gendered' in the modern period, so gender itself became more clearly identifiable as an aspect of social class.[6] This, too, is a point which relates to the analysis of gender in schools since 1964.

This phenomenon is made all the more puzzling by the fact that this period has seen a growing awareness of women's rights, resulting in significant legislation, and has seen a growing focus on issues which are central to the participation of women in the public sphere. This had not always been the case. The 1952 Income Tax Act confirmed that a wife's income belonged in law to the husband: it was not until 1991 that separate taxation for man and wife was made universal. The women's movement during the immediate post-war period contained within it several strands, one of the most influential being the 'welfare feminism' espoused by campaigners such as Eleanor Rathbone, who had campaigned for many years for family allowances payable to women. This objective was achieved in the 1945 Family Allowances Act, by which the State confirmed the popular assumption that homemaking was an appropriate role for mothers. Now financial support was provided for the return of women from the wartime workplace to the home. So the abandonment by the Civil Service in 1945 of the ban on the employment of married women and the slow progress towards equal pay, finally achieved through legislation in 1970, have to be seen as part of a rather confused and even self-contradictory set of official responses to the clearly recognised need for some kind of State regulation of the conditions under which women entered the public sphere immediately after the war. On the one hand, some legislation was intended to make it easier for women to find employment (although the coming of equal pay for equal work may have inadvertently made it harder for women to compete for jobs); on the other, women's child rearing responsibilities were never far from the minds of legislators.

During the 1960s, what has been called 'a new generation of feminists'[7] began to appear, and their lobbying resulted in legislation which focused more precisely on key issues affecting female participation in the public sphere. The legalisation of abortion in 1967, the 1969 Divorce Reform Act, the 1970 Equal Pay Act, the 1975 Employment Protection Act which gave women the right to six weeks of paid maternity leave, and, in the same year, the granting of women's' entitlement to occupational pension schemes and the banning of sexual discrimination in the workplace, all seemed to hold out hopes of a resolution of long-standing impediments to sexual equality. But again, the day-to-day implementation of each of these new measures has involved side-effects which have not been helpful to the women's movement and the net result has not been a dramatic improvement in the ability of women to participate fully in the public sphere. In some cases the new rights of female employees may have made employers less willing to hire or to promote them, and this may well be one factor which helps explain the growing monopolisation by men of senior positions in education in recent years, which was pointed out in Chapter one.

This, then, is the rather gloomy scenario against which we must assess the developments which have taken place in schooling in respect of gender, and

99

it is a background which at once makes what has actually happened within our educational system far more comprehensible.

At the start of our period, during the 1960s, the growing call for a levelling-up of educational opportunities for girls was heard within the well-established framework that, since girls' future career prospects were necessarily different from those of boys, then the education they received should be limited accordingly. This was one of the underlying considerations which had led John Newsom, in his influential book on *The education of girls* in 1948, to argue for at least three years of separate schooling between the ages of twelve and fifteen.[8] This, too, had been the tenor of a succession of official reports since then. In 1959, for example, the Crowther Report had distinguished between the needs of intellectually able girls for whom it was difficult to devise 'any education specifically related to their special interests as women', and, on the other, the majority of girls whose 'direct interest in dress, personal appearance and problems of human relations should be given a central place in their education'. Accordingly, the Report concluded that 'the broad distinction between boys' and girls' interests...is rightly reflected in curriculum planning....For a good many girls wage earning is likely to seem a temporary preoccupation.'[9]

This theme was picked up in the 1960 Albermarle Report on *The youth service in England and Wales*, which drew attention to the changing pattern of women's lives, adding that 'the shortening of the period between school and marriage leaves less time for the girl to acquire social maturity and technical competence at her job as a home-maker....The Youth Service should make good some of these deficiencies.'[10] In the same vein, the 1963 Newsom Report *Half our future* emphasised the contrasting approach of the two sexes to scientific and technological subjects in school:

> A boy is usually excited by the prospect of a science course...He experiences a sense of wonder and power...the locomotive he sees as a man's response: the switch and throttle are his magic wands...the girl may come to the science lesson with less eager curiosity than the boy, but she too will need to feel at home with machinery.[11]

A. M. Wolpe has suggested that these Reports were written in the shadow of a society and an economy which needed 'an adaptable, pliable and docile female labour source, with only marginal skills'.[12]

Be that as it may, the growing anticipation of a fuller participation by females in schooling and in higher education, which suddenly became fashionable during the mid-sixties, failed to break away entirely from these stereotypes. Although Lionel Robbins clearly saw females as a key part of the untapped pool of ability in higher education,[13] the Report which bore his name in 1963 failed to focus on the contrasts in educational achievement between the sexes, and what it had to say on this topic was largely in the spirit of much which had gone before. The Robbins Report identified early school leaving and a tendency for girls to cluster on teacher training courses as key determinants of the underachievement of women in universities, but then went on, rather complacently, to foresee an expansion of opportunities for females within a gendered employment market:

> training for many of the occupations open to girls does not, at present, fall within the definition of higher education adopted in our Report. But rising professional requirements may in future lead to more girls entering these occupations by means of full-time courses in higher education. Moreover, we discuss in later chapters various developments in higher education (such as new language courses) that may prove particularly attractive to girls. Many who now undertake no further study may, in future, wish to do so.[14]

At the same time, a study published by the Women's' Group on Public Welfare on *The education and training of girls* emphasised that:

> girls' different future roles in society may require a different approach to problems of vocational training.... Women still have their functions to perform as wives; helpers and supporters of their menfolk; and as mothers, trainers and teachers of the coming generation.[15]

Against this background, the realities of boys' and girls' education during the mid-sixties were far from straightforward. The majority of middle-class children attended single-sex grammar schools, while more than half of the children of the manual working class found themselves in mixed secondary modern schools. But the number of comprehensive schools was growing quickly and most of these were mixed. Further, the situation varied from area to area, depending on the social class composition of the region and on the policies of the local education authority. It was also becoming clear at this time that many girls were significantly ahead of boys of the same age at various points in their school career (one survey suggested that, in reading and in physical and psychological maturation, the gap was as great as two years at some stages)[16] yet they continued to leave at an earlier age and to underachieve in external examinations, particularly at eighteen years of age. One factor contributing to this may have been the policy adopted by some local education authorities of actively marking down girls in eleven-plus examinations to ensure a balance of numbers between the sexes in grammar school entry. This problem was exacerbated by the fact that a few local authorities continued to make available more grammar school places for boys because of the historical imbalance in the number of places available in such schools. The outcome was, as we have seen, that in 1964 only a quarter of university entrants were female, while women made up two-thirds of the student population of the teacher training colleges.

Yet, at this time, there were two issues to do with gender which preoccupied the educational press. First, the continuing governmental campaign to get qualified women teachers back into the classroom after having children received almost unqualified support. In March 1965, Tony Crosland, the then Secretary of State for Education, placed an open letter in the *TES* setting a target of 100,000 female recruits to teaching.[17] As the same journal put it in May, 1965, 'the first priority is to get the woman returner back'.[18] LEAs were encouraged to provide part-time teaching employment for young mothers; some, such as Enfield, introduced emergency training schemes for mature female graduates. During the winter of 1964/5 the Bristol authority ran an advertising campaign in the depths of winter, timed to attract housewives who were housebound and depressed. There was no public questioning of the time-honoured assumption that women in general, and young mothers in particular, were the most suitable recruits for primary school teaching. Some echoes of long-held prejudices were heard in the public debate on this problem: Dr D. G. Christopherson, Vice-Chancellor of the University of Durham, commented in one public address:

> The fact is that almost any employer – and headmasters, headmistresses and local authorities are no different from other employers in this respect – will not employ a married women so long as anyone else is available. The thought of possible absences due to children's illnesses is too prominent in their minds.[19]

Meanwhile, the drift towards co-education in the growing number of new secondary schools continued. By the late sixties, as Madelaine Arnot has pointed out:

> The two systems had diverged significantly, with the majority of the comprehensive schools offering co-education, and the majority of private secondary schools retaining their single-sex status.[20]

It was this which triggered the second issue of interest to the press and this was the perceived risk of sexual promiscuity and of teenage pregnancies in mixed educational settings. During January of 1965, for example, the *TES* ran a number of articles expressing this concern.[21] It was a preoccupation which reflected a deep Puritan streak in modern Britain and which did nothing to enhance the prestige of co-education.

Beyond this, the drift towards mixed schooling was seen at the time as largely unproblematic, and even by some contemporaries as being the key to an ending of long-term gender inequalities. As early as 1961 Dame Kathleen Ollerenshaw went on record saying that 'it is largely true...that women have won the battle for educational opportunity with men.'[22] This sense of a situation which was gradually and inexorably tilting in favour of sexual equality was also to be found in the work of R. R. Dale who, between 1969 and 1974, produced three important volumes charting and supporting the shift towards co-education. By 1971 he was able to conclude that:

in spite of the entrenched prestige of the single-sex 'public' schools . . . an educational revolution is now taking place in the schools of England by which it seems probable that most of the children will soon be educated in co-educational secondary schools.[23]

Three years later, the first admissions of girls to public schools seemed to confirm this judgement and enabled Dale to see the outstanding issues as largely administrative in nature:

Today, the climate of opinion has veered round and it is rapidly becoming accepted policy to make schools co-educational. One by one, even the bastions of single-sex education . . . are becoming co-educational or flirting with the concept.

Attention should be given to problems which will become more acute. It is of the essence of co-education that the two sexes should be treated equally. This entails a balance in the numbers of boys and girls, masters and mistresses, in the school and . . . the restyling of the senior mistress as head mistress.[24]

Hardly surprisingly, this was a view which was echoed from time to time in the official publications. The 1977 Green Paper on *Education in schools*, for example, referred blandly to 'the disappearance of the old stereotypes of the sexes, based on a traditional division of labour between men and women.'[25] Similarly, Caroline Benn and Brian Simon, writing at the end of the 1960s, were convinced of the growing success of mixed comprehensive schools:

in the early days there were quite a few who felt that the type of comprehensive most likely to 'succeed' was the single sex. This was partly because these had been developed out of grammar schools. . . . Since so many mixed comprehensives have now succeeded so well – including academically – this view no longer prevails. In some ways it is the single sex schools that are now on the defensive.[26]

But what quickly became apparent to those who were prepared to look a little more closely was that the mixed schools, particularly at secondary level, involved and often insisted on new divisions between boys and girls. Benn and Simon showed how, from the outset, about a half of mixed comprehensive schools were failing to throw all of their courses open to both sexes:

There were about a dozen subjects altogether not open to boys, among them catering and clothes design. There were over a dozen subjects in mixed comprehensives that were not open to girls, among them engineering and gardening.[27]

It is interesting to note that these researchers also found clear evidence of pupils choosing to sit in different parts of the classroom by sex in mixed schools, a reminder of the way in which pupil behaviour and attitudes reinforced the distinctions made by the schools themselves.

What seems to have been developing during this period was a system which was in reality more effective than the one it replaced at imposing upon pupils a 'gendered' view of their roles. As Madelaine Arnot has pointed out, these new mixed schools inadvertently, by their very existence, conferred greater snob value on the single-sex schools, particularly the Direct Grant schools which recruited in the main from a small slice of the population.[28] This factor alone goes some way towards explaining the stress that was placed on the separation of the sexes in mixed comprehensives. As Arnot has shown, the combined attitudes of parents, teachers, career officers, employers and finally of the students themselves resulted, almost inexorably, in 'an experience of schooling which was gendered from start to finish.'[29]

As this became realised, the first stirrings of disquiet were heard from within the teaching profession. One NUT pronouncement in 1975 emphasised that:

> society has changed radically... the pressures to give full equality to men and women in their work, their places in society and their responsibilities and commitments should be reflected in and catered for by the schools. To educate children in groups, segregated on the basis of difference of sex, is to effect an artificial separation which bears little or no relation to life at home or to society in general... a pattern of education based on such separation and founded on concepts of allegedly distinguishable and incompatible needs of boys and girls no longer serves the interests either of society or of children.[30]

The growing awareness of the shortcomings of this new educational settlement was linked to and derived from a new wave of feminism which was given focus by the publication in 1971 of Kate Millett's *Sexual politics*. This was the book which probably did more than any other to promote the male monopolisation of power as a political issue; as Millett summarised it:

> Our society like all other historical civilisations, is a patriarchy. The fact is evident at once if one recalls that the military, industry, technology, universities, science, political office and finance – in short every avenue of power within the society, including the coercive force of the police, is entirely in male hands.[31]

The emergence of this new radical feminism led directly to a closer look being taken at the ways in which schooling contributed to the maintenance of a patriarchal society, both in England and more widely. At a United Nations World Conference for Women held in Mexico in July 1975, a 'World Plan of Action' placed on governments the responsibility to ensure that it was possible for women to share fully in social, economic, cultural, civic and political life. The women's movement had become truly international in scale, and developments in England were in part a response to this broader movement.

In respect of schooling, what this meant was the appearance of research such as that undertaken by Jenny Shaw, who argued that schools were 'major agencies for maintaining the dominant (sexist) culture'.[32] She showed that the opening-up of access to school subjects traditionally reserved for the other sex had resulted not only in single-sex groups in otherwise mixed schools, but in a redefinition of the subjects themselves:

> When boys take girls' subjects the meanings quickly change; thus cookery becomes a prelude to a career in catering for boys, whilst as taught to girls it is still intended as a general domestic skill.[33]

Other researchers, such as Glenys Lobban and Sarah Delamont, began to investigate the range of influences which induced children to take a 'gendered' view of their future roles. Lobban looked at primary school reading schemes and showed how, in the main, girls were forced from an early age to read about boys.[34] Similarly, Sarah Delamont, in *Sex roles and the school* published in 1980, argued that a range of influences from toys and clothes through to more direct in-school practices, taught children from the very first years to develop gendered views of their environment.[35]

During the 1970s, a growing awareness of a skills shortage in industry led to a renewed focus on the problem of getting girls on to science, engineering and mathematical courses. In 1973 the Union of Women Teachers told the Commons Select Committee on Sexual Discrimination that:

> perhaps the greatest single contributory factor to the position of women as second class citizens in the matter of employment has been the lack of opportunity for girls in schools to participate in the technological developments of recent years.[36]

In the same vein, the unfortunately named Manpower Services Commission called in 1977 for a new approach to the teaching of:

> mathematical, scientific and technical knowledge, enabling boys and girls to learn the essential skills needed in a fast-changing world of work.... Girls should broaden and modernise their aspirations and ... feel confident of success in unfamiliar fields of science and technology.[37]

One four-year project, 'Girls into science and technology', ran from 1979 until 1984 and followed the subject choices of 2,000 girls who entered school in 1980. As part of the project, female technologists and scientists visited schools to provide role models for girls and the resulting publications offered a diagnosis of why girls turned away from the sciences and gave suggestions on how schools might reverse this trend.[38] In 1980, too, the DES produced a Report dealing specifically with *Girls and Science*, and this concern was kept to the fore when the Equal Opportunities Commission made 1984 its WISE year, a year of encouraging women to pursue careers in science and engineering.

Yet evidence continued to pile up suggesting that these initiatives had little, if any, effect. Alison Kelly, Jan Harding and Judy Samuel, all produced research reports during the early eighties suggesting that the teaching of science, on a day-to-day basis, was as discriminatory against girls as had ever previously been the case.[39] As Madelaine Arnot showed, the MSC Training Opportunities Programme had very gendered results, with in 1981 females accounting for 97 per cent of all students on shorthand and typing courses, 88 per cent on clerical courses and 74 per cent of those on hairdressing and cleaning courses. There were similar maldistributions in the career choices of male and female graduates into the 1980s, which Arnot also highlighted.[40]

A new insight into the processes at work was provided in 1981 by Michelle Stanworth, whose work on *Gender and schooling* was among the first to show how boys tended to hog classroom time and teacher attention in mixed classrooms.[41] In the same year, Margaret B. Sutherland's *Sex bias in education*[42] added to the growing volume of literature which examined the interplay of school and home influences which lay behind the disadvantages experienced by girls in schooling and employment. The argument was taken further in 1983 by Sarah Delamont, who argued that schools were among the most conservative social forces in the matter of labelling by sex. She argued that curricular practices and teaching strategies, the use of gendered uniforms (often vigorously enforced), and male dominated staff hierarchies, all contributed to the process of gendering through education. She concluded gloomily:

> in the past decade schools have shown themselves to be more conservative about sex roles than either homes or wider society.... The official voice of the school is claiming that male work is economically crucial and female work is frivolous.[43]

In 1985, Michelle Stanworth returned to this theme, arguing that:

> the current dynamic of classroom interaction does nothing to undermine the stereotypical views of appropriate spheres for men and women.... No matter how conscientious and capable female pupils are, they are perceived by their teachers to lack the authoritative manner and the assertiveness which many teachers seem to believe to be the pre-requisites of 'masculine' occupations.[44]

In the context of a body of writing such as this, it is hardly surprising that writers such as Madelaine Arnot came to see much of the earlier research on this subject as unsatisfactory. In 1983 she attacked R. R. Dale for his failure to see the extent to which his advocacy of mixed education had been constructed within a gendered view of society. She wrote:

for Dale, the advantage of mixed schools can be found precisely in their reproduction of life in a bisexual heterosexual world, in which men dominate and women learn to complement and subordinate themselves to men. With this image of 'normality' in mind, it is hardly surprising that co-educational schools are seen as nowhere near the ideal from a feminist position.[45]

This was but part of a developed critique of schooling articulated during the 1980s by authors such as Madelaine Arnot, who argued that the school system had developed historically to serve a patriarchal society, that it needed to sustain the idea of domesticity which had developed during the nineteenth century in order to justify separate and distinctive educational experiences for girls. Further, she suggested, the two key results of this process were that the school system was obliged to deepen social class distinctions between girls and, by and large, remained the key social influence militating against their aspiring to a set of life chances and experiences equivalent to those of boys.[46] It was a powerful and damning critique, but one which was by the mid-eighties embedded in a voluminous research literature.

Despite this growing understanding of the continuing discrimination against girls in schools, the issue remained politically contentious, and girls' access to parity in education continued to be frustrated by a succession of governments, either through ignorance, neglect or occasionally downright opposition. It is, perhaps, hardly surprising that there were many who saw this growing feminist literature as a threat. The fact that several of these authors drew ideas and insights from Bowles and Gintis, Bordieu and other writers who were popularly seen as being of the Left politically, merely added to the sense of threat felt by conservatives of whatever ilk. Beyond this, the application of these feminist insights to education involved an indictment of established practices in schools and colleges which many practitioners, who saw themselves as committed to the establishment of a more equal society, found it difficult to take. These considerations may go some way to explain the growing distance between the implications of this research literature and the response of successive governments.

Whereas the trend, at governmental level, during the 1960s had been to encourage women into employment (and this was particularly marked, as we have seen, in respect of staffing the schools), during the early seventies a growing sense of economic crisis, together with a sudden drop in the birth rate, forced this issue on to the back burner. As Rosemary Deem has pointed out:

The Sex Discrimination Act did not in any case promise to be very useful in relation to education...it focused mainly on ending discrimination in entry to mixed schools and on direct discrimination in the kinds of courses offered to pupils, without considering other elements in the form of schooling or, for example, the whole issue of how gender and gender relations are represented in the curriculum.[47]

Beyond this, several elements in the policies of the 1970s worked against the establishment of equal opportunities for women. The reorganisation of teacher training, which saw the absorption of many teacher training colleges into the new polytechnics as well as a significant downturn in the numbers being trained, impacted on the one sector of higher education which offered most to females. At the beginning of the decade there were 14,600 men and 31,800 women training to teach in the colleges. By the end of the decade, there were only 7,900 men and 13,700 women in the same sector (including those colleges which had been absorbed by polytechnics).

Set against this was the increase in the number of females aspiring to places at universities, a trend which had been accelerated by the Robbins Report and which continued through the 1970s. At undergraduate level there were, in 1970, 99,400 men and 70,700 women, an increase which reflected the steadily increasing number of qualified females emerging annually from the schools.[48] But it was an increase which was only accomplished at the cost of a continuing gendering of undergraduate courses. By the end of the decade there were roughly twice as many women as men enrolled on language and literature courses and on education courses at the universities, whereas at the start of the decade numbers had been roughly equal. The appearance of more women in other university faculties was in many cases only achieved at the cost of new patterns of recruitment being established course by course. So, during the 1970s, the predominance of females on courses in the biological sciences was confirmed. Although more women began to appear in mathematics and physics classes, they remained in these subjects a minority of all students.

There was little at governmental level to retard or even to monitor these trends. From the mid-seventies onwards the theme of family became increasingly dominant in political discourse. Margaret Thatcher told the Conservative Party Conference in 1977 that 'we are the party of the family',[49] and from 1979 onwards there were those around her who were prepared to spell out the implications of this emphasis. Patrick Jenkin, the Secretary of State for Social Services, went on record immediately after his appointment as saying that: 'If the good Lord had intended us to have equal rights to go out and work, he wouldn't have created man and woman.'[50] Within a year he elaborated the point in a radio broadcast:

the balance between the national needs for women's directly productive work and the need for them to look after their family is now shifting.... As the need for women's paid work outside the family evaporates...we may expect a gradual return to the education of women for domestic labour....Most of the advances achieved by women since 1944, both inside and outside education, have occurred in periods of full employment.[51]

By 1982, Margaret Thatcher was able to claim that 'the battle for equality is almost won'.[52] After the 1983 General Election, the Parliamentary Sex Equality Group was not resuscitated. The issues of women's rights and of girls' schooling found themselves once again at the bottom of the political agenda.

Oscillating political fortunes are but part of the explanation for the irony of gender and education in recent years. The underlying reality of this period was that a system of schooling which offered different experiences to boys and girls, and which conferred on them differential life chances, actually fitted with the developing social and economic structure. Changing patterns of lifestyle and of employment necessitated the continuing subjugation of women in low paid, part-time and casual employment and their continuing prime responsibility for child care. Much of the political rhetoric reflected this reality and was derived from it. The fact that there had been, over a long period, a divide between the educational experiences and life chances of middle-class and working-class girls was another factor which worked to debilitate the women's movement during this modern period and to lessen the likelihood that it would lead to truly radical changes, either in the structure of the education system or in its day-to-day workings. It is worth noting that it was agitation by working-class women in the late sixties, first on the issue of safety on trawlers in Hull, then among the sewing machinists at the Ford plant at Dagenham, campaigning for equal pay, and by women bus conductresses in London who wished to become drivers, which led to the Equal Pay legislation.[53] Although most middle-class feminist authors were sensitive to the issues raised by their sisters on the shop floor, the contrasting lifestyles of women in different social classes, sustained by differing patterns of education, made the adoption of a common programme which would encapsulate all women's issues at best unlikely. Those who wrote about women's issues were mostly from middle-class backgrounds, had themselves been through higher education and, understandably, saw the issues around selectivity and discrimination in access to the most privileged educational institutions as important. Some, if not all, of their concerns were met by the expansion of higher education during the period covered by this book. But to be born poor and female in one of the old industrial areas of Britain during this modern period was to risk the worst effects of class and gender disadvantages combined. It is the failure of the English education system to resolve this problem which lies at the heart of this chapter.

6

A NEW EUGENICS
ETHNIC MINORITIES AND EDUCATION

> Why have inner city problems worsened in our own lifetime? We know some
> of the answers. New towns, at great cost, 'decanted' the younger, more
> energetic and ambitious native-born English from their urban communities,
> thereby creating a vacuum filled by the mass import of people from backward
> countries, to meet an alleged labour shortage.
>
> (*Daily Telegraph* leader, 2 December 1985)

This quotation captures an important facet of the reality of education for
ethnic minorities in modern Britain. The racialisation of education, and with
it the marginalisation of ethnic minorities, reflects – despite many claims to
the contrary – a new eugenics which has underpinned many aspects of social
policy.

The impact of eugenic theory on educational policy during the early
twentieth century is well documented. Francis Galton and his followers
developed theories of 'race' and heredity which legitimised the development
of intelligence tests and which also gave credence to the establishment of
separate educational tracks for different social groups. The widespread
adoption of 'tripartism', for example, by local education authorities after the
Second World War, which was posited on theories of fixed intelligence, was,
as I have argued elsewhere, due in part to the pervasive influence of
eugenicists.[1]

The events of the Second World War, and in particular the discrediting of
racial theory which followed the revelation of Hitler's policies towards the
Jews, may have seemed to render eugenic theories obsolescent. The
collectivism which the war fostered in England, and which was reflected
in the policies of Clement Attlee's governments, was hardly a fertile soil for
eugenicists. Attempts during the fifties and sixties to break down the
selective system and to introduce comprehensive schools, as well as
initiatives in progressive and child-centred education, may be seen as
evidence of the strength of support for this collectivism in educational
circles.

But despite the popular mood, the post-war years saw a resurgence and a
reworking of eugenics which was to have a major impact in the field of

education, particularly in respect of the treatment of ethnic minorities. First, the Royal Commission on Population, announced in 1943, gave members of the Eugenic Society a chance to bring the question of declining population back into the public spotlight. In a carefully worded memorandum to the Commission on behalf of the Eugenics Society, C. P. Blacker stressed that, while Galton had 'believed that the different branches of the human race were unequally equipped with the inborn characters that produce and sustain highly organised civilisations, it was no part of his outlook that biologically inferior races should be persecuted or suppressed.'[2] One of the Commissioners, Carr-Saunders, pressed Blacker privately to emphasise in his evidence the need for policies which would 'halt the deterioration in the genetic heritage of the race.'[3] A number of witnesses to the Royal Commission who were sympathetic to the work of the Eugenics Society pointed out their concerns about differential fertility and declining intelligence. If the Report, which appeared in 1949, went part-way to confirm the fears of the eugenicists, it did help to condition British society to a generally negative response when the post-war labour shortage led to the recruitment of immigrant workers and their families.[4]

While critics of the Eugenics Society, such as Lancelot Hogben, attacked it as being permeated by the credo of the Third Reich, the central set of ideas which it espoused were still current. As Richard Soloway has put it:

> None of this meant that eugenical, hereditarian presuppositions about class, and increasingly race, as immigrants came into the country from India, Pakistan, Africa and the West Indies, did not continue to permeate the thinking of a great many successful, well-placed Britons. They were, however, like members of the Eugenics Society themselves, more cautious and restrained in expressing their beliefs and were in any event uncertain as to how they could be implemented in some concrete way without stirring up charges of class prejudice and racism.[5]

Further, the close post-war collaboration of Lionel Penrose, as Galton Professor of Eugenics at University College, and his friend J. B. S. Haldane, meant that a new 'reform Eugenics', focused on genetics and in particular the study of defective chromosomes, became fashionable.[6] Penrose was violently opposed to the propagandist work of Blacker and his group, and sought to distance himself from them. But these tensions within the eugenics movement did not prevent the emergence during the post-war period of views which were to be widely publicised and which were to colour the treatment of ethnic minority pupils in British schools.

Julian Huxley and Frederick Osborn drew attention to the relatively high fertility of socially deprived groups, particularly low-income blacks in the United States, and used the 1952 Population Council to argue for population control through widely available contraception. Under their influence during the 1970s the Repository for Germinal Choice was set up in

California and began to collect sperm from Nobel prizewinners (William Shockley being the only named donor).[7] In England, in response to this, Francis Crick mused on the feasibility of a licensing scheme which might limit the number of children allowed to 'genetically unfavourable' parents.[8] Although the majority of educational psychologists (who were a quickly growing band in post-war England) moved away from the theories of fixed intelligence which underpinned much of the immediate post-war educational policy, a few, most notably Cyril Burt, clung to their hereditarian beliefs. Earlier in the century Burt had published on the differences between ethnic groups in measured intelligence: his echo in the United States was Arthur Jensen, whose 1969 article in the *Harvard Education Review* pointed out that, on average, blacks scored 15 per cent lower on IQ tests than whites. 'The possible importance of genetic factors in racial and behavioural differences has been greatly ignored', argued Jensen. He made it clear that he thought that genetic endowment might play a significant part in the explanation of this contrast.[9] In England, Hans J. Eysenck was emerging as the main champion of hereditarianism. During the late sixties and early seventies, Eysenck propagandised his view that the kind of social problems which had long been evident in North America were becoming felt in Britain as a direct result of immigration from former British colonial territories. He, too, emphasised 'considerable scholastic backwardness and low IQ scores among coloured children'.[10] Meanwhile, in the US, William Shockley became the main proponent of the race/intelligence argument, urging the National Academy of Sciences to consider the possibility that the population of the United States was in genetic decline.[11]

Although it was politically astute for those politicians who sympathised with these ideas to remain quiet on the subject, a few were prepared to raise this issue as one for public debate. Enoch Powell's populism during the 1960s deepened feelings on both sides of the debate; Powell repeatedly drew attention to the disproportionate number of 'coloured births', using terms like 'bastardisation' and 'mongrelisation' to emphasise his claims.[12] It was, though, Keith Joseph's unguarded statement to the Birmingham Conservative Association in 1974 which revealed the growing attachment to these racist views of those within the hard right of the Conservative Party. Joseph warned his audience that 'the least fitted mothers – the unmarried, deserted, divorced, those of low intelligence and low education' were parenting more than a third of the next generation.[13] Although he did not specially refer to ethnicity, the implications were obvious.

There can be little doubt that this discredited, but still widely popular, set of ideas offers the key to our understanding of the treatment received by ethnic minority pupils in British schools since the 1960s. Only by appreciating the appeal of an essentially racist view of humankind and its potential can we fully understand how the well-established 'integrationist' approaches to ethnic minority pupils came to be rudely swept away.

Znaniecki's seminal work on *Modern Nationalities* argued that formal education systems are among the most important agencies in promoting the assimilation of immigrants. But he warned that:

> a very different and more serious conflict emerges when a dominant nationality, though imparting its own culture to ethnic foreigners, does not admit them to participation as full members, because it considers them racially inferior. While European rulers in colonial territories transmitted some of their culture to a minority of natives, the purpose was to facilitate their rule, not to increase the size of their own nationality by incorporating those foreigners, since the latter were usually considered hereditarily unfit to become full members of the dominant society.[14]

Although rather crudely over-generalised, this remark captures precisely the essence of what was to occur in Britain during the period covered by this book. At both national and local level, the official rhetoric was assimilationist, and remained so, but the widespread acceptability of eugenic ideas meant, first, that in practice there was a steady drift away from assimilation towards the adoption of other policies, and, second, that as the perception of a 'problem' grew more pervasive during the seventies and eighties, even official pronouncements re-emphasising the importance of integration were more and more posited on the view that this must involve a reaffirmation of 'Englishness' and a marginalisation of the cultures of the ethnic minorities. And this, of course, fitted precisely with the rise of the Radical Right politically, and generated a key part of its rhetoric. What had been dismissed during the 1960s as the rabble-rousing of extremists, steadily became a part of acceptable political discourse.

Attempts to use the education system to integrate the children of immigrant families had a long pedigree in Britain, so it is hardly surprising that the first response to an upturn in immigration from the Commonwealth took this form. Between 1870 and 1914 the existing Jewish communities in England were supplemented by over 120,000 new arrivals from Eastern Europe. By 1902, there were sixteen board schools in the East End of London, educating over 15,000 pupils, which were virtually run by the Jewish community. They supplemented the Jewish voluntary schools which, in London alone, were educating over 5,000 children. All of these schools served the function of integrating Jewish children to English society.[15] Similarly, within the education system, the responses to Belgian refugees in Soho in 1914 and to those fleeing from Germany during the inter-war years were integrationist. In 1947, the Polish Resettlement Act confirmed that schooling was to be a key element in the acculturation of refugees from Eastern Europe. By 1950 the Polish Education Committee was responsible for over 5,000 pupils in schools of one kind or another. Similarly, the reaction to a new group of immigrants from Eastern Europe, following the

1956 uprising in Hungary, was unequivocally integrationist. So, although legislation such as the 1905 Aliens Act was specifically designed to limit the numbers coming into the country, the response at government level and of those working within the education service to newly-arrived immigrants was, for much of the twentieth century, unequivocal: they saw their responsibility to be the assimilation of their pupils into an English way of life, which, it went without saying, was thought to be in various ways superior to that which immigrant children had left behind. For twenty years after the end of the Second World War, this remained the dominant response to immigration.

From the start, reactions to the upturn in the number of new arrivals from Commonwealth countries from the late 1940s onwards reflected this tradition. But at the same time, perhaps because the fact of colour rendered these new immigrants visible from the outset, and partly because of the residue of the Eugenics movement, what was happening was also unequivocally construed as being a problem, and this view soon came to predominate.

The perception of immigration as a whole as being problematic was shared by both major political parties and became evident at government level while Clement Attlee was Prime Minister. At the very moment that his Government was enacting the 1948 Nationality Act, conferring identical rights on all Commonwealth citizens, Attlee wrote privately to one of his own backbenchers: 'if our policy were to result in a great influx of undesirables we might, however unwillingly, have to consider modifying it'.[16] Already, behind the scenes, the government was using administrative devices to control immigration, and soon to control immigrant communities themselves.

The events of the late fifties and early sixties effectively guaranteed that the treatment of ethnic minority pupils in schools was to become one of the key issues of the period. Although the Conservative Government rejected the idea of immigration control as a matter of principle in 1955, it did begin to keep formal records of the arrival of Commonwealth citizens in that year. But events soon conspired to force the government into action in this issue. Oswald Moseley participated in the 1959 election, contesting Kensington North; his British Movement being a successor to the British Union of Fascists. Disturbances in 1958 in Notting Hill and Nottingham were construed by the press as being 'race riots'. But at that time it was widely assumed that little could be done about this through the education system and that the implications for educators were minimal. A *TES* leader at the time of the Notting Hill disturbances commented:

> To say that curbing racial strife is basically a task for education is merely shuffling out of the difficulty. What schools can do, they do. There is little more that education can do about it at all. The need for

progress is outside the school. No-one is saying it is easy. But society is not taking one step towards stopping more Notting Hills by saying that this is another job for the teachers.[17]

It was the fears of widespread public disorder which emanated from this that led even moderate Tories such as Boyle, Macleod and Butler reluctantly to consider immigration controls. Butler described the drafting of the 1962 Commonwealth Immigration Act as 'the most unpleasant thing I have ever had to do in my public career'.[18] As Ian Grosvenor has shown, Harold Wilson 'vowed to repeal the Act if he came to power, but in the event, did not change the law and sought to apply it even more rigorously.'[19] Yet the passage of this legislation was to bring about precisely the situation it sought to prevent. The threat of a legal ban led to a sudden upturn in the numbers of Commonwealth immigrants in the months before its enactment. The fact that the legislation allowed the entry of dependants resulted in a swift increase in the numbers of children from Commonwealth countries, thus generating a demand for school places. Further, the existence of legislation led many who had initially thought of only temporary residence in Britain to reconsider their position and start to think of themselves as permanent residents. Meanwhile, the steady increase in the 'white collar' sector of the economy (from 31 per cent of the workforce in 1951 to 36 per cent in 1961) meant that a growing proportion of the white population found itself with the opportunity to use the education system for new purposes, using paper qualifications to gain entry to secure, middle-class employment, while the newly-arrived immigrants were forced to fill the manual jobs and more menial positions which the indigenous white population was increasingly unwilling to staff. Also, the drift towards commuting and owner-occupation characterised the white population, and the clustering of ethnic minority groups in the old urban centres, which, as we have seen, was largely forced on them for economic reasons, meant that the social distance between them and white middle-class society was greater from the outset than it might otherwise have been.

The generally *laissez-faire* attitude of government to the ethnic minority communities already established in Britain was shown by its lack of responsiveness to detailed programmes which were outlined at the start of the 1960s. Anthony Richmond, for example, proposed not only legislation to prohibit racial discrimination, but the dispersal of immigrant school-children as well as educational programmes aimed at minimising prejudice among the indigenous school population. This was completely ignored by the Government of the day.[20] What the events of the late fifties and early sixties did achieve was to strengthen the political consensus on these issues: the main direction of policy became one which sought to relegate 'race' to the periphery of political debate through uncontroversial legislation and policies which were intended to marginalise the 'problem' of relations between ethnic groups. Schooling proved to be particularly susceptible to this approach.

An important recent thesis by Ian Grosvenor has argued that a racist view of black settlement coloured several aspects of government policy, and that education was particularly susceptible to this trend. In his view, the racialisation of education in Britain and, thereby, the increased racialisation of society as a whole, resulted from both national government and local government policy. He argues that, since the early sixties, 'educational policy has complemented the State's construction of black people as a "problem".... Education has been a crucial agent in the racialisation process.'[21] It was the catalyst of the 1962 Act which resulted in clear policy definition along these lines during the mid-sixties.

Certainly, at local level, a racist view of both immigration and of its educational implications was soon evident. The West Midlands was an area where feelings ran particularly high. At the time of the 1964 election, Harold Gurden, MP for Selly Oak, Birmingham, was campaigning strongly for further immigration controls, and in Smethwick, Peter Griffiths achieved notoriety for the racist tenor of his statements.[22] Their views originated in part in the concerns of local educationalists. In June 1963, the TES reported the views of the Chief Education Officer for Smethwick under the headline 'Every immigrant child a problem'. C. E. Robin claimed that there were already 447 immigrant children in Smethwick schools whose native language was not English. ' "Each one", Mr Robin reports, "is a major problem in his school" ', the journal reflected gloomily.[23] Four months later the TES returned to Smethwick, this time reporting the CEO as saying that 'English does not automatically mean integration or even peaceful coexistence: but these things cannot be secured without English.... English then, in the primary and secondary school, is the key to our immigrant problems.'[24] Similarly, in the following year, the headteacher of a Birmingham primary school reported to the LEA that Caribbean-born children 'were of lower mentality, dull and backward. But there are dangers of classifying them as ESN before they have had time to adjust.... No tests appear to be completely culture free. Results are affected by inability to understand simple instructions, lack of interest, poor concentration, emotional upsets and a generally unsatisfactory attitude to work.'[25] These concerns were neatly summarised by Roland Moyle, the MP for Lewisham North, who claimed in the Commons that 'the whole system of education is becoming distorted in the direction of trying to accommodate children, many of whom cannot speak the language, to the English way of life.'[26] In brief, it became usual to typify immigrant pupils as falling so far short of the standards of English pupils that they constituted a major educational problem.

This perceived problem had several facets, each of which generated its own racist discourse. On the one hand, the effort to recruit extra teachers was often construed in offensive terms. A draft advertisement prepared by the Birmingham LEA in 1965 read:

> Birmingham children are white and they're black.
> Immigrants come: we can't send them back.
> Really we'd like to, but now that they're here,
> Millions who multiply year after year,
> It's our job to teach 'em to live just like us,
> Nicely and soberly without any fuss.
> God knows how we'll do it, we'd all like to cry.
> Have you the desire to give help and to try?
> And teach in our schools? We'll see you get paid.
> May we please employ you to give us your aid?[27]

Another concern was the cost of immigrant pupils. The CEO for Birmingham wrote in 1968: 'if we assume that immigration is costing us something between one quarter and one half million pounds a year... the question arises: at whose expense, higher rates than we need otherwise have paid, or postponement of betterment in the education service'[28] Ian Katznelson has identified a third element in the contemporary concerns. This was the growing belief among teachers that the standards of non-immigrant pupils were falling in schools with a high proportion of immigrants.

> In 1967 the Inner London Education Authority published the report of a study of 52 primary schools, where immigrant pupils formed more than one third of the school population. Two thirds of the headteachers questioned felt that there had been some fall in the intelligence of their non-immigrant pupils.... This change had been due to the fact that the ablest families had been moving out of the area.[29]

The phenomenon of 'white flight', as it became popularly known, was a growing reality and was accelerating the demographic changes we have already identified.

Thus, when Enoch Powell said in his most reported speech on this subject in 1968 that 'I am filled with much foreboding. Like the Roman, I seem to see the River Tiber foaming with much blood', he was merely transferring to the national stage the concerns and the rhetoric of a growing number of local politicians and local authority officials.[30] His claim in 1972 that British society was witnessing 'the transformation, during our own lifetime... of towns, cities and areas that we know into alien territory' was merely the concern of these urban bureaucrats writ large.[31] It is neither possible nor necessary to distinguish local and national thinking on this issue: the two are inextricably interwoven.

Hardly surprisingly, the first response of educationalists was to identify a 'cultural deficit' among immigrant pupils which needed to be met, in the first instance by programmes for the teaching of English. In 1960, Birmingham became the first local authority to employ a full-time teacher of English for newly-arrived immigrant pupils. Within a decade his staff numbered over a hundred. Under Edward Boyle, the Ministry of Education identified the two major strands of policy. The publication of *English for immigrants* in 1963 gave government reinforcement to the responses already being made by some local education authorities to immigration.[32] This Ministry campaign was taken up by 45 Community Relations Councils and was unthinkingly implemented in schools.[33] It became usual, in the big cities particularly, for newly-arrived immigrant pupils to be placed initially in reception centres or in withdrawal classes where the intention was to make them ready for full participation in the life of an English school as quickly as possible. John Eggleston has referred to the recipients of this provision as 'trainee whites'.[34] Although seen as increasingly questionable, this strand of policy remained in place for several years. As late as 1977 one correspondent to *Multiracial school* was calling for 'a dose of systematic language teaching, preferably carried out in the monastic security of a special class or centre.'[35]

The second strand of Government policy also became apparent at that time. When, in October 1963, Edward Boyle met privately with protesting parents in Southall, Middlesex, he told them that he thought the principle of segregation was 'wrong and dangerous'.[36] Shortly after this meeting, Boyle addressed the House of Commons: 'I must regretfully tell the House that one school must be regarded now as irretrievably an immigrant school. The important thing to do is to prevent this happening elsewhere.' He was referring to Spring Grove school in Huddersfield, and he went on to spell out what was to become a cornerstone of policy for the next few years:

> If possible, it is desirable on education grounds that no one school should have more than about thirty per cent of immigrants....It is both politically and legally more or less impossible to compel native parents to send their children to school in an immigrant area if there are places for them in other schools.[37]

So, while the employment of extra teachers of English was one way of meeting the 'problem', another was to disperse ethnic minority pupils around the schools of any one local authority. If the extra teachers of English worked in a number of schools, they would become catalysts in this process. It was in this vein that *English for immigrants* had recommended the dispersal of immigrant pupils as well as the provision of specialist teaching help.

During this period, the Commonwealth Immigrants Advisory Council, which had been set up to advise the Home Office on policy, supported assimilation strongly. Its Second Report, in February 1964, emphasised that:

> a national system of education must aim at producing citizens who can take their place in a society properly equipped to exercise rights and

perform duties the same as those of other citizens. If their parents were brought up in another culture and another tradition, children should be encouraged to respect it, but a national system cannot be expected to perpetuate the different values of immigrant groups.[38]

The Report took a very negative view of the impact of too many ethnic minority pupils in any one school, emphasising that:

> the whole character and ethos of the school is altered.... The presence of a high proportion of immigrant children in one class slows down the general routine...and hampers the progress of the whole class, especially where the immigrants do not write or speak English fluently. This is clearly in itself undesirable, and unfair to all the children in the class.[39]

This racially discriminatory view of schooling and of the pupils passing through urban schools was given teeth in June 1965 when Circular 7/65, *Immigration from the Commonwealth*, advised local education authorities to institute a one-third rule. In a passage entitled 'Spreading the children' it proposed that:

> It will be helpful if the parents of non-immigrant children can see that practical measures have been taken to deal with the problems in the schools, and that the progress of their own children is not being restricted by the undue preoccupation of the teaching staff with the linguistic and other difficulties of immigrant children....Such arrangements can more easily be made, and the integration of immigrants more easily achieved, if the proportion of immigrant children in a school is not allowed to rise too high. The Circular 7/65 suggests that about one-third of immigrant children is the maximum that is normally acceptable in a school if social strains are to be avoided and educational standards maintained. Local Education Authorities are advised to arrange for the dispersal of immigrant children over a greater number of schools in order to avoid undue concentration in any particular school.[40]

A number of local authorities, notably Bradford, West Bromwich and Southall, began to 'bus' black students, although the reverberations of the Watts riot in Los Angeles in the same year and the furore over integration of ethnic minority students in Alabama meant that all concerned quickly became aware of the political sensitivity of what was being attempted. Largely for this reason, bussing never really took off, although the DES was still defending it as a viable policy as late as 1971. It became clear, when the Select Committee on Race Relations pronounced against bussing in 1973, that some LEAs were still moving ethnic minority pupils away from their home areas, and it took an injunction brought by the Race Relations Board against the Ealing authority in 1976 to end the practice altogether.[41] In retrospect, this policy stands as an indictment of the deeply racist nature of the way in which the State in Britain construed immigration. In practice, it meant that pupils from immigrant communities were made to feel part of an inferior minority. Its abandonment meant that the drift towards all-black inner-city schools continued unchecked. Either way, the prevalence of an essentially eugenic view of human society meant that the education system could do little more than reflect the deepening divisions of the 1960s.

Although there was broadly a consensus between the major political parties on the question of how to respond to the phenomenon of immigration during these years, the statement made by the Labour Home Secretary, Roy Jenkins, in a widely-reported address on 22 May 1966, certainly marked the beginnings of a new approach. He emphasised that 'I define integration ... not as a flattening process of assimilation, but as equal opportunity, accompanied by cultural diversity in an atmosphere of mutual tolerance.'[42] It was in this spirit, in the same year, that the Local Government Act (Section 11) provided local authorities with supplementary funding to cope with 'the presence within their areas of substantial numbers of immigrants whose language and customs are different from the rest of the community'. Now, at precisely the moment that the Labour administration was shifting towards policies of positive discrimination for those living in the run-down inner cities (the Educational Priority Areas were designated in the following year), resources were to be made available to rework the curriculum in those schools with significant numbers of ethnic minority pupils. During the following 20 years this Section 11 money, as it became known, enabled a variety of initiatives in the educational arena. A plethora of conferences and courses for teachers on the 'problems' posed by ethnic minority pupils was organised. Local Authorities appointed advisors with the remit of focusing on the particular needs of inner-city schools. Funding was available to provide ESN support for slow-learning pupils, many of whom were black.

In terms of broader policy towards the growing ethnic minority communities in Britain, the Labour Party in power found itself being driven towards a stance which was very similar in practice to that of the Conservative Party, and this reflected the extent to which eugenic ideas were influencing thinking across the political spectrum. Although Wilson had referred to Peter Griffiths as a 'parliamentary leper' in the Commons, the sudden increase in the number of Kenyan Asians arriving jolted the integrationist rhetoric of his Government. Roy Hattersley argued that 'without limitation, integration is impossible',[43] and Richard Crossman wrote in his diary that 'ever since the Smethwick election it has been quite clear that immigration can be the greatest political vote loser for the Labour Party if one seems to be permitting a flood of immigrants to come in to blight the central areas of our cities'.[44] At the same time that the 1965 Race

Relations Act set up the Race Relations Board, a White Paper argued strongly for extending controls on Commonwealth immigration. In 1967 the publication of W. W. Daniel's *Racial discrimination in England*,[45] at the same time as the alarmist propagandising of Enoch Powell, placed the government under pressure to enact further. The Commonwealth Immigrants Act and the Race Relations Act, both passed in 1968, were the result. On the one hand, the newly-established Community Relations Commission worked for the successful integration of the ethnic minorities, while the limitations set on the numbers of new arrivals reassured those who saw in immigration a threat to 'Englishness'. Now 'close connection' became the criterion for entry to Britain. In 1971 this was tightened further by a new Immigration Act passed by the in-coming Conservative Government. This introduced the concept of 'patriality'.

The late sixties and early seventies became a period marked by the adoption of policies which were of crucial importance for the conditions under which immigrant communities lived. The attempt to 'interrupt the cycle of deprivation'[46] led to the designation of Educational Priority Areas in 1967, and in the following year to the Urban Aid Programme initiated by the Home Office. A Home Office Circular at this time referred to a variety of interrelated criteria to be applied. They included housing, unemployment levels, juvenile crime, family size and the presence of ethnic minority communities. Similarly, the Select Committee on Race Relations and Immigration produced a Report in 1969 on *The problems of coloured school leavers*. Echoing earlier eugenic pronouncements, it referred to black youths as 'a social time bomb'. Its recommendations anticipated what was to become a main thread of educational policy during the next few years: 'We advocate teaching about the countries from which immigrants in any particular town come. This would help bring immigrant children into the life of the school'.[47]

Multiculturalism, then, was to be the new rallying cry of the 1970s, and was promoted particularly strongly by the DES. In 1972 it was decided not to issue a Schools Council pack on race, but instead to use the materials for a publication on *Education for a multicultural society*.[48] The 1975 Bullock Report, *A language for life*, was strongly multiculturalist in tone, emphasising that 'no child should be expected to cast off the language and culture of the home as he crosses the school threshold'.[49] In 1977 the DES's Green Paper, *Education in schools: a consultative document*, stressed that 'Our society is a multicultural, multiracial one ... the curriculum should reflect a sympathetic understanding of different cultures and races'.[50]

In that year the Inner London Education Authority became the first of many to produce policy statements endorsing a cultural pluralist perspective, and Inner London and Manchester became two of the most vigorous authorities in developing multicultural programmes in their schools. Chris Mullard has neatly summarised the thinking behind these initiatives:

121

In contrast to the assimilationist's view of our society as being politically and culturally homogenous, its advocates maintain that our society consists of different groups which are culturally distinctive and separate. Therefore, within a plural society there exists a positive commitment to difference and to the preservation of group culture, traditions and history.[51]

During the 1970s the British Government advertised in the Indian sub-continent for Asian teachers, publicising a shortfall of 14,000 teachers in British schools. But, as Paul Ghuman has shown, the relatively small number of Asian and Afro-Caribbean teachers who did succeed in gaining employment were met by racism from many of their fellow teachers and were marginalised, both in terms of promotion and the location of their employment.[52] As part of the drift towards a system which was divided on ethnic lines, the vast majority of immigrant teachers found themselves involved in the special programmes and multicultural education projects which were largely funded by Section 11 money. For this reason their employment proved to be particularly insecure when Section 11 funding was cut back in the 1980s.[53]

But by the end of the decade, what some came disparagingly to call the curriculum of the three Ss (saris, samosas and steel bands) was under heavy attack. During 1980 and 1981 disturbances in the St Paul's area of Bristol, Brixton in London, Toxteth in Liverpool and Handsworth in Birmingham highlighted the disaffection of black youth and the extent to which it was being marginalised in British society. Multicultural programmes in schools came to be seen as, at best, naive, and at worst, racist. J. Williams observed in the *British Journal of Sociology* that 'very few theories can have suffered so short an optimistic phase', identifying institutional racism as the key factor which distorted multicultural education from the outset.[54]

Several commentators stressed the extent to which multicultural education had, in reality, subordinated the ethnic minorities. R. Street Porter pointed out that, in practice, minority groups are allowed complete freedom to define their own cultural identity 'only in so far as this does not conflict with that of the white indigenous community'.[55] One ex-employee of the Inner London Education Authority argued in a letter to the *TES* that the racism engendered by multicultural education programmes was one cause of the disturbances in Brixton.[56] Even more pointedly, Chris Mullard, one of the leading critics of multiculturalism, argued that:

As interpreted in practice ... multiracial education has appeared to become an instrument of control and stability rather than one of change, of the subordination rather than the freedom of blacks in schools and in society as a whole. In the context of schools ... multi-racial education programmes have in fact integrally contributed to the increased alienation of black youth.[57]

Mullard extended this attack in his *Racism in school and society*, where he argued that the real function of multicultural education was to 'contain black resistance', and that it functioned as 'none other than a sophisticated form of social control'.[58] Yet, despite this, both national government and local authorities were loth to abandon multiculturalism completely, and, as late as the summer of 1981, an *Education Digest* was seeking to identify ways of developing new approaches to the multicultural curriculum.[59]

The official response was, increasingly, to seek to ensure that multiculturalism worked in practice and was implemented in such a way as to meet these criticisms. Although when, in 1973, the Select Committee on Race Relations and Immigration had asked for the establishment of a separate fund to meet 'the special needs of ethnic minority groups', the Home Office had refused, by the end of the decade there was an increasing willingness to respond. The Select Committee returned to the issue again in 1977, concerned at 'the poor performance of West Indian children in school'.[60] In response to this pressure, shortly before leaving office, Shirley Williams set up a Committee of Enquiry to review the needs and attainments of children from ethnic minority groups. Significantly, the Committee was instructed to recognise 'the contribution of the schools in preparing all pupils for life in a society which is both multiracial and culturally diverse'.[61] Some critics have seen this as a deliberate attempt to steer a path between the growing pressure from the extreme right for an education which would initiate all pupils to a common British culture, and the equally strongly felt view on the left that the key role of the schools was to concentrate on anti-racist education.[62] But, whatever the political context, it was certainly the case that the 1981 Rampton Report and the 1985 Swann Report, both of which were produced by this Committee, had the effect of reinvigorating the multicultural lobby.

Although the Rampton Report came out strongly in favour of anti-racist initiatives in schools, its main contention was that the role of educators remained the establishment of a multicultural society:

> a curriculum which takes account of the multiracial nature of society is needed for all schools, not just those in which there are ethnic minority pupils. It is important to make clear that a curriculum which reflects the multiracial nature of society should not be seen as something different or extra to be added on to the existing curriculum. . . . A good education cannot be based on one culture only.[63]

This chimed with a report submitted to the Schools Council in the same year which showed a growing contrast between the indifference to multicultural education of schools in the 'white highlands' and the acceptance by an increasing number of inner-city schools that 'an awareness of Britain's multi-ethnic society should permeate the curriculum as a whole'.[64]

As Carrington and Short have shown, a number of initiatives during the early eighties kept the multicultural lobby alive.[65] The Schools Council asked all of its subject boards to take into account multicultural issues under pressure from the National Association for Multiracial Education. Tutors on teacher training courses were encouraged to extend their knowledge of the issues involved: examination boards became increasingly sensitive to multiculturalism when devising curricula and examinations. But probably the last major blast for multiculturalism was the publication in 1985 of the final report of the Committee of Enquiry into the Education of Children from Ethnic Minority Groups. Now chaired by Lord Swann, it was unequivocal in tone:

> We consider that a multiracial society such as ours would in fact function most effectively on the basis of pluralism which enables, expects and encourages members of all ethnic groups, both minority and majority, to participate fully in shaping the society as a whole within a framework of commonly accepted values, practices and procedures, whilst also allowing, and, where necessary, assisting the ethnic minority communities in maintaining their distinct ethnic identities within this common framework.[66]

Beyond this, the Swann Report stressed that racism, whether institutional or individual, should be identified and countered.

In this last recommendation, the Swann Committee was reflecting the extent to which the debate was moving on during the 1980s. In 1981 the Parliamentary Home Affairs Committee on Race Relations had asked schools to examine both their formal and informal curricula to ensure that they were not inadvertently transmitting racism and were actively seeking to combat it. This was increasingly the tenor of the decade as the awareness of the extent to which the educational system was marginalising black students became more widely realised. The setting-up of a Black Students' Action Collective in a South London school in the mid-seventies was just one of several initiatives which led the ILEA between 1981 and 1983 to consult widely with the parents of ethnic minority pupils in order to develop 'an unequivocally anti-racist policy'. Similarly, in 1985, the National Association for Multicultural Education rechristened itself the National Antiracist Movement in Education. It was becoming clear, too, that black students were far more likely than their white counterparts to be excluded from school. One CRE report showed that, in Birmingham, a black pupil was four times as likely as a white child to be suspended from school.[67] Antiracism was becoming the dominant issue and a growing number of local authorities was initiating antiracist policies which covered all employees, including teachers. One such was Berkshire, where an 'Education for equality' campaign was sponsored in local schools.

This was made all the more relevant by the clear evidence that Thatcher's Governments were in reality committed to policies whose main purpose was to placate the enduring strain of racism which marked some of her grassroots support. In the run-up to the 1979 election she talked of 'being swamped by those coming in' and promised to 'allay people's fears on numbers'. The 1981 Nationality Act followed in short order. It strengthened the existing 1971 legislation by removing the right of those born in Britain to have an automatic claim to British citizenship. 'Patriality' was now redefined in a way which discriminated against non-whites. This set the tone for much of the detailed educational policy towards the existing ethnic minorities which was to follow. In the same way that Mark Carlisle, as Secretary of State for Education, made no positive response to the claims of the Rampton Report that a large part of the explanation for the underachievement of black pupils lay in racism, Keith Joseph rejected much of the Swann Report. He argued that 'antiracist interventions from the national state were neither desirable nor necessary', and went on to attack the 'self-appointed apostles of anti-racism who threaten ... to subvert our fundamental values and institutions'.[68] This was in line with much that emanated from the Department of Education at this time. Two years earlier, Joseph had implored teachers of History to stress 'the shared values which are a distinctive feature of British society', and Bob Dunn, his Junior Minister, argued in 1984 that

> It is essential that schools should foster and teach the language of this their adopted homeland. Our duty is clear. Whatever else we may also do in our schools, we must teach British History, customs and Christianity. Thus we will avoid the perpetuation of two classes of citizen.[69]

The survival of an essentially eugenic view of modern society could not have been more clearly demonstrated.

Further disturbances, most notably at Broadwater Farm, Tottenham in London, and in Handsworth, Birmingham, in 1985 were evidence of the difficulties still attaching to relations between ethnic groups in Britain. The popular fears which were aroused by these incidents were fuelled by a tabloid press only too willing to propagandise issues which should properly have been the subject of more measured debate. The think tanks and pressure groups from which the New Right took its ideas had proliferated during the seventies and eighties, and the question of 'Englishness' was high on their agenda. The Freedom Association, the Social Affairs Unit and the Centre for Policy Studies were all antagonistic to policies which seemed to threaten the national identity, so educational initiatives aimed at relations between ethnic groups and at the opportunities available to young blacks were high on their hit list. Several groups appeared during the early eighties to coordinate what were, in reality, largely white, middle-class parental fears. Among them were the Parental Alliance for Choice in Education, the Campaign for Real Education, and Parents for English Education. Members of the Hillgate Group, Anthony Flew and Ray Honeyford were among the more vocal right-wingers who made sure that their own opposition to multicultural education became part of the agenda of these groups. As Chris Gaine has summarised it:

> They had an effect in the construction of a 'debate' about nationalism, and in the Education Reform Act itself, with its 'Christian' assemblies, its abolition of the ILEA, and its marginalisation of race-related measures.[70]

What made all of this particularly pervasive was the fact that the press was all-too ready to propagandise the issues raised. When, in September 1986, a white boy murdered a Bangladeshi in the playground of Burnage School in Manchester, the local authority set up a committee of enquiry. While the council was still deliberating how best to proceed, the *Manchester Evening News* published the final chapter of the lengthy report and immediately put the issue into the public domain. This gave Anthony Flew and members of the Centre for Policy Studies an excuse to go public with blanket indictments of anti-racist educational initiatives. The popular newspapers had a field day. The *Sun* led with 'Anti-racist rules fail our kids'. The *Daily Mail* attacked the 'dangerous obsession with race which is endemic to certain left-dominated education authorities', while the *Daily Telegraph* concluded that 'Anti-racist policy led to killing'.[71]

In the same year the anti-racist policies of one London borough received a similar working-over. In October the *Mail on Sunday* turned its attention to the borough of Brent in a swingeing attack. Under the headline 'Race spies shock' it stated:

> Race Commissars in a left-wing borough are recruiting 180 Thought Police to patrol schools for prejudice. And they will be paid for out of a five million Government grant intended to promote racial harmony. But teachers in the London borough of Brent – who say they already work in climate of fear – believe the classroom spies will cause lasting damage in the drive for equality and will lower educational standards even further. Government Ministers, who are powerless to prevent taxpayers' money being used, are worried that it could rapidly be copied by other inner-city councils.[72]

Kenneth Baker, the then Secretary of State, responded to this with a television appearance in which he expressed his 'concern' at the article. He commissioned a special HMI investigation of this issue, and, despite its impartiality, used its publication to talk of 'the most disturbing report I have ever read'.[73] This elicited a *Daily Express* headline: 'Flushing out the fanatics'. The sense of paranoia which this induced in local authorities is shown by the fact that, in the following year, the Association of London Authorities commissioned *It's the way that they tell 'em*, a publication devoted to the exposure of press distortions of anti-racist policies.[74]

By the late eighties this polarisation of the debate on ethnic minorities in schools was having a clear effect on policy implementation. In the autumn of 1986, new Home Office guidelines on Section 11 funding limited it to support for the teaching of English as a second language, the provision of bilingual teachers for young children and of teachers capable of introducing ethnic minority pupils to existing school curricula. The 1988 Education Reform Act took this further, not only breaking up the ILEA, much of the opposition to which had stemmed from its initiatives in ethnic minority provision, but also defining the National Curriculum in narrow terms and placing further restrictions on the use of Section 11 funding. Ian Grosvenor has shown how attempts to modify the National Curriculum to make it more sensitive to the needs of ethnic minority pupils were quashed:

> A second amendment proposed incorporating into the Act a sentence from the DES publication *Better Schools* (1985) calling for all pupils to be educated to 'understand and acquire a positive attitude to the variety of ethnic groups in British society'. It was defeated.[75]

The Act went on to assume that 'the nation is politically and culturally indivisible'. Nor was there any sign at the end of the decade of a turn of the tide. In 1990 the Brent Development Programme for Racial Equality was scrapped, starved of funding and Government support. During the same year, John MacGregor, the then Secretary of State, ruled in response to lobbying from parents in Cleveland that 'parents can select schools on "racial" grounds and a parent's right to choose should override "race relations" legislation'. Ian Grosvenor has described this as a policy which has contributed to 'the continued subordination, isolation and alienation of black citizens in Britain'.[76]

All of this was in accord with the wider drift of policy. In August 1988, legislation was introduced to restrict immigration further by forcing Commonwealth males to prove that they could support their families. Second wives of polygamous marriages were explicitly excluded. At the end of 1989, the Conservative Government resisted international pressure and restricted the number of Vietnamese refugees entering Britain to 20,000. Norman Tebbitt led the successful opposition to a proposal to grant the right of settlement in Britain to Hong Kong Chinese. The tone of Conservative policy on this issue was captured by John Townsend, MP for Bridlington, who said that 'England must be recaptured for the English'.[77]

Ian Grosvenor offers a challenging summary of the impact of these policies on the British education system. He argues that

> education policy since the early 1960s has complemented the State's construction of black people as a 'problem'. Analysts of successive governments' response to the presence of black pupils in state schools generally identify three phases of development in education policy:

assimilationist, integrationist and cultural pluralist. There is an inherent weakness in this analysis in that it draws attention to the elements of change in policy rather than signifying the elements of continuity. These identified shifts in policy are more imagined than real: they exist in the sphere of articulation rather than in practice. In reality government policy towards black children in schools has been characterised since the 1960s through to the 1990s by an enduring commitment to assimilation as a policy goal. From an assimilationist perspective black children are seen as alien and a problem element in 'our' schools. Further, the problems of black children are seen to 'lie deep within their respective cultures'. These cultures are themselves reconstituted through political and educational discourses as competing 'ethnic identities' on the basis of which resources are allocated and policy determined. Consequently, multicultural and antiracist initiatives have been viewed as solely appropriate to so called multicultural schools and as irrelevant to 'white' schools. In this sense education policy must be regarded as a central force in the generation and reproduction of a discourse . . . which links 'race', colour and culture in such a way as to fix a national identity in which to be British is to be white.[78]

In sum, the effects of these policies over the thirty-six year period covered by this book were not simply to alienate and marginalise black youth within the education system, but also to generate significant contrasts in employment opportunities, which, in their turn, worked to deepen the rifts in the fabric of British society. This process operated in two ways. First, differential outcomes in terms of formal examination results were reflected in patterns of access to higher education. While the relative success of some ethnic minorities opened up the prospect for Britain's Asian communities,[79] the inability of other groups to compete on equal terms within schools led inevitably to under-representation in higher education. Further, there was growing evidence of foot-dragging by tutors in the older universities when challenged to initiate access courses for ethnic minority and mature students during the 1980s. Those few Afro-Caribbean youths who made it to the more prestigious institutions often did so at the cost of alienation from their own communities and families, in just the same way that white working-class entrants to the universities in the early twentieth century had faced a future which involved leaving behind their social roots. Since this period saw an intensification of the linkages between higher education, the acquisition of formal qualifications and access to secure employment in the professions and in the higher echelons of commerce and industry, the results in terms of employment patterns were immediate and profound. The failure of the education system to offer a fair start to ethnic minority pupils meant, inexorably, the intensification of their disadvantages in the employment market. Even worse, clear patterns became evident within the universities and colleges of further education; while it became fairly usual to see Asian students on courses in Law, Business Administration or Medicine, it was less common although not unknown to see them in other university faculties. Within the FE colleges, there was a similar clustering of ethnic groups. Courses in Car Maintenance became a regular target for Afro-Caribbean youths: those which led to sedentary work less so. This process became more marked during the period under review and demands fuller research than it has so far merited.[80]

Second, for those young people who did not aspire to higher education, it was the ethnic minorities which found the greatest difficulty in getting work and, once employed, in keeping it. Andy Forbes has sought to explain the dynamic which resulted in many black students leaving school without the formal qualifications or training to ensure they found work:

> The traditional model of British education was held in high esteem by the first Afro-Caribbean and Asian immigrants.... There was still a clear *prima facie* association of this traditional type of schooling and socio-economic success. People who successfully completed 'O' levels and 'A' levels and went on to polytechnics and universities, still got better jobs than those who did not. In many instances, ethnic minority parents and children reacted with anger and dismay to curriculum innovations and demanded a return to traditional methods.[81]

Mairtin Mac an Ghaill has confirmed that, by the 1980s, black students were becoming all too ready to link the anti-academic-work culture of their schools to high unemployment rates in their localities. As one black student put it:

> They are making us unemployable, or fit for the worst jobs white people don't want. All black and Asian kids feel this at different levels. It leads a lot of kids to give up, but some of us at school . . . see what's going on but we get through somehow.[82]

Several researchers have confirmed the results in terms of access to employment. S. Dex has shown that, by the early eighties, while the overall employment rate for school leavers in Bradford was 66 per cent, only 28 per cent of Asian school leavers were finding work.[83] Jackson's study of youth unemployment showed similar patterns elsewhere.[84] K. Roberts, in his definitive study of *School leavers and their prospects*, published in 1984,[85] argued that qualifications, clustering in the inner cities, lack of appropriate contacts, and discrimination, were the key factors leading to the relative failure of black youths in the job market. While Asian youth was often likely to retreat into family-based entrepreneurial activity, West Indian youth was more likely to drift into long-term unemployment. The bitterness of young Afro-Caribbeans was intensified by the fact that, as the period wore on, it became increasingly likely that they were doing better than their white classmates in school, but were still the victims of discrimination when it came to finding work. This irony enables one final twist to the application of eugenic ideas to an analysis of late twentieth century education. It is neatly summarised by K. Roberts:

> The superior performances of ethnic minority youths in many inner city schools are not difficult to explain. Inner city whites are a residue, many families with the means and motivation having departed. In contrast, the parents of present day Asian and West Indian school leavers are mostly first generation immigrants, and include many talented and ambitious people. Why else would they have crossed the oceans?[86]

This is a nice counterpoint to the quotation with which this chapter began. Whether or not we are about to see a reworking of eugenics which turns it against the less successful whites, there is ample evidence that the continuing strength of eugenic ideas is a key to our understanding of the ways in which the education system defined the social roles of ethnic minority students between 1964 and 1990.

7

BUREAUCRATISATION AND THE GOVERNANCE OF EDUCATION

Although bureaucratisation has been of major concern to social theorists, little if anything has been written from a historical perspective about the bureaucratisation of the English education system in the recent past. Yet, arguably, the transformations which have taken place in the scale, internal working and administration of our schools, colleges and universities have been among the most significant influences on their social functions, their overall impact on society and the extent and nature of their responses to wider social and economic change.

But, first, what exactly do we mean by 'bureaucratisation' in this context? Ralf Thorstendahl, who has sought to analyse the development of this phenomenon in North West Europe in this century, sees bureaucratisation as 'A kind of historical by-product ... which ... during the last hundred years has become central'.[1]

He identifies four key sources of power in modern society: alongside violence, capital and knowledge he sees organisational power as being itself one of the motors of social development. He describes bureaucratic power as:

A kind of authority which has been developed for use in bureaucracies, especially the public service. Its first variety is acquaintance with norms that are recognised as valid for society in general as well as norms with a limited scope within the bureaucratic apparatus.[2]

Organisational power is one of the key characteristics of the emerging middle classes. In an insightful analysis of middle-class formation in modern Britain, Mike Savage and his co-researchers have reflected on the kinds of explanation offered by historians of the nature and functioning of the middle class.[3] By definition, Marxist analyses see middle-class professionals as little more than the agents and functionaries of a capitalist class. Their role may be to 'de-skill' the working class by taking the 'thinking work' away from them: a distinctive middle class 'responsible for the conception of work' may need to operate as a bureaucracy to achieve this end. But this interpretation of bureaucratisation sees it as necessarily subordinating the bureaucrats to the true controllers of social development. Similarly, Weberian theories see the middle classes as:

> functionaries for the processes of domination. . . . In modern societies it is the role of the middle classes as bureaucrats that is given greatest emphasis. Weber saw bureaucracies as the embodiment of an impersonal, rational authority, in distinction to traditional or charismatic authority based on personal characteristics. . . . The middle classes have a distinct role as functionaries within bureaucratic processes.[4]

It was in this vein that C. Wright Mills identified the years following the Second World War as a crucial period of bureaucratisation which imposed new lifestyles and new pressures on the emerging middle classes.[5] As Savage *et al.* point out, all such theories tend to see the middle class as a lieutenant class, with bureaucratisation as one of the key weapons available to it to perform its functions.

Their own preference is to see the middle classes as social collectivities worthy of study in their own right. This approach necessarily stresses the importance of bureaucratisation as a key device enabling the social closure and power structures which legitimise and perpetuate these classes. But they also stress that in the last few years there are increasing grounds to query the view of Abercrombie and Urrie that 'service class places are places within bureaucracies and are likely to become increasingly so'.[6] They argue that

> the dominant economic and social trend is the declining significance of bureaucratic hierarchies in economic organisations. While it remains true that many professionals and managers continue to work within large organisations, the type of work they do and the career strategies they use seem to be departing from those associated with older bureaucratic hierarchies. . . . Of particular note here is the growing inter-organisational mobility, even for managerial workers who have tended to progress through an internal labour market. In our view it is the declining significance of organisational assets that is of major significance in altering the terrain on which middle-class formation takes place in the contemporary period.[7]

Be that as it may, there can be little doubt that schooling is one arena where the growing significance of bureaucratisation can be readily perceived, especially in the most recent historical period. The education system was never conceived of as a bureaucracy in its own right, although from the early years of the provision of popular education, a small but growing bureaucracy was set up to administer it. The Education Department of the nineteenth century has evolved into a much larger and more pervasive central authority in recent times, just as the local education authorities which replaced the school boards have grown in size and taken on ancillary functions which were far from foreseeable at the outset. But bureaucratisation, in the sense in which it is used here, means far more than the development of an administrative system to support and supervise the working of schools, universities and colleges. These institutions have themselves become increasingly bureaucratised. Not only have the numbers of ancillary and secretarial staff multiplied, but the day-to-day functioning of all those involved in education has become steadily more susceptible to and controlled by bureaucratic norms.

A direct spin-off from this bureaucratisation of the education system has been the emergence of new and more powerful modes of regulating what goes on day by day, both at the individual classroom level and in respect of the running and administration of whole institutions. It is for this reason that this chapter deals also with the changing governance of education: the control systems and power structures at work by the late eighties were in part a direct result of this growing bureaucratisation, and it is appropriate to deal with the two together. The central argument of this chapter is that this process, which has been particularly marked since the mid-sixties, has impinged on and helped to redefine the social functions of education. The task here is to describe and analyse the process.

It is possible to identify immediately six ways in which the growth of educational bureaucracies had an impact on the working of the system. First, and perhaps most pervasive, any group which is bureaucratised (and this applies to professional groupings particularly) is, by definition, more susceptible to a hierarchical view of its own functioning. Bureaucracies are by their very nature power hierarchies, and those who work within them become acolytes of hierarchical power relationships. Second, following from this, career routes become more clearly defined and career progression tends to depend on a steady and predictable progress through this kind of hierarchically arranged bureaucracy. There is some evidence, as I will argue, that the education system was particularly susceptible to this trend. Third, there can be no doubt that bureaucratisation impacted profoundly on the day-to-day working of schools, colleges and universities. By the end of our period, a host of working practices at every level had been permanently transformed and a main cause of this was the bureaucratisation of the system. Fourth, and no less significant, these new bureaucracies had the effect of confirming and reinforcing gender contrasts, both among students and particularly among the providers of education. Fifth, it is possible to argue, and the present author believes it to be the case, that this newly transformed education system became one which was particularly adept at preparing its students for those modes of employment which were themselves bureaucratised. The whole business of increasing accreditation for entry to higher education and the workplace meant that there was a particularly close symbiosis between bureaucratised educational institutions and a particular set of employments and career routes within which these new practices were

133

becoming widespread. In other words, analysts of social class formation in modern Britain should consider schooling as one of the ways in which the emergent middle classes promoted their own ends and their own values. The education system became, as never before, the agency through which they confirmed their newly won position. Children and young people from particular social backgrounds were perceived to be successful within a bureaucratised education system, learnt how to operate effectively within such systems in the schools, and, in so doing, enhanced their own chances of moving successfully into particular modes of employment. This was a direct and powerful result of bureaucratisation. Finally, as the converse of this last point, there can be little doubt that bureaucracies, in many areas of public life, and not least in education, worked to confirm the exclusion of those social groups which were not themselves in bureaucratised employments and were, by and large, in disadvantaged positions within society. To the extent that they failed to take on board the styles and modes of operation of these newly bureaucratised systems, the old working class and the unemployed remained, and were clearly observed to be, outside the norms of what a growing number came to see as the natural ordering of society.

Between 1964 and 1990, evidence of the process of bureaucratisation can be seen at every level within the education system. At the start of the period, the universities were still, by and large, unaffected by the trend towards bureaucratisation. Below the level of university Senates, committee structures were embryonic. One result of the sudden post-Robbins expansion was that this changed dramatically. Two key catalysts can be discerned. First, the expansion of teacher training in newly expanded Colleges of Education involved the establishment of Bachelor of Education degrees, validated, in most cases, by the nearest university. This involved the establishment of formal administrative structures to oversee developments. By 1970, for example, the University of Birmingham had assumed responsibility for these awards in thirteen local colleges, and a Department, largely administrative in function, had been set up to run this new part of the University's work. Within a few years, such administrative expansion was generalised through the work of the CNAA, quickly overtaking the University of London as the largest degree-awarding institution in Britain. CNAA validation became the route followed by the nascent polytechnics, and this involved the establishment of administrative structures to oversee the fairness and comparability of awards in differing institutions. It became more usual, and more widely accepted, for the introduction of new degree courses to involve a greater amount of paperwork than had been the case previously. At the same time, the role of the University Grants Committee itself developed, as successive Governments struggled to control the expansion of the university system.

So, although the ratio of administrative to academic staff remained at roughly one to fourteen throughout the period,[8] the net result of the expansion of the system was that the roles of administrators changed perceptibly, impinging increasingly on the day-to-day working of academics by acting as the agents of increasingly interventionist Government policies. One increment in that progression was the effect of the 1968 student unrest, which led many universities to examine closely their internal management, and to set up more sophisticated committee structures – often at that time involving student representation – to bring this about. The outcome was that by 1990 there were over 10,000 administrative staff in employment in the universities of Great Britain.[9] During the 1980s the establishment of administrative support systems to monitor the quality of taught courses, the introduction of staff appraisal, the development of equal opportunities policies (all thoroughly defensible in their own right, and mirroring practice in other parts of the economy) were only a few of the areas in which university life became steadily more bureaucratised. Yet this process did not result in the equalisation of opportunity. In reality the opposite proved to be the case.

There is a deep irony about these developments which is worth pointing out. An administrative system which might have been expected to ensure widespread public confidence that degrees from differing universities and different departments were of equal worth certainly had not had that effect by the late eighties. Similarly, if it could have been expected that a bureaucratised system would be one which led to more precise detection of the origins of social class inequalities in access to the universities and in some kind of levelling-out of the chances of young people from contrasting social backgrounds entering them, this, too, proved to be illusory. Further, by the late eighties, the upper echelons of the academic hierarchies were predominantly male in British universities and the secretarial and support routes were almost exclusively female. The AUT reported in 1990 that only one Vice-Chancellor (2 per cent!) was female. Further, the clearly identified grades which had developed within this bureaucratised system could be seen to be discriminatory against females. In 1990, while 32 per cent of contract research staff were female, only 14 per cent of lecturers were, 6 per cent of senior lecturers and 3 per cent of the Professoriat in British universities.[10] It would be hard to find a clearer example of a bureaucratised system confirming inequalities, and further research is needed to identify both why this was the case and the processes through which it occurred.

The trends at school level were not dissimilar, although for those working within the system, bureaucratic interference may have come to seem ubiquitous by the end of the 1980s. The motor of significant bureaucratisation in this part of the education system was, first, the growth in the size of secondary schools particularly, and second, the growing impact of external policy on routine practice. During the mid-sixties, there were few ancillary staff in the schools and their functions were usually confined to secretarial support for one or two individuals in positions of power. Even the new comprehensive schools at this time had few ancillary and support staff, and the power hierarchies within them were accordingly slight. A large school might have one head, possibly two deputy heads, and a few staff who took on pastoral duties as heads of houses within a house system or in some cases heads of year. Within a few years these structures were being elaborated. Heads of house and heads of year were complemented by identified staff who took responsibility for upper and lower schools, examination entries, careers advice and external liaison of one sort or another. Beyond this, the growing army of specialist and ancillary staff employed by the local authorities meant that schools were obliged to identify and process students with particular needs: behavioural problems, learning difficulties and other special educational needs, the teaching of newly arrived immigrants, as well as the establishment of pastoral systems which would enable pupils to thrive in the school environment, were among the challenges all of which imposed their own administrative demands. Social workers, educational advisers, child psychologists and specialist and peripatetic teachers all became common features of school life.

Beyond this, external pressures resulted in the systematisation of a host of practices which had previously been informal in style. The writing of termly reports became more systematised, as did the conduct of regular meetings with parents. At the behest of government during the 1980s, records of achievement, profiling of student progress, staff appraisal and the publication of inspectors' reports all added to the administrative load of the schools. Perhaps unsurprisingly, in view of the impact of rate capping and central government financial cuts, the number of support staff employed in the education service fell significantly during these years. Central Statistical Office returns showed that the figure of 253,000 full-time support staff employed in education in England and Wales in 1975 fell to 209,000 by 1986. The fall in the number of part-time staff was less marked.[11] This meant that many of the tasks which had previously been undertaken by secretaries accrued to the teachers themselves, and the preparedness to undertake these extra duties became one of the criteria for successful advancement through this bureaucratised hierarchy.

It followed naturally that career routes for teachers became more clearly charted, and that deviations from the career track became less acceptable. Although this could never be voiced formally when selection and promotion procedures were taking place, it seems that females who took advantage of maternity leave could have been marginalising themselves from the promotion track, especially when this came to be seen as involving a steady, and preferably unbroken, progress from successful classroom teacher to departmental headship and further pastoral and responsibility posts, before approaching deputy and eventually full headship. In other cases there were, doubtless, many female teachers who stayed in post during the early years of parenting but were unable to commit fully to career advancement given the demands of child rearing. This constraint was felt far less by males, for whom the arrival of children often meant a greater sense of obligation to ensure financial security through career advancement. What made the dynamic of this intraprofessional career routing all the more powerful was that it came to be seen as linked to the acquisition of appropriate further qualifications, often in Educational Management, achieved through attendance at institutions of higher education of one sort or another. During the sixties and seventies there was enough money within the system for significant numbers of teachers to be seconded full-time for one year to gain extra qualifications. During the 1980s this became less common, and most teachers were forced into part-time routes for in-service courses. In brief, what was occurring historically was that the popular judgement of what constituted a successful teacher was being almost imperceptibly reworked, so that by the late eighties it had come to mean something quite different from its connotations at the start of the period covered by this book. In the process, females were further marginalised, and the statistics of those appointed to school headships which are given elsewhere in this book certainly bear out this view.

In considering the extent and nature of bureaucratisation within the education system during these years, it would be wrong to overlook the sweeping changes which took place in its administration at both national and local level. In 1964 the establishment of the Department of Education and Science meant that, for the first time, a central government agency existed with responsibility for oversight of the whole formal educational provision in England and Wales. Now even the University Grants Committee came under its purview. The DES took on a wide range of duties, including the establishment of minimum educational standards, control of the cost of the education service and advice to the Treasury on appropriate levels of central and local government expenditure. Beyond this, the support of direct grant institutions, the determination of policy on teacher training, the encouragement and sponsorship of educational research and the administration of superannuation schemes were all included in its brief. It is hardly surprising that a complex committee structure had soon developed to make this possible. By the mid-eighties there were four schools branches, and each had numerous divisions within them, so that a specialist section existed for every aspect of the work of schools. Four further branches supervised further and higher education: the finance branch also had four divisions, while other branches took responsibility for teachers, educational research, statistics, pensions, teacher supply and training, information and legal matters.[12] The Department had a more elaborate committee structure than had existed at any previous period for the oversight of education.

During its first twenty years the DES was subject to a number of pressures which each had an impact on its functioning. Peter Gordon et al. have suggested that, during the 1960s, the Department came under increasing pressure to justify the demands it was making of the Treasury, which in return 'insisted that the Department define its objectives and more clearly establish priorities and anticipate needs. This required changes in style, intelligence-gathering and awareness.... The Inspectorate, threatened by a range of local authority advisers, now began to look for new roles'.[13] One device used by the DES during its early years to bring pressure for curriculum reform was the Curriculum Study Group, which was set up in 1962 and which, two years later, was converted into the Schools Council. For thirteen years, with the warm support of William Alexander and the Association of Education Committees, the Schools Council flooded the schools with suggestions on both the organisation and content of teaching. But the demise of the AEC in 1977, and the closing down of the Schools Council in 1984 by Keith Joseph, left the DES seriously weakened in its ability to bring about curriculum reform through cooperation.

This coincided with other developments which worked to modify the style of the DES and to accelerate its bureaucratisation. During the sixties and seventies, the DES was willing to work through its Inspectorate to bring about change through consultation. The Assessment of Performance Unit, set up in 1974, was headed by an HMI, and the *Yellow Book* of 1976 which precipitated the Ruskin Speech and the 'Great Debate' on education was, in part at least, compiled by Inspectors. But the growing reliance on the Downing Street Policy Unit and on backroom advisers such as Sir Bernard Donoghue, first evident under Jim Callaghan as Prime Minister, resulted in the marginalisation of the Inspectorate, and, during the 1980s, in the Inspectorate becoming the defenders of professional autonomy against policies which were increasingly dictated by unelected gurus working in Government 'think tanks'.[14] The publication of the reports of Inspectors from January 1983 onwards may have heightened their visibility, but it also worked to circumscribe their role.

Another element in the changing role of the DES was the introduction of the block grant system in 1964. This new financial arrangement meant that, although the needs of spending departments and local authorities were individually costed, funds were disbursed in a lump sum, with local authorities being given discretion to distribute the monies as they wished between all of their activities. Hardly surprisingly, DES officials opposed this new arrangement on the grounds that it gave too much power to the local authorities and threatened educational development: the Association of Metropolitan Authorities was to become a staunch defender of these block grant arrangements. In 1982 an attempt from within the DES to restore specific grants was squashed in Cabinet.[15] There can be no doubt that this arrangement eroded the basis of the 1944 settlement and made the DES itself more susceptible to an interventionist government, particularly in the straightened economic circumstances of the 1980s. Funding patterns were helping to define the bureaucratic role of the Department.

During the 1970s there were complaints that the DES had too much power to devise policy in secret (this was the main criticism contained in a 1976 OECD Report), and also that it was becoming too much of a postbox between local authorities and teachers' unions.[16] By the mid-eighties neither charge was possible. The DES had become the instrument of a Government determined to impose its own educational settlement. It was used increasingly to announce and to implement policies which were not negotiated with the professional organisations and were not liked by them. In order to do this, the bureaucratic hierarchy which, as we have seen, had developed within the Department had to be deployed to the full. In this respect, one spin-off from bureaucratisation was a tilt towards coercion.

At local government level, too, there was a marked shift towards the delivery of policies which had been devised elsewhere. In this sense, LEAs were also becoming increasingly part of a bureaucratised system. The first element in this process was the ironing-out of administrative anomalies. First, the London area divisional executives were abolished from 1965. By increasing the size and influence of the Inner London Education Authority, this measure made it a readier target for an interventionist government twenty years later. This was but part of a more general trend, though, which was signalled by the 1969 Redcliffe–Maud Commission on Local Government. The Commission's proposals resulted in the number of local education authorities being reduced from 146 to 104, as small authorities in the metropolitan areas were merged. At the very moment that this was being implemented, the 1972 Baines Report led many authorities to introduce systems of corporate management, under which it was far more difficult for individuals or pressure groups to exercise influence on decisions. This trend was confirmed by the Widdicombe enquiry into the conduct of local authorities in 1986 which further hobbled the work of LEAs by making it illegal for co-optees, or indeed anyone other than an elected councillor, to participate in key decisions. The professional representatives who for almost a century had played an important part in the work of the LEAs were thus put out of the game.[17]

Beyond this, the steady attenuation of the powers of the local authorities has been one of the most marked features of the education system since the mid-sixties. Their role as key elements in the policy-making process was eroded, first through a starving of resources, which became a drought after the introduction of rate-capping in 1983. The diversion of funds through agencies such as the MSC further weakened the LEAs. But administrative changes proved an equally effective way of curtailing their powers, as Gordon *et al.* have shown:

> LEAs have become involved in a keener scrutiny of public performance. Examples are the Tameside High Court case of 1977 where the Secretary of State challenged an LEA which proposed to retain selective

schools, the rights given to individuals for redress of grievances, such as the Local Government Act 1974 . . . the Sex Discrimination Act 1975, the Race Relations Act 1976 and Admissions Appeals which were set out in the 1980 Education Act.[18]

Finally, the introduction in 1986 of City Technology Colleges, which were to be outside of the LEA provision, the provision in the 1988 Act that schools could opt out of LEA control, and the abolition of the ILEA, sounded the death knell of local authority influence in education. By 1990 the LEAs were in an analogous position to that of the School Boards in the two years following the Cockerton judgement. Their future remains uncertain at best. What is clear, though, is that they, too, had become, as never before, bureaucracies charged with the task of implementing the policies of others. Weakened central and local government agencies meant the enhanced power of government itself to impose its policies through an administrative system which was increasingly bureaucratised but, at the same time, strangely weakened.

But if we are to seek the one area of activity which has contributed most significantly to the bureaucratisation of education during the period under review, it is probably school governorship, in which there has been a major transformation. Although the 1944 Act had stipulated that schools had to have either managing or governing bodies, their functions during the following thirty years remained in reality largely honorific. The Ministry's guidance on the implementation of the 1944 Act did not mention the possible inclusion of parents on governing bodies. By the late eighties, with financial and managerial responsibility devolved to individual schools to a far greater degree than had ever been the case before, governing bodies had become one of the most powerful influences on what went on in schools and, as often as not, the key participants were the elected parents. How did this transformation come about and what were its implications?

The moribund state of governing bodies was commented on by the 1967 Plowden Report, which took the view that 'the whole subject of school management requires reconsideration', emphasising their concern that at primary school level almost a third of the headteachers they had surveyed thought that managing bodies were of little or no help, and only 40 per cent thought that they were helpful. In some urban areas, one managing body was at work for as many as twelve schools, and even in those rural areas where there was a managing body for each school, there was rarely, if ever, parental representation.[19]

At both primary and secondary level, the duties of governing bodies seemed to be largely honorific, involving appearance at prize-giving ceremonies and the occasional grand tour of the premises, and the confident expectation that their functions would be limited to rubber-stamping the decisions of the headteacher. In a situation in which the role of governors was generally perceived to be either honorific or social, parental involvement was neither expected nor demanded. If parents did become involved as school governors it was, as often as not, through the accident that their involvement in local politics led to them being seen as a suitable representative of their interest group for the school which their own children attended. This situation was posited on the reality that day-to-day decisions as well as most of the broader strategic issues concerning the school were delegated to the headteacher. This 'traditional' style of school governorship, which had persisted for much of the twentieth century, was only possible in a concatenation of power which saw central and local government and the school staff themselves as the three agencies with any real influence over what went on in schools. These were the 'professionals', the expert providers and arbiters of a good education. In the last resort, the teacher knew best.

In the brief period between the appointment of the Taylor Committee by Reg Prentice in 1975 and the passing of the 1988 Education Reform Act, this power structure, together with the assumptions which underpinned it, was rudely swept into the dustbin of history. Why was it possible for such a tried and well-established set of relationships to be cast aside so quickly, and seemingly with so little opposition? Three explanations spring to mind immediately, although the reality may have been more complex. First, the need to expand the teaching profession quickly during the late sixties in response to demographic change, and the trend for more pupils to stay on at school beyond the minimum leaving age, did much in the long term to 'demystify' teaching as a growing number of recruits to the profession were drawn from a wider social catchment. Second, the rise of the Radical Right, which is commented on elsewhere in this book, with its demands for greater accountability, was bound to have implications for school governorship. The lessening of public confidence in the ability of the teaching profession to keep its own house in order forced change in this area. A third key factor was that this lobbying was an ironic echo of the progressive lobby, which, through the whole period since the Second World War, had been calling for a closer involvement of teacher and parent. In this vein the Plowden Report, perhaps the official document of the post-war era which embodied most completely a progressive ideology, had outlined a minimum programme of cooperation with parents, seeing understanding and collaboration between parents and staff as crucial to the smooth running of a school. Similarly, the 1972 Halsey Report called for increasing parental involvement as one of the keys to a realisation of the programme outlined by the Plowden Committee.[20] The irony is that, on the one hand, these progressives were seeking to strengthen the power of the teacher by establishing more effective links with parents. As the thinking of the Radical Right became more widely known, it seemed that what was demanded was a parental watchdog as much as positive cooperation. But the apparent similarity in these two politically opposed programmes made it difficult for progressives within the education system to mount effective opposition to this part of the new agenda, and even attenuated their wish to do so.

During the mid-seventies a growing number of reports drew attention to the question of school governorship. The National Association of Governors and Managers undertook two surveys and showed that less than a quarter of the LEAs in England and Wales had any parental representation at all on governing bodies. Although the Sheffield Authority had, in 1970, set up separate governing bodies for all of its secondary schools and actively encouraged community and parental participation, it was out of step with the practice of most authorities; even the small minority which did allow for the appointment of one token parent on school governing bodies made no provision for any adequate consultation with the rest of the parent body.[21]

It was the Taylor Report,[22] published one year after the Auld Report on the William Tyndale affair,[23] which put the reconstruction of school governing bodies firmly on the political agenda. It appeared at almost the same moment as a study prepared for the Royal Commission on Local Government under the title of *School management and government*, which showed that, even as late as 1977, only nine counties and eleven county boroughs had any kind of parental involvement in school governing bodies, 'in some case through representative, in others through cooperative governors. Where a school has a parent–teacher association, it will normally put forward a name acceptable to the head, but where no such body exists it may be left to the head to suggest a suitable parent'. It is clear that at this time many heads retained almost feudal control over the nature of parental involvement in the schools. The Taylor Committee was to be the catalyst of change. Its Report confirmed that 'the extent to which managing and governing bodies carried out the functions assigned to them in rules and articles was slight'. The work of the Taylor Committee was founded on several assumptions; one of them was that the roles of central and local government which had been confirmed by the 1944 Education Act would remain unchanged, and that new schemes for governing bodies, which would allow parents to play a larger part, would operate within that framework. It must be said, in retrospect, that if governing bodies had been reconstituted in that context, then the outcomes would have been very different. Where the Taylor Report did challenge the 1944 settlement was in the recommendation that every school should have its own governing body, with balanced representation of the local authority, the staff of the school, parents and the local community. It was also foreseen that the governing body should play a fuller role in 'setting the aims of the school ... - considering the means by which they are pursued ... keeping under review the school's progress towards them and ... deciding on action to facilitate such progress'. There was evidence of a developing lobby for more radical initiatives in the note of dissent which was appended to the Report. This suggested that governors should have more control over the school's financial arrangements and ultimately be more accountable for the school's pattern of expenditure.

The Labour Government of the moment responded to the Taylor proposals with a White Paper in December 1978 on *The composition of school governing bodies.*[24] This echoed the Report, calling for individual governing bodies for each school, and for better consultation between governors, teachers, local authorities and the community. But the subsequent legislation, enacted in 1980 after Thatcher's coming to power, emasculated many of the Taylor Report's detailed recommendations. Falling back on the argument that 'there is still no agreement about what the formal powers of governing bodies should be', the Secretary of State argued in the Commons that his intention was simply to ensure that 'the right people' found their way on to governing bodies, rather than to completely re-jig their powers and responsibilities. This, he argued, would be enough to accomplish the changes that were needed.[25] Accordingly, the 1980 legislation focused on the need to recruit both teacher representatives and parents to governing bodies, which remained, for the time being at least, under the control of the local education authorities.

But although the legislation gave guidance on the balance of representatives on governing bodies, it stopped short of precise prescription. Various models were made available. While the Taylor Report had called for parental elections to governing bodies, the Act left methods of appointment to the discretion of local authorities. By 1980, recommendations on the training of school governors had disappeared completely. With the exception of infant and junior schools at work on the same site, each school was now to have its own governing body. As is argued elsewhere in this book, this first phase of Thatcherite Government was preservationist in its approach to educational issues, and was certainly not ready to make root and branch alterations to familiar practices.

So, the arrangements which pertained during the early eighties have to be seen in retrospect as transitional. Parents were now elected as a matter of course to governing bodies which began, in some cases, to take a lively interest in curricular issues. For many of those involved, the experience constituted a political education, and it was one which carried with it its own dynamic, making further developments more rather than less likely. The experience of coping with rate capping and externally imposed budget limitations sensitised a growing number of parents to the politics of education. Some contemporary research suggested that there had been in reality little change in the distribution of power. In many cases headteachers still controlled the agenda and the level of involvement of governing bodies in the day-to-day affairs of their schools.

As the Thatcher Governments moved during the mid-eighties towards more interventionist educational policies, portents began to appear of further developments affecting governing bodies. The 1984 Green Paper on *Parental*

143

influence in school was followed by *Better schools* in the next year, and both anticipated the enhanced powers to be given to governors by the 1986 Education Act (No. 2).[26] It was this legislation which transformed both the composition of governing bodies and the duties they were expected to perform. The Act required LEAs to draw up instruments of government for their schools which brought about a numerical balance between parent and local authority representatives, the exact numbers depending on the size of the school. The largest schools were to have five parents and five local authority representatives, and the smallest two of each. Parents were now required to be elected. As well as ensuring teacher representation on governing bodies, this legislation demanded that co-option should be made from among 'the local business community'.

But it was perhaps in its definitions of the organisation and functions of these new governing bodies that the 1986 legislation was most breathtaking. First, it was made clear that the conduct of the school was now unequivocally under the direction of the governing bodies, which were required to keep up to date a written statement on the secular curriculum proposed to them by the local education authority, as well as a separate written statement of their policy on sex education. In the case of aided and special agreement schools, the curriculum was to be under the direct control of the governing body. Governors now had to make available to parents formal statements of the syllabuses to be followed by pupils, together with any other information which might be required on the educational provision made by the school. Beyond this, there was a requirement for an annual meeting of parents, properly convened, at which the governors would present a formal report of their work over the previous year, including a financial statement and, for secondary schools, such information on the performance of pupils in external examinations as was required by the 1980 Education Act. Governing bodies were now to liaise with local authorities on the numbers of pupils to be admitted each year. They were now required to play a part in the appointment of senior staff, and their power to suspend anyone working at the school was confirmed. Further, it became the responsibility of school governors to forbid the pursuit of partisan political activities and the promotion of partisan political views, and to guarantee the balanced presentation of opposing political views within the schools for which they were responsible. Not least, they were also instructed to 'take such steps as are reasonably practicable to secure that where sex education is given ... it is given in such a manner as to encourage those pupils to have due regard to ... the value of family life'.

The Education Reform Act which was passed two years later[27] went even further, placing yet more obligations on the governing bodies of schools. They were identified, along with the local authorities and the Secretary of State, as the responsible parties whose duty it was to deliver the new National Curriculum. It was made clear that governing bodies shared with

LEAs the duty of ensuring a daily act of collective worship which would be 'wholly or mainly of a broadly Christian character'. The requirement to make available on request the record of the academic attainment of pupils was extended to include the results of the new 'Key Stage' tests introduced by this legislation. Perhaps most important was the delegation of each school's annual share of the LEA budget to the governing body, which now became responsible for budgeting and for the staffing and equipment needs of their school: 'the governing body...shall be entitled...to spend any sum made available to them...as they think fit for the purposes of the school'. The responsibility of governing bodies in this area was confirmed by Schedule Three of the Act, which specified the powers of appointment and dismissal now delegated to governing bodies, giving teeth to governors to exercise this new-found initiative as they saw most fit. Finally, governing bodies were identified as the responsible body which had the power to initiate procedures for the acquisition of Grant Maintained status.

The implications of these changes were immediately apparent. By specifying this list of new responsibilities, Thatcher's Governments not only moved governing bodies to the centre of the policy-making process within schools, permanently altering the power balance between parents and teachers in the process, but also guaranteed that the system as a whole would be further bureaucratised. The struggle to wrest power from the local education authorities and to devolve it more closely on the schools themselves (although there was no hint of any weakening of the grip exercised by central government on the education system as a whole or any of its constituent parts) transformed semi-permanently the day-to-day management of schools; for any individual to be effective, he or she would now need to work through a more fully articulated committee structure.

The new arrangements also involved a heightened competitiveness between schools which was to take on some strange forms. In the Autumn of 1989, the Manor High School in Nuneaton offered a starter pack to all new pupils which included a voucher for a reduction of ten pounds on the purchase of a Triton shower unit from the Payless DIY store in the town. This particular initiative stemmed from the involvement of a local shower manufacturer in the school's governing body. When interviewed, he told the *TES* that 'we must go into the market place and compete with other schools'.[28] This extreme and untypical example reminds us that, with these transformed power structures in place, increased competitiveness between schools came to mean the offer of new inducements and the suggestion of new criteria for educational success and satisfaction. Changing patterns of involvement in the running of schools meant, among other things, changing perceptions of what exactly constituted a good education.

How then do we summarise the impact of bureaucratisation on the English education system during the period since 1964? First, there is little if any evidence that these transformations have worked to improve the lot of the disadvantaged. Systems which might have been expected to guarantee greater fairness have not resulted in significant gains for the underprivileged, for ethnic minorities or for women. Indeed, in respect of gender, it seems that this newly bureaucratised system has ironically been more effective at perpetuating the disadvantages suffered by females. In terms of both career hierarchies and the routes through the education system, any gains experienced by women have been offset by impediments to their participation on equal terms which have in no way lessened.

It does seem to be arguable that, as society itself has become more bureaucratised, the education system has played a key role in generating a bureaucratic class and, in the process, has itself been subtly modified in several ways. Changed practices in education and changing perceptions of the constituents of a good education have enabled the schools and colleges to be the arbiters, as never before, of who exactly would be the successes in a bureaucratised workplace. Hardly surprisingly, it has proved to be those students from backgrounds which were sympathetic to and familiar with these trends who did best. Bureaucratisation has enabled the education system to confirm its function as the most important agency for the maintenance and transmission of intergenerational advantage. In modern England the emergent middle classes have taken hold of the school system and have fashioned it in a form which suits their ends, and which ensures, by and large, the success of their own children. It may be, historically, that bureaucratisation is the process which has enabled the middle classes finally to assert their primacy over groups with longer-established power bases in land ownership or capital. If that is so, then education has been one of the vital tools used.

8

A NEW POLITICS OF
EDUCATION?

In 1964, at the start of the period under consideration in this book, the consensus between the two major political parties that education was a proper target for investment by the State, and that much of that investment should properly be directed to the alleviation of social class distinctions, remained firmly in place. By the end of the 1980s a new set of priorities had emerged, with the focus increasingly upon value for money, competition and differentiation between schools and sectors, and on the power of the consumer (usually construed as the parent) to exercise choice in the selection of schooling. How did this come about, and to what extent did it represent a sea-change in the politics of education? Did these newer themes have any long-term pedigree, or were they the product of a new politics which had emerged during the seventies and eighties? These are the questions to be addressed in this chapter.

It is usual to see the publication of the first *Black Paper* in 1969[1] as a starting point for the emergence of Radical Right views on education, coming, as it did, in the wake of the student unrest of the previous year and reacting, too, to the perceived permissiveness of the 1960s, reflected in both student mores and in teaching styles. But, as some authors have shown in recent publications, several of the ideas and attitudes reflected in the *Black Papers* were not new. Although the foundation of the Centre for Policy Studies by Keith Joseph and Margaret Thatcher in 1974 is seen by many as one of the key intellectual starting points of New Right influence, it is worth reminding ourselves that there were a number of pressure groups which shared the aim of opposing collective solutions to social problems with much longer pedigrees. The Economic League was set up as early as 1919; Aims of Industry in 1942; Common Cause in 1952 and the Institute of Economic Affairs in 1957. Although none of these was precisely targeted at educational issues, they prepared the ground for the new organisations of the 1970s within which New Right policy objectives were clarified. These included, as well as the Centre for Policy Studies, the Freedom Association, the Salisbury Group, the Adam Smith Institute and the Social Affairs Unit.[2]

There must also be a question mark over the contrast identified at the start of this chapter between the educational policies of the period of 'Keynesian social democracy', extending from the end of the war into the 1970s, and those of recent years, when there has been a clear attempt to implement the ideas of the New Right. As Clyde Chitty has pointed out, the post-war consensus 'did not cover the whole spectrum of political opinion'[3] and it did not prevent fierce conflict between the parties on educational issues. As early as 1950 it was becoming evident that opposition to comprehensivisation, especially that which threatened existing grammar schools, was focused within the Conservative Party; this was the case in Middlesex in 1949 and at Ashford in Kent the following year. In 1954, the realisation that the proposed Kidbrooke comprehensive school threatened the Eltham Hill Girls' Grammar School, and a similar threat to the Bec Grammar School, focused thinking within the Conservative Party on this issue.[4] Yet, by the early sixties, Harold Wilson was promising that the grammar schools 'will be abolished over my dead body'[5] as the imperative to win votes drew the Labour Party away from out-and-out advocacy of comprehensive reorganisation. This followed the sideways drift of the Conservative Party towards support for some kind of comprehensivisation and its acceptance, during Edward Boyle's tenure of the Ministry of Education, of an ongoing programme of reorganisation. Thus, on the question of comprehensive reorganisation, the battlelines of much subsequent dispute were laid down in the 1950s, and the consensual position which was reached during the early sixties may have been no more than a brief interlude.

Long-term reservations on the Right about the value of popular education were reflected in other aspects of policy. It was during the early fifties that R. A. Butler, as Chancellor of the Exchequer, had pressed his Minister of Education, Florence Horsburgh, to consider the reintroduction of fee paying for secondary schooling, the lowering of the compulsory leaving age to 14, and the restriction of the numbers of children under five being funded by the State to receive some form of education.[6] In part, this was no more than a reversion to what had been almost a reflex action for Chancellors at moments of economic crisis. But the targets which Butler proposed to Horsburgh suggested an underlying reservation about the value of mass education provided at the expense of the State.

Another question mark has been thrown over the nature of the 1960s settlement by critiques such as that developed in *Unpopular education*. Here, four main criticisms of the dominant policies of the 1960s are developed:

the contradictoriness of Labour's repertoire; the absence of a direct educational relation to the working class; the non-popular character of the 1960s alliance; and the limits of a narrowly statist politics, focusing almost exclusively on access.[7]

This criticism links the two ways in which we might question the newness of the New Right. On the one hand, we are arguing, there were elements in policy and thinking between 1945 and 1964 which prefigured New Right ideas: on the other, there is a longer-term residue. But if we pursue the analysis quoted above, offered by the CCCS in 1981, much of the nature of this residue may be attributable to the ways in which State education developed in Britain, to its links with Labour Party and social democratic policy, and to a particular view of the working class which, by the sixties and seventies, was becoming increasingly obsolescent. In other words, something had to give: the understandings and conventions of educational policy which were current for much of the twentieth century and dominant after the Second World War were no longer tenable, or were, at least, susceptible to attacks which suggested that alternative policies were more appropriate. To understand this, we need to look a little more closely at this long-term residue.

Both the structure and the administration of the English education system have reflected, over a long period, ambivalent attitudes towards popular education. That ambivalence was evident at the time of the 1870 Education Act, when there were clear reservations about the extent to which the State should take direct responsibility for schooling. This stemmed in part from mid-nineteenth-century views on the role of government generally, but also from conflicting views on the value and extent of popular schooling. It was, after all, only ten years since the Reverend James Fraser had advised the Newcastle Commission, at the conclusion of his work for them as an Assistant Commissioner, that it was neither possible nor desirable 'to keep the peasant boy at school till he was 14 or 15 years of age. We must make up our minds to see the last of him, as far as the day school is concerned, at 10 or 11'. Summarising the strict limits which should be placed on an elementary schooling, he concluded grimly:

> I have no brighter view of the future or the possibilities of an English elementary education floating before my eyes than this. If I had ever dreamt more sanguine dreams before, what I have seen in the last six months would have effectually and for ever dissipated them.[8]

Andy Green has outlined the ways in which the 1902 legislation effectively created two education systems which placed a ceiling on the opportunities available to most working-class pupils, with no proper access to secondary education and a leaving age of 15 for elementary schools.[9] This reticence to launch or fully support an education system for the working poor was seen in the closing years of the nineteenth century, and has been a repeated theme of policy more recently. It is interesting to note that, as the State took on responsibility for secondary schooling at the start of the twentieth century, Robert Morant sought to convince the Treasury that by issuing regulations on the curriculum he could control the likely expenditure and establish a model of secondary schooling to which only a

149

minority of pupils would be able to aspire.[10] Similarly, recent research has suggested that the 1944 Act was concerned as much about restricting the opportunities available within the State-provided system of secondary education as it was to universalise it.[11] An education system which, over a long period, has perpetuated these social class distinctions may be particularly susceptible, in a period of economic transition, to policies which bring the effectiveness of that State provision into question and which also have the effect of limiting the demands which schooling makes of the public purse. In this sense, the policies of the New Right are, if not an extension of earlier practices, at least in some senses in context and therefore more acceptable at the time and more explicable in retrospect.

Another element which made the education system more susceptible to these political pressures was the coming of affluence during the post-war period, and, with it, of 'consumerism'. Between 1951 and 1983, real income doubled. The growth in the number of salaried occupations and this general increase in disposable income resulted in a steadily increasing proportion of the population being able to exercise choice in many areas of life which had not previously been questioned. Owner-occupation meant enhanced choice of location. As people came to exercise greater control over which suburb they inhabited, the nature of the schooling available in different parts of cities and conurbations became a factor influencing these decisions, especially for young parents. But, beyond this, the growing range and number of luxury goods and of different leisure pursuits undoubtedly worked to redefine citizenship. Whereas, in the early twentieth century, to participate in society meant either a pooling of scarce resources or an acceptance of austerity for most people, now the freedom to select became paramount. Increasingly, suppliers of services as well as sellers of goods found themselves accountable to their publics. Professionals and experts, whose work had previously been above question, began to find themselves involved in justification of what they were about. Schoolteaching, never seen as more than a marginal profession, proved to be particularly susceptible to these trends.

Compounding this was the increasing preparedness of the press to feed off these changing appetites. The collapse of the middle-brow newspaper market (the *News Chronicle*, the *Daily Herald*, the *Sunday Dispatch* and the *Empire News* all disappeared during the early 1960s) and the rise of the tabloid press (in 1964 the *Herald* was relaunched as the *Sun*) generated a situation in which it was far easier for the press to propagandise a particular viewpoint. Further, the rhetoric of newspapers such as the *Daily Mirror*, which had long campaigned for the elimination of poverty, was dislocated by the coming of affluence, so that, for survival, the press found it necessary to minister to, and even define, the fears and aspirations of the newly emerging middle class. Increasingly high on their agenda was the worry that the school system might fail to equip their children to aspire to their own newly won lifestyles. It was in this spirit that figures such as Rhodes Boyson, a *Black*

Paper author, was seen by the *Daily Mail* as 'caring passionately about standards', while opponents of the *Black Paper* movement were dismissed as 'political fanatics'. Even the *Daily Mirror* was drawn into this critique, proclaiming in 1976 that 'the brutal truth is that standards have fallen'. This newspaper greeted the 'Great Debate' in the same year with the banner headline 'Crisis in the classroom'.[12]

What, then, were the steps to the demolition of the social democratic consensus, such as it was, during the late sixties and early seventies? The policy developments of the 1960s must be seen as providing the immediate context. There was a steady upturn in the number of plans coming forward for comprehensive reorganisation, and much of the policy of the Labour administration made the steady extension of comprehensivisation appear inexorable. Alongside this, the increasing acceptability of positive discrimination, hinted at in the Newsom Report and actually implemented in response to the Plowden recommendations, seemed to those on the Right to offer a new and frightening vision of what egalitarianism might come to mean in practice. Further, the swift expansion of post-school education triggered by the Robbins Report was quickly seen by some civil servants as having dire financial consequences, and for many traditionalists within the universities it raised the old spectre of more meaning worse. In combination, these factors led to an increase of 50 per cent in educational expenditure as a proportion of gross domestic product. The student unrest of the late sixties seemed to a few observers only to confirm that this expansion of the education system was bound to have dire consequences.

At much the same time there developed a growing realisation of the relative weakening of the British economy. Consequently, the continuing rhetoric of growth, seen in publications such as *Education: a framework for expansion* (1972), coincided with the reality of an increasingly fierce programme of cuts. This publication looked forward confidently to the system continuing to expand during the following ten years 'as it must if education is to make its full contribution to the vitality of our society and economy', Yet, only one year previously, it was Margaret Thatcher, as Minister of Education, who had been turned to by Prime Minister Heath for a hundred million pounds' worth of savings from the education budget. Ironically, the item which earned her most opprobrium, the ending of free milk for primary school pupils, was estimated to have saved her no more than £8 million towards this target.

With the dramatic rise in world oil prices during 1973 and 1974, the demands for prudence in public-sector spending became more pressing. This generated a situation which, as the Centre for Contemporary Cultural Studies has put it, 'eroded belief in the social democratic educational settlement'.[13] Not only were unemployment, economic growth rate, world market share and inflation chronic indices of economic problems, but new analyses began to suggest that one underlying cause was the unrestrained

151

growth of the public sector of the economy. In November 1975 an influential analysis by Bacon and Eltis suggested that 'armies of teachers, social workers and civil servants' were putting pressure on the productive sector and diverting investment away from potentially more fruitful areas of the economy.[14] Education, which was coming to be seen as unsuccessful in sustaining Harold Wilson's 'white hot technological revolution', became a natural target for cuts and criticism.

Most of the writing around education during the fifties and sixties had seen it as being unequivocally a public good. A succession of sociologists debated how its benefits might be more fairly bestowed; official publications such as the 1963 Newsom Report and the 1967 Plowden Report shared a similar perception. Angus Maude's *Education: quality and equality*, published in 1968, suggested that it was time for Conservatives to think through which of the recent initiatives were permanent and which were reversible. This shift in tone was confirmed by the publication of the first *Black Paper* in March 1969. Although this publication was directed mainly at what was seen as an incipient crisis within the universities, triggered by the appearance there of growing numbers of the 'academically unfit', a fair proportion of the blame for this state of affairs was attributed to the comprehensive schools, even though only a small minority of university students at this time had in fact been through the comprehensive sector. Before the end of the year the second *Black Paper* had placed the issues of falling standards in schools and the renewal of the debate on fixed intelligence at the heart of its agenda.[15] A year later, in November 1970, a third *Black Paper* focused its attention on progressivism and the impact of comprehensivisation.[16]

These publications received a mixed reception, being seen by most teachers and educationalists as bearing little relationship to the significant educational debate, which was still seen by most professionals as the broadening of access and the ability to benefit from a State-provided system. To these educational professionals, the *Black Papers* seemed no more than a desperate attempt to put back the clock and to challenge trends which were in many ways inexorable. But, within the Conservative Party, these ideas were beginning to take hold. The second *Black Paper* was timed to coincide with the start of the 1969 Conservative Party Conference, and it received wide publicity. The impact of these first three *Black Papers* is also shown by the fact that 80,000 copies had been sold by 1971. It is significant, too, that in March 1970 a number of the contributors to the *Black Papers* were invited to Westminster to give evidence to the Commons Select Committee on Education. Here they mounted a blistering attack on progressivism in teacher training, a portent of education policy which was as yet unformulated. What is significant in the context of this chapter is the fact that these early *Black Papers* were all 'preservationist' in tone; that is, they appealed to moderation and commonsense against the supposed extremism of the supporters of comprehensivisation. Their programme did not go beyond the maintenance or resuscitation of all that could be rescued from the tripartite post-war settlement, the argument being that this particular form of State schooling had given the best chance of identifying the most able (the future leaders of society) and was ultimately, in this respect, fairer to inner-city children than the comprehensive schools which were now being introduced. These pamphleteers of the late sixties and early seventies laid down this one enduring plank in what was to become the platform of the New Right, but perhaps their greatest significance lay in the fact that they began to articulate a Conservative philosophy in this area of social policy which had been so monopolised by socialist and social democratic writers and thinkers in the years since 1945. It is worth noting, too, the fact that their writing drew so much scorn from the Left. Trapped in the conviction of their own intellectual superiority, the supporters of comprehensivisation grossly underestimated the extent to which these authors preyed on the fears of the new middle classes; their complacency fuelled the sense of betrayal which swept through the teaching profession when, a few years later, policies which reflected these fears began to be enacted.

It is interesting that, in power between 1970 and 1974, the Conservative Party pursued educational policies which reflected this 'preservationism'. The paradoxes inherent in Conservative thinking at this time were encapsulated in the manifesto for the 1970 election which, on the one hand, reflected the consensus politics of the previous twenty years by committing the Party to end selection at eleven, but also included a promise to withdraw Circular 10/65. At the same time this manifesto spoke of the need for greater parental choice and enhanced freedom for the private sector. But perhaps the single factor which did most to mould the face of future education policy was the selection of Margaret Thatcher as Secretary of State for Education. The significance of her appointment was not spotted by the *TES*, which saw Mrs T. as no more than the token woman in Edward Heath's team:

> New Prime Ministers always have a quite understandable tendency to play safe in their first Cabinets. And Mr. Heath will doubtless feel that he ought to have a woman somewhere in his team.[17]

Margaret Thatcher's appointment marked an attempt by Edward Heath to placate the right wing of the Conservative Party; it resulted in the promotion of a number of issues which were to remain central to the programme of the Radical Right. In her first few months in office, Thatcher withdrew Circular 10/65, confirming the question of comprehensive reorganisation as by far the most sensitive in the education arena. She went on to withdraw subsidies on school milk and school meals and to raise the question of student loans with the NUT. In July 1971 she proposed that museums should now charge entrance fees and two months later refused to investigate the state of slum schools at the request of the NUT. In November she announced an annual subsidy of two million pounds to the Direct Grant schools. The extent to which these policies were judged at the time to be controversial is shown by the fact that 40,000 students descended on London in protest, that all of her public appearances soon began to be hounded by demonstrators, and that the *Sun* labelled her 'the most unpopular woman in Britain'.[18]

The difficulties which confronted Thatcher during this early period in office undoubtedly did much to define the programme which she herself was to pursue as Prime Minister a few years later. Heath's refusal to drop her from his Cabinet forced her into unwelcome compromises during her final three years at the DES. Plans for student loans were dropped. More significantly, she found herself obliged to accede to a growing number of requests from local authorities for comprehensive reorganisation. Shortly before the end of her term of office, 3,612 proposals had been received. The result was that she presided over an increase in the number of comprehensive schools from 1,250 in 1970 to 2,677 in 1974. This unprecedented growth in numbers reflected the momentum of the comprehensive lobby at this time, and the power of the local authorities. This, too, goes a long way to explain her assault on the LEAs as Prime Minister.

Early in 1972 the National Foundation for Educational Research produced a report which suggested that illiteracy rates in secondary schools were surprisingly high, perhaps as many as 70,000 out of 850,000 pupils being affected. This gave Thatcher the chance to pounce upon the standards issue, setting up the Bullock Committee and thereafter never allowing the question of literacy and numeracy levels to be sidelined. In these ways the politics of Thatcher's period as Secretary of State worked to move the Radical Right from 'preservationism' towards more proactive policies.

Equally significantly, the realities of policy during these years were cloaked by a public rhetoric of expansionism which was never fully reflected in reality. Within a few months of the announcement of Heath's programme of cuts in public expenditure, the White Paper *Education: a framework for expansion* spelt out what Brian Simon has called 'a profoundly... radically expansionist programme'. Thatcher's speeches at the time reflected this mood. Educational expenditure was set to rise by £1,000 million over ten years (a 50 per cent increase). Yet the industrial and economic crisis of the autumn of 1973 swept away these illusions. The 'Barber cuts' of £200 million imposed in December left only the Government's nursery schools programme in place; for the rest, the expansionism of the whole post-war era became, at a stroke, a memory.

The mid-seventies proved to be a catalyst for New Right approaches to educational issues as the tried formulae were made to look increasingly inappropriate. First, the continuing economic crisis of the period eroded the power of governments to return to expansionist policies and also generated an employment situation in which schools were all-too-easily perceived as failing to provide the recruits needed by industry. The problems which had led to the 'Winter of Discontent' and Edward Heath's demise as Prime Minister continued to beset the Callaghan Government which replaced Heath's. The nadir is probably marked by the recourse to the International Monetary Fund in March 1976, resulting in a dramatic drop in real wages and living standards and in a growing willingness of government to resort to monetarist solutions to economic problems. Education became an increasingly likely target for economies. Educational expenditure, seen as a percentage of GDP, peaked in 1975/6 at 6.3 per cent: by the late eighties it had fallen back to below 5 per cent, a figure comparable to that of the late sixties.

Second, there were clear signs in the mid-seventies of a reaction against the progressivism which had been preached by numerous educationalists since the Second World War. In 1975 there was enormous press interest in the case of the William Tyndale Junior School in Islington, whose teaching staff was operating a wildly libertarian and quite untypical curriculum. The Auld Report, in the following year, used the school as a lever for a general indictment of progressive teaching methods, and was seized on by the media to suggest that progressivism was widespread. In the same year the Bennett Report from the University of Lancaster also enabled the press to suggest the superiority of formal teaching methods at the primary stage. In March 1977, a BBC 'Panorama' programme pilloried the day-to-day routines of the Faraday Comprehensive School in West London. These episodes enabled the popular identification of several key issues: schools were seen as undisciplined and badly organised, contributing to a general social and economic malaise. It was increasingly becoming the role of parents to monitor what was going on and to ensure standards. As the *Daily Mail* put it in January 1975: 'Most parents are frightened that if they make too much fuss their children will suffer'.[19]

Third, with Rhodes Boyson as co-editor of the *Black Papers* from 1975 onwards, a new programme was articulated by authors such as Caroline Cox, Edward Norman and Stuart Sexton, all of whom were to become increasingly involved in policy-making within the Conservative Party. By the time the last *Black Paper* appeared in 1977, parental choice, a national curriculum, testing at ages seven, eleven and fourteen, the publication of test results, and an emphasis on the core curriculum, were being articulated as key elements in educational policy. Further, Edward Norman was arguing that it was the job of the schools to introduce pupils to Britain's fundamentally Christian culture; pluralism, as well as Marxism, was now a target for attack.[20]

This was also the moment when New Right thinking began to percolate into the Conservative Party as a whole. Boyson used the Conservative Political Centre to produce pamphlets such as *Parental choice* (1975), aimed at grassroots Conservative supporters. The Centre for Policy Studies, set up in 1974 by Keith Joseph and Margaret Thatcher, quickly became a focus for these new ideas, its Education Study Group providing a platform for figures such as John Marks and Caroline Cox. By 1975 even the journal of the Conservative Research Department was starting to echo the ideas of the *Black Papers*, and in the same year the pressure group FEVER began to lobby actively for the use of vouchers in education, echoing ideas first voiced by Milton Friedman as early as 1955. Thatcher's assumption of the leadership of the party in the same year meant that any future Conservative administration would have the question of educational reform at the heart of its agenda and would be sympathetic to this lobbying.

It is perhaps ironic that it was under James Callaghan as Labour Prime Minister in October 1976 that New Right preoccupations were first brought into governmental thinking. The detail of events and influences has been fully documented by Clyde Chitty, and there is no need to rehearse them here. But it is worth remarking that the events surrounding the leaking of the *Yellow Book* and the Ruskin speech in October 1976 show that the Prime Minister, who now took a personal interest in the education issue, was drawing in part on the views of civil servants, and in part on those of Bernard Donoghue at the Downing Street Policy unit. This anticipated what, by the 1980s, was to become Margaret Thatcher's appeal to the electorate over the heads of HMIs and civil servants, drawing increasingly on themes developed within the 'think tanks' which were articulating New Right ideas.[21]

The Ruskin speech, and the 'Great Debate' which followed it, emphasised the extent to which the schools should ensure educational standards and the effective use of resources. In the process, it became increasingly clear that the education professionals (the phrase 'educational establishment' was used for the first time by Callaghan at Ruskin) were to be increasingly answerable to their public. One reason for the emergence of these themes at this time was that the mid-seventies saw a fundamental and sudden transformation of the labour market for young people. An education system which put most of its products into employment with few qualifications at sixteen years of age as semi-skilled or unskilled workers was suddenly seen as dysfunctional. The jobs which this social group used to fill disappeared; suddenly much higher skill levels were sought by employers. It was all too easy in this situation to explain economic problems as the result of the failings of the education system.

Now the themes of the New Right began to be echoed in day-to-day policy. The 1977 Taylor Report called for closer involvement of parents in the running of schools; many local authorities set about implementation, although they were not required to do this until the first piece of educational legislation to be brought in after the Conservatives were returned to power, the 1980 Education Act. In November 1977, Circular 14/77 invited local authorities to review six aspects of their school curricula, including the transition from school to work; it was made clear that this was intended to ensure that the education system was meeting 'national needs'. Further, the *Yellow Book* had argued that the MSC was better placed than the DES to respond quickly to the changing needs of the 16–19 age group. In the event the Job Creation Scheme which the MSC initiated in October 1975 proved to be only the first of several programmes which, by the end of the decade, had established the MSC as a provider of novel and potentially influential modes of education.

Before moving on to look more closely at the impact of the New Right after Thatcher's accession to power, it is important to emphasise that, by the time she became Prime Minister, it was already possible to discern two strains in the thinking of the New Right which were, ultimately, to make it impossible for 1980s Conservative governments to devise an educational programme without its own profound internal inconsistencies.[22] On the one hand there were those Neo-Liberals, deeply influenced by Freidrich von Hayek, who believed in a completely deregulated free market society and who saw the family, as it had evolved in Western Europe, as the key agency for social regeneration. Their views were neatly summarised by Peter Clarke in 1975, who argued that those elements within the Conservative Party who believed in the need of the State to intervene were the real enemy. Ranged against them were those Neo-Conservatives who, from 1977, worked through the Conservative Philosophy Group and the Salisbury Group to argue for increased central control. One of their spokespersons was Roger Scruton, who claimed that 'the concept of freedom cannot occupy a central place in Conservative thinking'. By seeking to take on board elements of the thinking of both groups, Thatcher obfuscated deep contradictions and committed her party to a set of policies which, in the final resort, could not hold, although this was far from apparent at the time to most observers.

In the event, the dominant theme of Margaret Thatcher's educational rhetoric during the 1979 election was preservationist: her claim that 'we are the Party of the roots of tradition' was not one she chose to deny in her policies on schooling. The appointment of Mark Carlisle to the DES after the election marked the start of a period in which education was given considerable priority. But during the first two years of office, legislation was in line with traditional Tory policy. Two Education Acts were quickly in place. One reversed the Labour legislation of a few years earlier which had sought to force comprehensive reorganisation on local authorities. A second introduced the Assisted Places Scheme and gave parents a role in re-jigged governing bodies as well as greater choice over the schools their children attended. As part of the drive to save expenditure on education, local authorities were no longer to be required to provide school meals, milk or transport to and from school. This was followed in March 1981 by a White Paper on expenditure which had the effect of cutting educational investment by 7 per cent. Brian Simon has estimated that, for capital expenditure, the cut was at the level of over 30 per cent.[23]

As unemployment rose steeply, and the summer of 1981 began to appear to be one of general protest, with teachers, students and other educationalists involved, Thatcher reshuffled her Cabinet. Defenders of the 'old' politics, such as Mark Carlisle, who had resisted the cuts to his Departmental budget, were jettisoned in favour of supporters of the new Conservative faith. Keith Joseph went to the DES. The fact that Thatcher appointed such a close ally to Education (she and Keith Joseph had founded the Centre for Policy Studies together in 1974) marks her perception that educational issues were moving closer to the heart of her agenda. Two important initiatives during Joseph's first years at the DES marked the transitional nature of the politics of education at this time. First, the MSC was used to introduce the Technical and Vocational Initiative in 1982, shortly after the announcement of a drive to ensure that each school had at least one microcomputer. This new emphasis on modernisation, and the need for the schools to link with the needs of the economy, coincided with public discussion of the need to focus on the core curriculum, although it is interesting that Joseph himself expressed reservations about governmental coercion in this area. Second, between 1981 and 1983, Keith Joseph made several attempts to get the question of educational vouchers considered by the Cabinet, a proposal which Edward Heath dismissed as 'crackpot' but which was popular with the Tory Right. Clyde Chitty has shown that it was pressure from senior civil servants at the DES which led Joseph to announce at the 1983 Conservative Party Conference that the idea of the voucher was, 'for the foreseeable future', dead. Thatcher's increasing reliance on 'think tanks' during the next few years stemmed in large part from the failure to persuade well-established civil servants of the appropriateness of the new direction of policy. It was during this period, too, that Circular 3/84 announced the assault on initial teacher training. This followed the more long-term drive to control higher education as a whole, a process which had been intensified by the 1981 cuts.

Several initiatives reflected Joseph's determination to strengthen central control of the education system. The abolition of the Schools Council was announced in April 1982. Not long afterwards the Central Advisory Councils for England and Wales were done away with, as was the Advisory Committee on the Training and Supply of Teachers. One by one, those bodies which might have represented the best professional opinion against the trend of governmental policy were either emasculated or brought to an end. Brian Simon sees the introduction of a single examination at 16-plus (also announced during Keith Joseph's period in office) as another example of centralisation at work. He argues, too, that the underlying rationale for this trend was a perceived 'need for explicit social engineering to cope with the dangers arising from over-education in a contracting labour market'.

At the beginning of 1984, Keith Joseph used the North of England Conference to turn the attack against the teachers themselves, questioning the professionalism of many of them and promising to look closely at their conditions of employment. It was probably this initiative, as much as anything, which triggered the teachers' industrial action in February 1985. This dispute, coming on the back of the miners' strike, was to prove a hinge point for Thatcher's educational policies because, although it brought the downfall of Joseph in May 1986, its resolution marked the end of any prospect of concerted or effective action from within the teaching profession to oppose the drift of policy. Kenneth Baker, who replaced Keith Joseph, appeared to be offering a compromise by throwing more money at the education system, but in reality the settlement he imposed on the dispute used the 1987 Teachers' Pay and Conditions Act to remove teachers' negotiating rights, to abolish the Burnham Committee and to impose draconian conditions of service, including the introduction of designated working hours for the teaching profession.

This capitulation by the teachers, resulting in part from the difficulties generated by a divisive trade union structure, was followed very quickly by a set of governmental initiatives on education which marked the highpoint of the influence of the Radical Right. The introduction of City Technology Colleges, to be funded in large part by private industry, was announced at the 1986 Party Conference. Within six months Baker had floated proposals for a National Curriculum, for a system of testing at key stages of schooling to judge the effectiveness of schools, and for the 'opting out' of schools which wished to free themselves from local authority control. In March 1987, financial responsibility for the running of schools was devolved to individual institutions.

Emboldened by her victory in the 1987 General Election, Thatcher promised that, in education, 'we are going to go further than we have ever gone before'.[24] It proved to be no idle boast. Within six months the terms of what became the 1988 Education Act were announced. Ideas which had been canvassed only a few months before now became key elements in a major piece of legislation. Rather than producing a White Paper, the usual device to encourage discussion of proposed legislation, the Government distributed four 'consultation papers' in July 1987, allowing only the two summer months for interested parties to respond. Despite this curtailing of normal democratic process, a flood of protests from educationalists and the general public appeared at the DES. This did not deflect the Government from its purpose, and the introduction, as the legislation was going through Parliament, of a major section which broke up the Inner London Education Authority, only had the effect of strengthening the Act. On its enactment in July 1988, those working within the education system found themselves in a quite unprecedented situation. Management was devolved to individual institutions; the new National Curriculum and tests at seven, eleven, fourteen and sixteen forced schools into a competitive stance for pupils, as their funding levels now came to depend in large part on the number of students recruited; the demise of the ILEA stood as an epitaph for the powers of local authorities generally. The choice of opting out was made, in the first instance at least, enormously financially attractive, as the newly competitive nature of the system was reflected in differing funding levels for different institutions. Social Democracy had given way to Social Darwinism, and it was to take several years before a shell-shocked teaching profession was able to show that, in the long term, many of these provisions were not fully workable. More immediately, by opening up opportunities to those who were ready to grasp them for their own career advancement, or in the interests of a relatively small number of children in one school against those of the majority, the Act introduced an element of managerialism into the running of schools which had previously been only latent. Now the image of the school in its locality became as important as the reality; its marketing became as significant as its day-to-day working.

Many within the education system (this author included) saw this as an unqualified loss, as the values towards which most teachers had worked throughout the twentieth century were undermined. How, then, does one summarise the impact of the New Right on English education? There are several key elements. First, the private sector, which had been inadvertently reinforced by Labour's ending of Direct Grant status in 1976, emerged from the 1980s greatly strengthened. The Assisted Places Scheme gave a cushion against the worst effects of economic difficulties to many parents and did not result in the schools being opened up to a much wider clientele. Further, the net impact of the governmental assault on higher education meant that the major universities became more, rather than less, accessible to students who had been educated outside the State system. The 'access' schemes run by most universities were, in the event, little more than a chimera, disguising the reality of a growing percentage of ex-public-school pupils in those universities towards the top of the various 'league tables' of performance. This fact alone did a great deal to confirm the desirability of private schooling, as it continued to offer an unfair chance to its alumni of entering the major professions, or indeed, in the conditions of the late eighties, the job market in any form.

Second, the steady opening-up of schools to parental influence, heralded by the Taylor Report, had a twin impact. First, it confirmed the shift towards that consumerism which was becoming so marked a feature of the system: schools were now obliged to listen to and, to some extent, be fashioned by their more vocal and committed parents. While this may have been in many ways a good thing, what was less desirable was that this process gave undue influence to schools in middle-class areas where there was little difficulty in recruiting parents who were often well connected within the local professions and who knew how to lobby effectively and how best to organise. This was not the case in the inner-city areas, where parents were often too busy pursuing other more immediate concerns to be able to contribute effectively to school management and were less likely to be able to win resources for their children's schools. This situation was a gift to the better-off suburbs.

Third, the profession as whole was made more accountable, and not always in ways that were desirable. From the early eighties the reports of Inspectors on the work of schools were made available for public scrutiny, and the introduction of staff appraisal as well as the demand for more thorough reporting on pupil progress, including records of achievement, and the auditing and monitoring of courses, meant that the work of the teacher lost much of its mystique. The profession was being made, as a conscious act of policy, accountable for its work. This not only reduced professional autonomy, but also meant a significant accretion of paperwork for schoolteachers, and by no means all were persuaded of the necessity for these extra duties. All of this meant a semi-permanent lowering of the status of schoolteaching as a profession, and this was reflected in lower staff morale, with a significant number deciding to leave the profession. Senior posts in particular imposed greater stress, with a consequent impact on the health of those involved, and fewer and fewer teachers, particularly within the public sector, served to what had traditionally been seen as the completion of their career at 65 years of age. The availability of retirement deals, as was increasingly common within the public sector of the economy generally, made early retirement a reality for significant numbers of teachers.

Fourth, the time-honoured tension between a liberal education and the need for schools to service economic development was renewed. The modernisers in Government circles (of whom the most prominent during the early eighties was probably Lord Young) saw to it that a plethora of new courses and new routes was established: Youth Training Schemes, Technical and Vocational Initiatives, and the City Technology Colleges. While these initiatives sought overtly to provide the basis for economic recovery by ensuring that school leavers (or some of them, at least) had the appropriate qualifications and training to enter the expanding high-tech sector of the economy, in reality they strengthened the 'tracking' element in English education. That is to say that the most prestigious schools, and in many cases the upper streams of comprehensive schools, remained relatively impervious to these trends. This technical training was, as a result, all too often a device by which pupils from particular social backgrounds were steered towards particular kinds of career route. Differentiation of schools by type and differentiation of courses within schools has always meant the discrimination of social classes and this was no less true during the 1980s than it had been at earlier periods.

Perhaps two elements stand out in any assessment of the impact of the New Right on education in England. First, there was a significant redistribution of power within the system. Central government, despite the claims that schools and parents were being offered greater autonomy, was in reality given greatly enhanced power to control and command the education system. Whether it was through the determination of funding levels, specific instructions on curricula or the control of recruitment numbers, the DES (later the Department For Education) became, more than ever before, the puppeteer of the education system. The key losers were the local education authorities, which were financially weakened and whose powers were eroded by statute. While the schools, and those managing them, may seem to have gained in autonomy – and in some senses they did – their powers were constrained within strictly defined limits, so that the style and social significance of their individual initiatives were largely predetermined.

Second, the chances that the education system would reinforce, rather than erode, the stratification of English society were increased by these changes. The private sector, which for over a century had buttressed the position of the upper and middle classes, was given help through the Assisted Places Scheme in particular to survive the economic rollercoaster of the 1980s, and emerged from the decade as strong as ever. Meanwhile, within the State sector, the new funding arrangements constituted a kind of Social Darwinism which made life harder for those teaching in the old industrial areas and inner-city suburbs but which worked for the prosperity of schools in more affluent areas. The 'pecking order' of schools and institutions of higher education, which had been informally recognised for over a century, was reinforced and made clearer. In a society in which the distinctions between those in work and the dispossessed were becoming steadily more marked, schooling was made a more efficient instrument for sorting the sheep from the goats. The problem for the teachers, who generally espoused one or other form of egalitarian rhetoric, was that the system was now overtly being dedicated to a set of social purposes which made their central objectives irrelevant.

To return to the question raised at the start of this chapter, it seems that, although the application of New Right policies to education led a host of writers to identify the turning points at which the post-war consensus gave way to a new polarisation, in reality what was happening was that old and tried themes of Conservative policy were being taken to new extremes. For over a hundred years there had been those who were anxious to ensure that differentiated routes were available for pupils from different social backgrounds: now this became a dominant element in policy. The determination of central government to superintend the curriculum had been apparent at least since Robert Morant's move to become Permanent Secretary at the Board of Education in 1902; what was new now was that, in a situation in which different views on school curricula were being canvassed, government was taking action to ensure that its version was accepted. In one sense, it seems that the move to weaken the local authorities was novel, since a succession of governments had acquiesced in trends and policies which originated at local level. But, even in this respect, it is worth reminding ourselves that, in 1902, a Conservative Government saw fit to abolish the

School Boards when they threatened to dictate policy, despite a body of professional opinion which saw a need for their continuation. What may well have been happening in this respect is the slow working-out of very long-term trends, in which the scale of the local bodies responsible for education grew slowly over time as regional policy became steadily more significant than local policy. So, just as the School Boards gave way to local authorities at the start of the century, it may well prove, in retrospect, that these same local authorities have outlived their usefulness and are soon to be replaced by regional bodies or some other organisation of greater scale. In this analysis, what may prove of greater significance historically is not the accident of exactly how these local authorities were put under pressure so much as the nature of the longer-term process of which this is evidence.

The policy shifts charted in this chapter have undoubtedly generated a transformed context for those working in education; the policy landscape today appears scarcely recognisable to those whose careers began during the era of consensus. While the education system today appears to be better fitted to the task of separating the sheep from the goats than was the case in the mid-sixties, we should not overlook the fact that its deeper social functions have merely been modified rather than transformed. Our school system has the effect of confirming pre-existing social structures and of predetermining life-chances and lifestyles; it has been so since the education system took on its recognisably modern form in the late nineteenth century, and it remains so today.

9

CONCLUSION

The issues which have been identified and dealt with in the separate chapters of this book each provide insights into the social functions of our modern system of education. But it is only through recognition of their interconnectedness that we can begin to approach understandings of the complex web of relationships through which the education system links to the wider processes of social change. Developments in social class formation, in suburbanisation and housing policy, in the ethnic composition of society, in gender relations and in patterns of employment, were inextricably interrelated and all-pervading; there was no aspect of life in modern Britain that was not touched by them. These changes became potentially destabilising during the period under review, threatening at times to lead to major social disruption and endangering the smooth transformation of the economy. That these changes were able to take place without major social or political unrest was in large part explicable by reference to the role of the education system. It is in this sense that we can conclude that, between 1964 and 1990, schools and colleges played an important part in determining and shaping the dynamics of social and economic change. As British society 'modernised' during these years (in the sense that it underwent the social and economic changes necessary for participation in the new global economy which was emerging), it also retained many of its underlying characteristics, not least its strong sense of social hierarchy, with only limited opportunities for movement between social classes, even though the bases of social class were themselves undergoing subtle but perceptible change. That all this was accomplished without major social disturbance was due in large part to the mediating role of the education system.

As was argued in Chapter one, the power of historical precedent to determine contemporary practice in education did not diminish during the period under review. Rather it was strengthened. The years which saw the coming of 'credentialism' (that is, the use of formal qualifications achieved through the education system for entry to a far wider range of modes of employment) also witnessed, as we have seen, a confirmation of the pre-existing structure of the education system and of much of its practice. This inherent conservatism within schools and colleges reflected their role as arbiters of who exactly were to be the beneficiaries of the skills and qualifications the teachers and lecturers had to offer. In a period of swift social change, too great a set of adjustments to educational practice and values would have weakened the power of the system to provide the intergenerational defence of social and economic advantage which, throughout the period since industrialisation, had been one of the key functions of education. It is, therefore, hardly surprising that these years of relatively swift social and economic transition did not see a major restructuring of education.

But beyond this, the swift growth of new technologies and the expansion of the tertiary sector of the economy, together with ongoing suburbanisation, the bureaucratisation of professional employment, the emergence of new mass media and of a new politics, in combination placed massive strains on the education system. So great were the upheavals that some commentators identified the birth of a 'post-modern' era. It is at just such moments of historical upheaval that the ability of an education system to confirm its own practices and values with reference to its past, and thereby to confirm social values more widely, becomes of particular importance. It is for this reason that we need hardly be surprised by the relative conservatism of the education system between 1964 and 1990. For the middle classes in particular, in a world where so much was changing, the ability of the more prestigious schools and colleges to offer an education which was by and large familiar and which transmitted a well-established value system, while at the same time guaranteeing the future prospects of their own sons and daughters, was of particular importance. This is why change was so relatively slow within the education system, and this, too, is part of the answer to the question of why education moved slowly but perceptibly towards the middle of the political agenda during these years.

While this relatively stable education system meshed with and was part of the other social developments identified in this book, it was unable, of itself, to generate economic transformation. One key reason for the fact that the economic revolution of this period occurred with little reference to the formal education system was that the schools remained committed to other ends, including the maintenance of social difference involving the preservation of established elite routes and the prestige of liberal studies. The responses made by the education system to economic transformation certainly helped determine the niches to be occupied by its products within newly established 'high-tech' industries, but did little to promote the development of those industries. As it became increasingly apparent that the education system was largely dysfunctional from the economic transformations taking place, it became so much easier for politicians, of whatever persuasion, to castigate the schools for their failure to meet national needs. However unfairly, teachers and educationalists became the whipping boys in the search for the causes of relative national decline. This accident, too, had the effect of turning education into a political football. Debates which had raged within education for over a century on the need for specialisation and differentiation, and the promotion of new technologies, now became more prominent in the political arena.

But it is difficult to see how it could have been otherwise when we consider the fierce pressures placed on educationalists by the wider social changes we have considered in this book. In the examination of the impact of suburbanisation on schooling, I have argued that, in several ways, the likelihood of educationalists being able to offer a fair start in life to their pupils was minimised as a result of the housing patterns which emerged in the years after 1964. At the same time, the chances which the comprehensive schools had of succeeding in one of their central objectives, that of cementing social cohesion, were also lessened. The rift between public and private housing sectors, the enormous regional contrasts in housing stock which developed, and the growing recognition of the significance of location as a determinant of lifestyle and social status, all impinged on the education system. The advantaged position of those who were fortunate enough to be owner-occupiers during the twenty years of house price inflation from the mid-sixties to the mid-eighties enabled them to use their local schools (both primary and secondary, grammar or comprehensive) to confirm the advantages which their children already enjoyed. In this process much of the rhetoric which surrounded the advance of the Radical Right politically was preordained.

If the schools could do little to overcome the social rifts generated by location and housing, they might, on the face of it at least, have been expected to play a more significant part in the eradication of the disadvantages under which women suffered, both in the workplace and at home. But, as we have seen, the evidence suggests that the outcomes were hardly, if at all, more encouraging. While the education system did succeed in bestowing formal qualifications on a significantly greater proportion of females during this period, and the coming of mixed secondary education may be viewed, from one perspective at least, as a solution to long-term discontents, both developments were achieved at the cost of stronger gender stereotyping, both in the school and in the workplace. The more women entered employment, the more career hierarchies appeared which seemed to rope them off from positions of real power. Sadly, this trend was anticipated in the schools, where the price of mixed education seemed to be the development of more rather than less well marked career tracks for boys and girls. Despite a plethora of projects and initiatives aimed at solving this problem and a clear determination on the part of many teachers, at both college and school level, to ensure that their work did not discriminate against females, the outcomes appear to have been otherwise. In this area, too, the education system was responding to, and working within, a society

166

in which gender remained, and seemed increasingly to be, one key element in the definition of social class.

The appearance of growing numbers of visible ethnic minority citizens in modern Britain also posed challenges to educationalists, and this phenomenon was similarly linked to suburbanisation and to changing perceptions of social class. Driven by housing policy and economic pressures to cluster in particular locations in the inner cities, young black Britons found themselves corralled into schools in which they quickly became a majority. The phenomenon of 'white flight', which resulted in part from the deep strain of racism which persisted and which was fuelled by the survival of eugenic ideas, soon meant that the education system became the repository of a hidden apartheid, by which many young people attended schools in which only their own ethnic group, or a selection of ethnic groups, was represented. If ethnicity was also one of the tokens of social class, the failure of the education system to do anything effective about this problem meant that the schools became, unwittingly, agencies for the redefinition of class and for the establishment of ethnicity as one of its tokens. In respect of ethnicity, as well as gender, the education system came to perform the role during the years under review of confirming social distinctions. Despite the efforts of literally thousands within the education system who would have been horrified to think that this was the net effect of their work, a society which was deeply divided against itself, both in respect of gender and of ethnicity, came to use its education system to reflect and even strengthen pre-existing trends.

In this analysis, the bureaucratisation of the workplace was of great significance, since it worked to formalise and to perpetuate processes which previously had been informal and unsystematic. By ensuring that positions of power and influence were accessible only through the acquisition of qualifications and often through the working-out of prescribed and preordained career routes, the process of bureaucratisation also ensured that those born into positions of relative advantage and in particular locations were far more likely to gain maximum benefit from the education system. In a very real sense during this modern era, the middle classes came into their own and used the education system to reinforce and secure their position. The achievement of what appeared, during moments of economic transformation and growth, to be a meritocracy was, in reality, one which defined merit in terms which suited those already advantaged. It is in this sense that what I am describing in this book may be seen as a social dynamic. It is the interrelatedness of all these elements which gives such power to the education system to preserve and sustain social hierarchies, social class and positions of advantage.

And, as I have argued throughout the book, this pattern of social developments was one in which it became almost predictable, in retrospect, that a 'Thatcherite' or 'New Right' political discourse would emerge and would become dominant. Although for those who lived through them, the Thatcher years may have appeared to be a period during which a new politics of education was being foisted upon a largely unwilling or sceptical public, in reality the policies which became suddenly fashionable, with their emphasis on competitiveness, individualism, cost-effectiveness and the demands of the consumer, all stemmed from a new social situation in which the education system was, as never before, able to reinforce the social order. By underlining social contrasts which already existed, and by ensuring, by and large, that those children who were born advantaged were able to sustain those advantages into the workplace, schools and colleges were performing an important social function. Some observers have pointed out the apparent contradiction of this new politics of education emphasising individual choice but at the same time insisting on tight central government control of the curriculum. True enough, in one sense, this conjunction is deeply ambiguous and problematic. But if we bear in mind the distinction that the education system was committed to the promotion of social change (the preparation of tomorrow's labour force for employment in a quickly changing workplace) and, at the same time, the defence of social stability, then the irony becomes more explicable. The social processing which the education system had long offered was confirmed through growing deference to the consumer, while, at the same time, close governmental oversight of curricula seemed to guarantee the relevance and effectiveness of what was on offer.

In all of these ways, then, the education system was central to the social and economic changes taking place during this period. And, equally, the tensions which were felt in wider society necessarily impinged on the life of the schools and colleges and did much to construct the debates which raged around them. If we pause to reflect on some of the more important issues which were played out in education at this time, we can see that they were reflections of wider social changes and concerns. The survival and redefinition of the private sector is an obvious example. Arguably, the greatest rift running through the education system remains to this day the divide between private and public sectors. The two most significant attempts to address this issue were, arguably, the ending of the direct grant system for over one hundred prestigious secondary schools in 1976, and the introduction of assisted places in 1980. Yet neither initiative did more than blur this divide, just as the introduction of grant maintained schools after 1988 worked to reinforce an educational hierarchy without disturbing this one central characteristic of the education system, the distinction between public and private. The fact that the private sector remains to this day exempt from the National Curriculum only reinforces the point. It is difficult to reach any other conclusion than that those who were most privileged in modern society retained a strong vested interest in seeing to it that the private sector survived and clung to many of its advantages (including the recognition of charitable status for many private schools, with the fiscal advantages which flowed from this) and many of its characteristics. There could be no more telling example of the essentially conservationist and defensive social role of our modern education system than the continuing perpetuation of this rift.

Similarly, if we turn to the primary sector, it was the struggle for control of the curriculum, described earlier in this book, which proved to be the major issue of concern. Tentative efforts to develop child-centred curricula and new approaches to the teaching of literacy and numeracy, and to link the work of the schools to the localities through the introduction of project work which threatened to change for ever the established curriculum of the primary schools, were all curtailed by the wider debate which gave a platform to those keen to promote a view of the historic functions of the primary schools. In this struggle for control, not only was the power of the teachers themselves to determine what was best for their pupils eroded, but the drift back towards an emphasis on the core curriculum, delivered in particular ways which were increasingly prescribed, became inexorable. It was the fact that the primary schools were seen as being able to provide 'modernisation' while sustaining well-established teaching practices which made them so susceptible to the increasing encroachments of external agencies, including central government.

In respect of curriculum, much the same was true of the secondary sector. Here, during the late sixties and early seventies, there were challenges to the structure of the curriculum as a whole. Some of the projects sponsored by the Schools Council, for example, brought into question the autonomy of separate subjects in the secondary schools, particularly in the social sciences. At the same time, there were lively debates, many of them arising from within the teaching profession, on aspects of teaching method, and vigorous efforts to promote change and curriculum development. By the late eighties these issues had been marginalised as new voices came to dictate what was done in the schools. It is a sad historical irony that a movement which might have done much to equip young people to meet the challenges and changing circumstances of the closing years of the twentieth century was muted by those elements in society who had most to fear from the changes which were under way. The appeal to the acquisition of basic skills, the core curriculum and to well-established methods of teaching had the effect of vindicating what was going on in some of the most prestigious schools, and certainly had the effect of confirming established patterns of recruitment to higher education, but that appeal may not have worked for the flexibility and adaptability which was to prove increasingly important to the changing conditions of global economic competition. Like the primary schools, the secondary sector became increasingly, as the period progressed, one of the defensive bastions of those in positions of power and privilege.

Two further developments, the drift towards comprehensive secondary schooling and the coming of mixed secondary education (which were themselves interrelated phenomena) both occurred in a situation which largely preordained the outcomes. Whether the defence of comprehensive reorganisation was a fair distribution of educational opportunity or the rebuilding of a sense of community, it was inevitable, in a society whose suburbs were becoming increasingly segregated, that the kinds of social cohesion and egalitarianism which were aspired to must remain a chimera. In the event, the contrasts between comprehensive schools in differing locations were to become as significant as the similarities between them. In a society which was becoming increasingly alert to the advantages which could be gained through the acquisition of qualifications, skills and even particular lifestyles during the years in secondary school, it was almost inevitable that decisions on housing location and on type of suburb would predetermine the outcomes of secondary schooling. As a wider wedge of the new middle classes found themselves with the affluence to exercise greater control over housing location, the schools themselves became one of the important determinants of which were the 'good' suburbs. Similarly, in respect of gender, the move towards mixed secondary education, which, as we have seen, seemed to hold out such high hopes to its supporters during the sixties and seventies, was soon seen to be taking place within a society which, despite the legislation, was in various ways exercising a tighter rather than a weaker grip on the separate identities of men and women. It is hardly surprising, then, that the schools themselves became more clearly tracked by gender during this period, and that the final outcomes were not an equalising of opportunities but a reinforcement of gender distinctions.

In respect of higher education, the period under review seems to have been one during which the changes which took place were little short of kaleidoscopic. During the mid-Sixties, only one in twenty young people made their way to university. By 1990 almost one in three followed this route. Beyond this, the swift expansion of higher education which was given the blessing of the Robbins Committee was quickly shaped through the introduction of a binary policy, clearly distinguishing the role of the new polytechnics from that of the universities. Only during the late eighties did the inexorable pressure of numbers result in the two sectors being brought increasingly close together, both in funding and administration, anticipating the merger which was to follow in 1992. At the same time, the agencies set up by government to oversee the workings of higher education were transformed, as the autonomy on which academics had prided themselves during the post-war era gave way to a situation in which many saw themselves, like the schoolteachers, as little more than the deliverers of approved messages.

While it is impossible to deny that these developments were enormously significant, it remains true that none of them eroded the academic prestige and social pre-eminence of the ancient universities and the relative esteem in which the older 'redbrick' colleges were held. Patterns of recruitment to a variety of professional career routes meant that a liberal education retained its value in the market place, hence the respect it was accorded. If engineering and the applied sciences became more popular and won a rather better social 'cachet' in terms of public esteem, this was not at the expense of a reversal of popular perception. As was argued earlier in the book, perhaps what was most remarkable was the resistivity of the universities and colleges to social change, and their continuing ability to mediate it effectively during this period, rather than any wholesale revolution in higher education.

Each of these examples, these cameos of the developments which this book has tried to explore more fully, brings home the extent to which change within the education system was inextricably linked with and responsive to wider social developments. It is impossible to escape the judgement that, between 1964 and 1990, the developing pattern of educational provision in Britain can be fully explained only with reference to its ability to provide a means of social stability by working to slow down those social transformations which were under way. This may not have been the conscious intention of the protagonists, but it certainly seems to have been the outcome. The essentially conservative functions of the British system of schooling meant that, in so far as it promoted social change, this was largely in the interests of retarding social mobility. This is a theme which I will seek to explore more fully in a later book. For the moment, suffice it to say that the evidence assembled here of the development of the education system in England between 1964 and 1990 brings home clearly the extent to which – as Brian Simon pointed out years ago – education is a social function and its history can only be studied with reference to the wider changes taking place in society. It is my belief that analyses of the dynamics of social change during this modern era must have the study of education at their heart. It is only by coming to terms with the essentially conservative role of our system of schooling that we can come to understand the workings and many of the key characteristics of modern British society.

NOTES

1 THE POWER OF THE PAST

1 The statistics presented in the tables in this chapter are drawn from the annual reports of the Department of Education and Science.
2 Walford, G., 'Girls in boys' public schools: a prelude to further research', *British Journal of Sociology of Education*, 4, 1983, p. 41.
3 Dyhouse, C., *Girls growing up in late Victorian and Edwardian England*, Routledge & Kegan Paul, London, 1981.
4 Purvis, J., (ed.), *The education of girls and women*, Proceedings of the 1984 Annual Conference of the History of Education Society of Great Britain, History of Education Society, Leicester, 1985.
5 Woods, A., *Coeducation*, Longman, London, 1903, and 'Questions concerning coeducation', *New Ideals Quarterly*, 5(1), 1931, 20–2.
6 Badley, J. H., writing in Woods, *Coeducation*, p. 2., quoted in R. Deem (ed.), *Coeducation Reconsidered*, Open University Press, Milton Keynes, 1984.
7 Grant, C., 'Can American coeducation be grafted on the English public school system?', in Board of Education, *Special Reports on Educational Subjects*, vol. 2, 1902, p. 27.
8 Public Record Office, Education files 12/119.
9 Royden, A. M., 'Doubts and difficulties', in A. Woods (ed.), *Advance in education*, Sidgwick and Jackson, London, 1919, p. 5.
10 Newsom, J., *Half our future*, HMSO, London, 1963, pp. 37 and 135.
11 Cited in J. Purvis, *Women and education*, Open University, E205, Unit 25, Milton Keynes, 1984, p. 43.
12 Ollerenshaw, K., *The girls' schools*, Faber & Faber, London, 1967.
13 Purvis, *Women and education*, p. 33.
14 *Ibid.*, p. 35.
15 Anderson, G., *The white blouse revolution: female office workers since 1870*, Manchester University Press, Manchester, 1988.

2 EDUCATION AND THE ECONOMY

1 On this, see Morris, D. (ed.), *The economic system in the United Kingdom*, 3rd edn, Oxford University Press, Oxford, 1985.
2 Martin, R., 'Industrial capitalism in transition: the contemporary reorganisation of the British space economy', in D. Massey and J. Allen, *Uneven*

redevelopment: cities and regions in transition, Hodder & Stoughton for the Open University Press, London, 1988, p. 216.

3 Hall, P., 'The geography of the fifth Kondratieff', in Massey and Allen, *Uneven redevelopment*, pp. 51–67.

4 Boltho, A. (ed.), *The European economy: growth and crisis*, Oxford University Press, Oxford, 1982; and Lawrence, R. Z. and Schultz, E. (eds) *Barriers to European growth*, The Brookings Institution, New York, 1987.

5 Lawrence and Schultz, *Barriers to European Growth*, pp. 2–12.

6 Landymore, P. J. A., 'Education and industry since the War', in Morris, *The economic system in the UK*, pp. 690–717.

7 Rubinstein, W. D., *Capitalism, culture and decline in Britain*, Routledge, 1993, pp. 1–2.

8 Weiner, M. J., *English culture and the decline of the industrial spirit*, Pelican, Harmondsworth, 1981.

9 Barnett, C., *The audit of war: the illusion and reality of Britain as a great power*, Macmillan, London, 1986.

10 McCulloch, G., Jenkins, E. and Layton, D. (eds), *Technological revolution? The politics of school science and technology in England and Wales since 1945*, Falmer Press, Lewes, 1985, p. 1.

11 *Ibid.*, p. 2.

12 *Guardian*, 24 July 1990, and *Independent on Sunday*, 30 September 1990.

13 Price, R. and Sayers Bain, G., 'The labour force', in A. H. Halsey (ed.), *British social trends since 1900*, Macmillan, London, 1988, p. 167. See also Ball, M., Gray, F. and McDowell, L., *The transformation of Britain*, Fontana, London, 1989, pp. 157–8, and Lewis, J., *Women in Britain since 1945*, Blackwell, Oxford, 1992.

14 Mazier, J., 'Growth and crisis: a Marxist interpretation', in Boltho, *The European economy*, p. 69.

15 Price and Sayers Bain, 'The labour force', pp. 162–201.

16 Halsey, *British social trends*, pp. 173–7.

17 Perkin, H., *The rise of professional society: England since 1880*, Routledge, London, 1989.

18 Massey and Allen, *Uneven redevelopment*, p. 53.

19 *Ibid.*, p. 203.

20 Marsden, W. E., *Unequal educational provision in England and Wales: the Nineteenth Century*, Woburn Press, London, 1987.

21 Sanderson, M., *The missing stratum: technical school education in England, 1900–1990s*, Athlone Press, London, 1994, p. 163.

22 *Ibid.*, p. 165.

23 *Ibid.*

24 *Ibid.*, p. 153.

25 On this, see Department of Education and Science, *Education for commerce*, Report on Education No. 15, HMSO, October 1964.

26 *Ibid.*, pp. 3–4.

27 DES, *National certificates and diplomas*, Report on Education No. 26, HMSO, November 1965, pp. 3–4.

28 Aldcroft, D. H., *Education, training and economic performance, 1944–1990*, Manchester University Press, Manchester, 1992, pp. 54–8.

29 McCulloch, G., *The secondary technical school: a useable past?*, Falmer Press, Lewes, 1989, pp. 123–33.

30 Sanderson, *The missing stratum*, pp. 167–8.

31 On this, see DES, *Education in the National Plan*, Report on Education No. 25, HMSO, October 1965.
32 *Ibid.*, p. 3.
33 *Ibid.*, p. 4.
34 'MSC: the first decade', An *Education* digest, 15 July 1983, p. 1.
35 *Ibid.*, p. 4.
36 McCulloch, *The secondary technical school*, p. 168.
37 *Times Education Supplement*, 17 February 1984; see also Simon, B., *Education and the social order, 1940–1990*, Lawrence & Wishart, London, 1991, pp. 498–504.
38 *Ibid.*, p. 500.
39 Sanderson, *The missing stratum*, pp. 169–74, and McCulloch, *The secondary technical school*, pp. 176–88.
40 Sanderson, *The missing stratum*, p. 172.
41 On this, see Stewart, W. A. C., *Higher education in Post-War Britain*, Macmillan, London, 1989, Chapter 9.
42 Aldcroft, *Education, training and economic performance*, p. 79.
43 Simon, *Education and the social order*, pp. 251–4.
44 Sanderson, *The missing stratum*, p. 155.
45 *Education: a framework for expansion*, Cmnd. 5174, HMSO, London, 1972, para. 118.
46 Kogan, M. with Kogan, D., *The attack on higher education*, Kogan Page, London, 1983, p. 23.
47 *The Times*, 4 September 1985. See also Stewart, *Higher education in Post-War Britain*, p. 226.
48 Sanderson, *The missing stratum*, p. 157.
49 This issue is discussed fully in Aldcroft, *Education, training and economic performance*, Chapter 6.
50 Mansell, J., 'The role of the further education sector in post-16 education', in C. Chitty (ed.), *Post-16 education: studies in access and achievement*, Kogan Page, London, 1991, pp. 113–23.
51 *Ibid.*, p. 122.

3 CONTESTED PEDAGOGIES

1 Jackson, B., *Streaming: an education system in miniature*, Routledge & Kegan Paul, London, 1964, pp. 14–16.
2 Taylor, P. H., *Expertise and the primary school teacher*, NFER-Nelson, Windsor, 1986, p. 10.
3 Simon, B., *Education and the social order, 1940–1990*, Lawrence and Wishart, London, 1991, p. 377.
4 Cunningham, P., *Curriculum change in the primary school since 1945*, Falmer Press, Lewes, 1988, p. 183.
5 Jones, D., 'Planning for progressivism: the changing primary school in the Leicestershire authority during the Mason era, 1947–71', in R. Lowe (ed.), *The changing primary school*, Falmer Press, Lewes, 1987, pp. 41–43.
6 Simon, *Education and the social order, 1940–1990*, p. 354.
7 *Ibid.*, p. 353.
8 *Ibid.*, pp. 353–4.
9 Central Advisory Council for England and Wales, *Children and their primary schools* (The Plowden Report), HMSO, London, 1967.
10 Cunningham, *Curriculum change in the primary school since 1945*, p. 156.

11 Dearden, R. F., 'The Plowden philosophy in retrospect', in Lowe, *The changing primary school*, p. 84.

12 Simon, *Education and the social order, 1940–1990*, p. 369.

13 Cunningham, P., 'Open plan schooling: last stand of the progressives', in Lowe, *The changing primary school*, pp. 54–6.

14 Cox, C. B. and Dyson, A. E. (eds), *Black Paper Two: the crisis in education*, Critical Quarterly Society, Hull, 1969, p. 98.

15 Pinn, D. M., 'What kind of primary school?', in *Black Paper Two*, p. 102.

16 Simon, *Education and the social order, 1940–1990*, pp. 444–6.

17 Woodhouse, J., 'Towards central control: Government directives on the primary curriculum', in Lowe, *The changing primary school*, pp. 131–52.

18 Simon, B., 'The primary school revolution: myth or reality?', in B. Simon and J. Willocks, *Research and practice in the primary classroom*, Routledge & Kegan Paul, London, 1981, p. 27.

19 Woodhouse, 'Towards central control', p. 140.

20 *Ibid.*, p. 141.

21 Benn, C. and Simon, B., *Half way there*, McGraw Hill, London, 1970.

22 *Ibid.*, p. 223.

23 Bruner, J. *et al.*, *A study of thinking*, Wiley, Chapman & Hall, London, 1956.

24 Bruner, J., *Toward a theory of instruction*, Belknap Press, Harvard, 1966.

25 Bloom, B. S. (ed.), *Taxonomy of educational objectives: handbook one, the cognitive domain*, Longman, New York, 1956; and Krathwohl, D. R., Bloom, B. S. and Masia, B. B., *Taxonomy of educational objectives: handbook two, the affective domain*, Longman, New York, 1964.

26 Fenton, B., *Teaching the new social studies in secondary schools: an inductive approach*, Holt, Rinehart & Winston, New York, 1966; and Fenton, B., *The new social studies*, Holt, Rinehart & Winston, New York, 1967.

27 On this, see Gordon, P., 'The Schools Council and curriculum: developments in secondary education', in Lowe, R (ed.), *The changing secondary school*, Falmer Press, Lewes, 1989, p. 55; also, Plaskow, M. (ed.), *Life and death of the Schools Council*, Falmer Press, Lewes, 1985.

28 Gordon, P., Aldrich, R. and Dean, D., *Education and policy in England in the Twentieth Century*, Woburn Press, London, 1991, p. 287.

29 On this, see Simon, B, *Education and the social order, 1940–1990*, p. 313.

30 Gordon, P. and Lawton, D., *Curriculum change in the Nineteenth and Twentieth centuries*, Hodder & Stoughton, Sevenoaks, 1978, pp. 74–7.

31 *Ibid.*, pp. 96–7.

32 Cox, C. B. and Dyson, A. E., *Black Paper Two: the crisis in education*, Critical Quarterly Society, London, 1969, pp. 57–62.

33 Simon, B, *op cit*, 555.

34 *Ibid.*, 492.

35 *Ibid.*, 493.

36 *The Times*, 25 September 1991.

37 Grimmitt, M., 'Evolving styles of religious education in England', *Word in life*, August 1981, pp. 136–43.

38 Simon, B, *op cit*, 548–9.

39 Hallam, R. N., 'Logical thinking in history', *Educational Review* 19, 1967; Hallam, R. N., 'Piaget and thinking in history', in M. Ballard (ed.), *New movements in the study and teaching of history*, Temple Smith, London, 1970; see also De Silva, W. A., 'Concept formation in adolescence ... with special reference to history', PhD thesis, Birmingham University, 1969.

40 Goldman, R. J., *Religious thinking from childhood to adolescence*, Routledge & Kegan Paul, London, 1964.

41 Board, C., 'Maps as models', in R. J. Chorley and P. Haggett, *Models in Geography*, Methuen, London, 1967; and Satterly, D. J., 'Skills and concepts involved in map drawing and map interpretation', in J. Bale *et. al.* (eds), *Perspectives in Geographical Education*, Oliver & Boyd, Edinburgh, 1973.

42 Chitty, C., *Towards a new education system: the victory of the New Right?*, Falmer Press, Lewes, 1989.

43 Johnson, R., 'Thatcherism and English education', *History of Education*, 18(2), 1989, pp. 91–122; and Centre for Cultural Studies, *Education limited*, Heinemann, 1991.

44 Campbell, M. B., 'Nonspecialist study in the undergraduate curricula of the new Universities and Colleges of Advanced Technology', University of Michigan Comparative Education Dissertation Series, No. 10, Ann Arbor, 1966.

4 SUBURBS AND SCHOOLS

1 Burnett, J., *A social history of housing, 1815–1985*, Methuen, London, 1986; Swenarton, M., *Homes fit for heroes*, Heinemann, London, 1981; Bowley, M., *Housing and the State, 1919–1944*, Allen & Unwin, London, 1945; and Melling, J. (ed.), *Housing, social policy and the State*, Croom Helm, London, 1980.

2 Perkins, H., *The rise of professional society: England since 1880*, Routledge, London, 1989, pp. 46, 82–3, 269.

3 *Ibid.*, p. 82.

4 Burnett, J, *A social history of housing, 1815–1985*; Cullingworth, J. B., *Town and country planning in Britain*, Unwin Hyman, London, 1988; Sutcliffe, A. (ed.), *Multi-storey living: the British working class experience*, Croom Helm, London, 1974; Berry, F., *Housing: the great British failure*, Knight, London, 1974.

5 *Ibid.*, p. 56.

6 Hopkins, E., 'Working class life in Birmingham between the Wars', *Midland History*, XV, 1990.

7 Robson, B. T., *Urban social areas*, Clarendon Press, Oxford, 1975, pp. 12–15.

8 *Ibid.*, p. 52.

9 Henderson, J. and Karn, V., *Race, class and State housing: inequality and the allocation of public housing in Britain*, Gower Press, Aldershot, 1987, pp. 127–39.

10 This is based on a distribution map of council housing in Birmingham which appears in Henderson and Karn, *Race, class and State housing*, p. 34, with additional information on the location of schools being drawn from the City of Birmingham Education Committee, *Year Book and Directory*, 1969.

11 Seaborne, M. and Lowe, R., *The English school: its architecture and organisation, 1870–1970*, Routledge & Kegan Paul, London, 1977, p. 162.

12 Robson, *Urban social areas*, p. 17.

13 Bradford, M., 'Education, attainment and the geography of choice', *Geography*, 326, 76(1), January 1990, pp. 3–16.

14 Moser, C. A. and Scott, W., *British towns: a statistical study of their social and economic differences*, Oliver & Boyd, London, 1961; see also Robson, *Urban social areas*, p. 18.

15 *Ibid.*

16 Jackson, B. and Marsden, B., *Education and the working class*, Routledge & Kegan Paul, London, 1962. See also Mays, J. B., *Education and the urban child*, Liverpool University Press, Liverpool, 1962.

17 Campbell, F., *Eleven plus and all that*, Watts, London, 1956.
18 Robson, B. T., *Urban analysis: a study of city structure with special reference to Sunderland*, Cambridge University Press, Cambridge, 1969.
19 Guratsky, S. P., *Owner occupation and the allocation of comprehensive school places: the case of Walsall*, University of Birmingham Centre for Urban and Regional Studies, Working Paper 90, 1982.
20 *Ibid.*, p. 3.
21 *Ibid.*, p. 26.
22 Simon, B., *Does education matter?*, Lawrence & Wishart, London, 1985, pp. 218–19.

5 BRIDGING THE GENDER GAP?

1 Ellis Cashmore, E., *United Kingdom? Class, race and gender since the War*, Unwin Hyman, London, 1989, p. 184.
2 *Report on social insurance and allied services* (The Beveridge Report), HMSO, London, 1942, p. 52.
3 Cited in White, C., *Women's magazines, 1963–68*, Michael Joseph, London, 1970, p. 142; and Carter, A., *The politics of women's rights*, Longman, London, 1988, p. 18.
4 Bowlby, J., *Child care and the growth of love*, Pelican, Harmondsworth, 1953.
5 Pennington, S. and Westover, B., *A hidden workforce: homeworkers in England, 1850–1985*, Macmillan, London, 1989, p. 153.
6 Crompton, R., 'The feminisation of the clerical labour force since the Second World War', in G. Anderson, *The white blouse revolution: female office workers since 1880*, Manchester University Press, Manchester, 1988, pp. 121–42.
7 Carter, *The politics of women's rights*, p. 51.
8 Newsom, J., *The education of girls*, Faber & Faber, London, 1948.
9 See Byrne, E. M., 'Education for equality', in M. Arnot and G. Weiner (eds), *Gender and the politics of schooling*, Hutchinson, London, 1987, p. 28; and Carter, *The politics of women's rights*, p. 37.
10 Albermarle Report, *The youth service in England and Wales*, Cmnd. 929, HMSO, London, 1960, p. 15.
11 The Newsom Report, *Half our future*, HMSO, London, 1963, p. 142, quoted by R. Deem, 'State policy and ideology in the education of women', in C. Ungerson (ed.), *Women and social policy: a reader*, Macmillan, London, 1985, p. 126.
12 Wolpe, A. M., 'The official ideology of education for girls', in M. Flude and J. Aider (eds), *Educability, schools and ideology*, Croom Helm, London, 1976.
13 On this, see Armytage, W. H. G., 'Robbins and the reproductive ratio', in *History of Education*, 16(3), September 1987, pp. 205–8.
14 The Robbins Report, *Higher education* (vol. 1), HMSO, London, 1963, pp. 17, 62–3.
15 Women's Group on Public Welfare, *The education and training of girls*, National Council for Social Service, London, 1962, pp. 15, 110.
16 Shaw, J., 'Finishing school: some implications of sex segregated education', in D. L. Barker and S. Allen (eds), *Sexual divisions and society: process and change*, Tavistock, London, 1976, p. 134.
17 *Times Educational Supplement*, 19 March 1965.
18 *Ibid.*, 21 May 1965.
19 *Ibid.*, 3 December 1965.
20 Arnot, M., 'A cloud over coeducation', in S. Walker and L. Barton (eds), *Gender, class and education*, Falmer Press, London, 1983, p. 71.

21 See particularly *Times Educational Supplement*, 2 January 1965 and 29 January 1965.

22 Quoted by E. M. Byrne, 'Education for equality', in Arnot and Weiner, *Gender and the politics of schooling*, p. 23.

23 Dale, R. R., *Mixed or single sex schools* (three vols), Routledge & Kegan Paul, London, 1969, 1971, 1974. This quotation is from vol. 2, p. 292.

24 *Ibid.*, vol. 3, p. 274.

25 Quoted by Tomes, H., 'Women and education', in G. Ashworth and L. Bonnerjea (eds), *The invisible decade: UK women and the UN decade*, Gower Press, Aldershot, 1985, p. 73.

26 Benn, C. and Simon, B., *Half way there*, Second edn, Penguin, Harmondsworth, 1972, p. 410.

27 *Ibid.*, p. 417.

28 Arnot, M., 'A cloud over education', in Walker and Barton (eds.), *Gender, class and education*, p. 80.

29 *Ibid.*

30 *Ibid.*, p. 82.

31 Millet, K., *Sexual politics*, Avon Books, New York, 1971, p. 25.

32 Shaw, *Finishing school*, p. 134.

33 *Ibid.*, pp. 139–140

34 Lobban, G. M., 'The influence of the school on sex role stereotyping', in J. Chetwynd and O. Hartnett (eds), *The sex role system*, Routledge & Kegan Paul, London, 1978.

35 Delamont, S., *Sex roles and the school*, Methuen, London, 1980.

36 Carter, *The politics of women's rights*, p. 36.

37 Wickham, A., 'Gender divisions, training and the State', in R. Dale (ed.), *Education, training and employment*, Pergamon, London, 1985, p. 158.

38 Whyte, J., *Girls into science and technology*, Routledge & Kegan Paul, London, 1986.

39 On this, see Kelly, A. (ed.), *The missing half*, Manchester University Press, Manchester, 1981.

40 Arnot, M., 'State education policy and girls' educational experiences', in V. Beechey and E. Whitelegg (eds), *Women in Britain today*, Open University Press, Milton Keynes, 1986, pp. 151–5.

41 Stanworth, M., *Gender and schooling: a study of sexual division in the classroom*, Women's Research and Resource Centre, Pamphlet No. 7, Hutchinson, London, 1981.

42 Sutherland, M., *Sex bias in education*, Blackwell, Oxford, 1981.

43 Delamont, S., 'The conservative school? Sex roles at home, work and school', in Walker and Barton (eds.) *Gender, class and education*, p. 93.

44 Stanworth, M., 'Just three quiet girls', in Ungerson, *Women and social policy*, p. 144.

45 Arnot, 'A cloud over education', p. 83.

46 *Ibid.*

47 Deem, R., 'State policy and ideology in the education of women, 1944–80', in Ungerson, *Women and social policy*, p. 132.

48 These figures are drawn from the DES's *Annual statistics of education*.

49 *Guardian*, 21 March 1980, p. 12.

50 Ashworth and Bonnerjea, *The invisible decade*, p. 3.

51 Deem, 'State policy and ideology in the education of women', p. 34.

52 Ashworth and Bonnerjea, *The invisible decade*, p. 3.

53 Bouchier, D., *The feminist challenge: the movement for women's liberation in Britain and the USA*, Macmillan, London, 1983, p. 57.

6 A NEW EUGENICS

1 R. Lowe, 'Eugenicists, doctors and the quest for National Efficiency: an educational crusade, 1900–1939', *History of Education*, 8, 1879, pp. 293–306; and R. Lowe, 'Eugenics and education: a note on the origins of the intelligence testing movement', *Educational Studies*, 6, 1980, pp. 1–8.
2 R. A. Soloway, *Demography and degeneration: Eugenics and the declining birth rate in Twentieth Century Britain*, University of North Carolina Press, Chapel Hill, 1990, p. 339.
3 *Ibid.*, p. 341.
4 *Report of the Royal Commission on Population*, Cmnd. 7695, HMSO, London, 1949.
5 Soloway, *Demography and degeneration*, p. 352.
6 D. J. Kevles, *In the name of Eugenics*, Pelican, Harmondsworth, 1986, pp. 213–15.
7 *Ibid.*, pp. 262–3.
8 *Ibid.*, p. 263.
9 A. S. Jensen, 'How much can we boost IQ and scholastic achievement?', *Harvard Educational Review*, pp. 162–3.
10 Kevles, *In the name of Eugenics*, p. 271.
11 *Ibid.*
12 Soloway, *Demography and degeneration*, p. 361.
13 *Ibid.*, pp. 352, 359.
14 F. Znaniecki, *Modern nationalities*, London, 1952, p. 71.
15 On this, see L. P. Gartner, *The Jewish immigrant in England*, London, 1960.
16 D. Dean, 'Coping with Colonial immigration', *Immigrants and minorities*, 6(3), November 1987, p. 73.
17 *TES*, 12 September 1958.
18 I. Katznelson, *Black men, white cities*, Oxford, 1973, p. 134.
19 I. Grosvenor, 'Education, history and the making of racialised identities in post-1945 Britain', PhD thesis, Birmingham University, 1994, p. 41.
20 Katznelson, *Black men, white cities*, p. 130.
21 Grosvenor, 'Education, history and the making of racialised identities', p. 78.
22 *Ibid.*, p. 139.
23 *TES*, 21 June 1963.
24 *TES*, 4 October 1963.
25 Grosvenor, 'Education, history and the making of racialised identities', p. 193.
26 *Ibid.*, p. 43.
27 *Ibid.*, p. 192.
28 *Ibid.*, p. 198.
29 Katznelson, *Black men, white cities*, p. 175.
30 Grosvenor, 'Education, history and the making of racialised identities', p. 139.
31 *Ibid.*, p. 143.
32 *English for immigrants*, Ministry of Education Pamphlet No. 43, HMSO, London, 1963.
33 C. Mullard, 'Multiracial education in Britain: from assimilation to cultural pluralism', in J. Tierney (ed.), *Race, migration and schooling*, Holt, London, 1982, p. 123.

34 B. Troyna, 'Can you see the join?', in D. Gill, B. Mayor and M. Blair (eds), *Racism and education*, Open University Press, Milton Keynes, 1992, p. 68.

35 A. James, 'Why language matters', in *Multiracial school*, Summer 1977.

36 *TES*, 18 October 1963.

37 *Hansard*, vol. 685, cols. 433–44, 27 November 1963.

38 *Second Report of the Commonwealth Immigrants Advisory Council*, Cmnd 2266, HMSO, London, 1964, para. 25.

39 *Ibid.*

40 DES, *The education of immigrants*, Circular 7/65, London, 1965, para. 42.

41 B. Carrington and G. Short, *Race and the primary school: theory into practice*, NFER-Nelson, 1985, p. 5.

42 R. Jenkins, *Address given by the Home Secretary to a meeting of voluntary liaison committees*, London, NCCI, 1965.

43 E. E. Cashmore, *United Kingdom? Class, race and gender since the War*, Unwin Hyman, 1989, p. 91.

44 S. Patterson, *Immigration and race relations in Britain, 1960–1967*, London, 1969, p. 73.

45 W. W. Daniel, *Racial discrimination in England*, Penguin, 1968.

46 Carrington and Short, *Race and the primary school*, p. 6.

47 B. Troyna and J. Williams, *Racism, education and the State*, Croom Helm, London, 1986, p. 22.

48 C. Gaine, *Still no problem here*, Trentham Books, 1995, p. 34.

49 DES, *A language for life* (the Bullock Report), HMSO, London, p. 453.

50 DES, *Education in schools: a consultative document*, Cmnd. 6869, HMSO, London, 1977, p. 41.

51 Mullard, 'Multiracial education in Britain', p. 129.

52 P. Ghuman, *Asian teachers in British schools*, Multilingual Matters, Clevedon Press, Bristol, 1995.

53 C. Ranger, *Ethnic minority school teachers*, CRE, London, 1988.

54 J. Williams, 'Race and schooling', *British Journal of Sociology of education*, 2(2), 1981, p. 221.

55 R. Street Porter, *Race children and cities*, Open University Press, Milton Keynes, 1978, pp. 80–1.

56 *TES*, 6 March 1981.

57 Mullard, 'Multiracial education in Britain', p. 131.

58 C. Mullard, *Racism in school and society*, University of London, Institute of Education Centre for Multicultural Studies, 1981.

59 *Education digest*, 12 July 1981.

60 Carrington and Short, *Race and the primary school*, p. 7.

61 *Ibid.*

62 Mullard, *Racism in school and society*.

63 DES, *West Indian children in our schools* (The Rampton Report), Cmnd. 8273, HMSO, London, 1981.

64 Schools Council, *Multicultural Education*, York, 1982; see also Carrington and Short, *Race and the primary school*, p. 9.

65 *Ibid.*, pp. 9–10.

66 DES, *Education for all* (the Swann Report), Cmnd. 9453, HMSO, London, 1985.

67 J. Bourne, L. Bridges and C. Searle, *Outcast England: how schools exclude black children*, Institute of Race Relations, London, 1994, p. 39.

68 Grosvenor, 'Education, history and the making of racialised identities', p. 99.

69 *Ibid.*, p. 98.

70 Gaine, *Still no problem here*, p. 51.
71 Grosvenor, 'Education, history and the making of racialised identities', p. 112.
72 Gaine, *Still no problem here*, p. 53.
73 *Ibid.*, p. 54.
74 Association of London Authorities, *It's the way that they tell 'em*, London, 1987.
75 Grosvenor, 'Education, history and the making of racialised identities', p. 117.
76 *Ibid.*, p. 125.
77 E. E. Cashmore, *United Kingdom?*, p. 100.
78 I. Grosvenor, ' "Race", racism and black exclusion', *Forum*, 37(3), Autumn 1995, pp. 81–2.
79 G. White, 'Black access to higher education', in P. D. Pumphrey and G. K. Verma, *Race relations and urban education*, Falmer Press, Lewes, 1990, p. 296.
80 *Ibid.*, pp. 295–307.
81 A. Forbes, 'The transition from school to work', in Pumphrey and Verma, *Race relations and urban education*, p. 286.
82 M. Mac an Ghaill, 'Coming of age in 1980s England: reconceptualising black students' experience', in Gill *et al.*, *Racism and education*, p. 48.
83 S. Dex, 'A note on discrimination in employment and its effects on black youths', *Journal of social policy*, 8(3), 1982, pp. 357–69.
84 M. P. Jackson, *Youth unemployment*, Croom Helm, London, 1985.
85 K. Roberts, *School leavers and their prospects*, Open University Press, Milton Keynes, 1984, pp. 52–5.
86 *Ibid.*, p. 53.

7 BUREAUCRATISATION AND THE GOVERNANCE OF EDUCATION

1 R. Thorstendahl, *Bureaucratisation in Northwestern Europe, 1880–1985*, Routledge, London, 1991, p. 33.
2 *Ibid.*, p. 13.
3 M. Savage, J. Barlow, P. Dickens and T. Fielding, *Property, bureaucracy and culture: middle class formation in contemporary Britain*, Routledge, London, 1992.
4 *Ibid.*, p. 3.
5 C. Wright Mills, *White collar*, Oxford University Press, Oxford, 1951.
6 N. Abercrombie and J. Urrie, *Capital, labour and the middle classes*, George Allen & Unwin, London, 1983, p. 119; see also Savage *et al.*, *Property, bureaucracy and culture*, p. 212.
7 Savage *et al.*, *Property, bureaucracy and culture*, p. 212.
8 Association of University Teachers, *Goodwill under stress: morale in British Universities*, AUT, London, 1990, p. 15.
9 *Ibid.*
10 *Ibid.*, p. 16.
11 Central Statistical Office, *Social trends*, No. 17, HMSO, London, 1987, p. 66.
12 On this, see P. Sharp and J. Dunford, *The education system in England and Wales*, Longman, London, 1990, chapter 3.
13 P. Gordon, R. Aldrich and D. Dean, *Education and policy in England in the Twentieth century*, Woburn Press, London, 1991, p. 83.
14 *Ibid.*, p. 95.
15 P. Gosden, *The education system since 1944*, Martin Robertson, Oxford, 1983, p. 195.
16 Gordon *et al.*, *Education and policy in England*, pp. 96–8.

17 On this, see Gosden, *The education system since 1944*, pp. 196–205; Gordon *et al.*, *Education and policy in England*, pp. 99–101; Sharp and Dunford, *The education system in England and Wales*, chapter 4.

18 Gordon *et al.*, *Education and policy in England*, p. 101.

19 The Plowden Report, *Children and their primary schools*, HMSO, London, 1967, pp. 414–16.

20 A. H. Halsey, *Educational priority*, HMSO, London, 1972.

21 National Association of Governors and Managers, *Parents and teachers as governors and managers*, NAGM, London, 1973.

22 DES, *A new partnership for our schools: the Taylor Report*, HMSO, London, 1977.

23 R. Auld, *The William Tyndale Junior and Infant schools*, ILEA, London, 1976.

24 DES, *The composition of school governing bodies*, Cmnd. 7430, HMSO, London, 1978.

25 See R. Rogers, *Crowther to Warnock: how fourteen reports tried to change children's lives*, Heinemann, London.

26 DES, *Education Act (No. 2)*, HMSO, London, 1986.

27 DES, *Education Reform Act*, HMSO, London, 1988.

28 'Shower of gifts entices parents', *TES*, 3 November 1989.

8 A NEW POLITICS OF EDUCATION?

1 Cox, B. and Dyson, A. E. (eds), *The fight for education*, The Critical Quarterly Society, Hull, 1969.

2 On this, see Griggs, C., 'The New Right and English Secondary education', in R. Lowe (ed.), *The changing secondary school*, Falmer Press, Lewes, 1989, pp. 99–125.

3 Chitty, C., *Towards a new education system: the victory of the New Right?*, Falmer Press, Lewes, 1989, chapter one.

4 Lowe, R., *Education in the Post-War years*, Routledge, London, 1988, p. 132.

5 *Ibid.*, p. 140.

6 *Ibid.*, p. 89.

7 Centre for Contemporary Cultural Studies, *Unpopular education*, Hutchinson, London, 1981, p. 163.

8 Maclure, J. S., *Educational documents: England and Wales, 1816–1967*, Methuen, London, 1965, pp. 76–7.

9 Green, A., *Education and State formation*, Macmillan, London, 1990, p. 306.

10 Lowe, R., 'Robert Morant and the 1904 regulations for secondary schools', *Journal of educational administration and history*, XVI(1), 1984.

11 Simon, B., 'The 1944 Education Act: a Conservative measure?', *History of Education*, 15(1), March 1986.

12 Centre for Contemporary Cultural Studies, *Unpopular education*, pp. 210–15.

13 *Ibid.*, p. 169.

14 *Ibid.*, p. 172.

15 Cox, B. and Dyson, A. E., *The crisis in education*, Critical Quarterly Society, Hull, 1969.

16 Cox, B. and Dyson, A. E., *Goodbye Mr. Short*, Critical Quarterly Society, Hull, 1970.

17 *TES*, 29 June 1970.

18 Simon, B., *Education and the social order, 1940–1990*, Lawrence & Wishart, London, 1991, pp. 405–30.

19 Centre for Contemporary Cultural Studies, *Unpopular education*, pp. 410–15.

20 Cox, C. B. and Boyson, R. (eds), *The fight for education*, Critical Quarterly Society, 1975; and Cox, C. B. and Boyson, R. (eds), *Black Paper, 1977*, Critical Quarterly Society, Hull, 1977.
21 Chitty, *Towards a new education system*, chapter three.
22 *Ibid.*, pp. 211–19.
23 Simon, *Education and the social order*, p. 480.
24 Chitty, *Towards a new education system*, p. 196.

BIBLIOGRAPHY

Government reports, policy statements and circulars have been omitted from this list in the interest of brevity, although full references are available in the Notes to those cited.

Abercrombie, N. and Urrie, J., *Capital, labour and the middle classes*, George Allen & Unwin, London, 1983.

Aldcroft, D. H., *Education, training and economic performance, 1944–1990*, Manchester University Press, Manchester, 1992.

Anderson, G., *The white blouse revolution: female office workers since 1870*, Manchester University Press, Manchester, 1988.

Arnot, M. and Weiner, G. (eds), *Gender and the politics of schooling*, Hutchinson, London, 1987.

Ashworth, G. and Bonnerjea, L. (eds), *The invisible decade: UK women and the UN decade*, Gower Press, Aldershot, 1985.

Bale, J., Graves, N. and Walford, R. (eds), *Perspectives in geographical education*, Oliver & Boyd, Edinburgh, 1973.

Ball, M., Gray, F. and McDowell, L., *The transformation of Britain*, Fontana, London, 1989.

Ball, S., *Politics and policy making in education: explorations in policy sociology*, Routledge, London, 1990.

Barker, D. L. and Allen, S. (eds), *Sexual division and society: process and change*, Tavistock, London, 1976.

Barnett, C., *The audit of war: the illusion and reality of Britain as a great power*, Macmillan, London, 1986.

Beechey, V. and Whitelegg, E. (eds), *Women in Britain today*, Open University Press, Milton Keynes, 1986.

Benn, C. and Chitty, C., *Thirty years on: is comprehensive education alive and well or struggling to survive?*, David Fulton, London, 1996.

Benn, C. and Simon, B., *Half way there*, McGraw Hill, London, 1970.

Berry, F., *Housing: the great British failure*, Knight, London, 1974.

Bloom, B. S. (ed.), *Taxonomy of educational objectives: handbook one, the cognitive domain*, Longman, New York, 1956.

Boltho, A. (ed.), *The European economy: growth and crisis*, Oxford University Press, Oxford, 1982.

Bouchier, D., *The feminist challenge: the movement for women's liberation in Britain and the USA*, Macmillan, London, 1983.

Bourne, J., Bridges, L. and Searle, C., *Outcast England: how schools exclude black children*, Institute of Race Relations, London, 1994.

Bowlby, J., *Child care and the growth of love*, Pelican, Harmondsworth, 1953.
Bowley, M., *Housing and the State, 1919–1944*, Allen & Unwin, London, 1945.
Bruner, J., *Toward a theory of instruction*, Belknap Press, Harvard, 1966.
Bruner, J. *et al.*, *A study of thinking*, Wiley, Chapman & Hall, London, 1956.
Burnett, J., *A social history of housing, 1915–1985*, Methuen, London, 1986.
Bush, T. and Kogan, M., *Directors of education*, George Allen & Unwin, London, 1982.
Carrington, B. and Short, G., *Race and the primary school: theory into practice*, NFER-Nelson, London, 1985.
Carter, A., *The politics of women's rights*, Longman, London, 1988.
Cashmore, E. E., *United Kingdom? Class, race and gender since the War*, Unwin Hyman, London, 1989.
Centre for Contemporary Cultural Studies, *Unpopular education*, Hutchinson, London, 1981.
Centre for Contemporary Cultural Studies (identified as Education Group II on the title page), *Education limited*, Unwin Hyman, London, 1991.
Chetwynd, J. and Hartnett, O. (eds), *The sex role system*, Routledge & Kegan Paul, London, 1978.
Chitty, C. (ed.), *Redefining the comprehensive experience*, Institute of Education, London, 1987.
——, *Towards a new education system: the victory of the New Right?*, Falmer Press, Lewes, 1989.
—— (ed.), *Changing the future: Reprint for education*, Tufnell Press, London, 1991.
—— (ed.), *Post-16 education: studies in access and achievement*, Kogan Page, London, 1991.
Chorley, R. J. and Haggett, P. (eds), *Models in geography*, Methuen, London, 1967.
Coffey, D., *Schools and work*, Cassell, London, 1992.
Cox, B. and Dyson, A. E. (eds), *Black Paper 1, 'Fight for education'*, Critical Quarterly Society, Hull, 1969.
——, *Black Paper 2, 'The crisis in education'*, Critical Quarterly Society, Hull, 1969.
——, *Black Paper 3, 'Goodbye Mr Short'*, Critical Quarterly Society, Hull, 1970.
Cox, B. and Boyson, R. (eds), *Black Paper 4, 'The fight for education'*, Critical Quarterly Society, Hull, 1975.
——, *Black Paper 5, 'Black Paper'*, Critical Quarterly Society, Hull, 1977.
Cullingworth, J. B., *Town and country planning in Britain*, Unwin Hyman, London, 1988.
Cunningham, P., *Curriculum change in the primary school since 1945*, Falmer Press, Lewes, 1988.
Dale, R., *Mixed or single sex schools* (3 vols), Routledge & Kegan Paul, London, 1969, 1971, 1974.
—— (ed.), *Education, training and employment*, Pergamon, London, 1985.
Daniel, W. W., *Racial discrimination in England*, Penguin, Harmondsworth, 1968.
Deem, R. (ed.), *Coeducation Reconsidered*, Open University Press, Milton Keynes, 1984.
Delamont, S., *Sex roles and the school*, Methuen, London, 1980.
Dyhouse, C., *Girls growing up in late Victorian and Edwardian England*, Routledge & Kegan Paul, London, 1981.
Ellis Cashmore, E., *United Kingdom? Class, race and gender since the War*, Unwin Hyman, London, 1989.
Fenton, B., *Teaching the new social studies in secondary schools*, Holt, Rinehart & Winston, New York, 1966.
——, *The new social studies*, Holt, Rinehart & Winston, New York, 1967.

Flude, M. and Ahier, J. (eds), *Educability, schools and ideology*, Croom Helm, London, 1976.

Flude, M. and Hammer, M. (eds), *The Education Reform Act, 1988*, Falmer Press, Lewes, 1990.

Gaine, C., *Still no problem here*, Trentham Books, Stoke on Trent, 1995.

Gartner, L. P., *The Jewish immigrant in England*, Longman, London, 1960.

Ghuman, P., *Asian teachers in British schools*, Clevedon Press, Bristol, 1995.

Gill, D., Mayor, B. and Blair, M. (eds), *Racism and education*, Open University Press, Milton Keynes, 1992.

Goldman, R. J., *Religious thinking from childhood to adolescence*, Routledge & Kegan Paul, London, 1964.

Gordon, P., Aldrich, R. and Dean, D., *Education and policy in England in the Twentieth Century*, Woburn Press, London, 1991.

Gordon, P. and Lawton, D., *Curriculum change in the Nineteenth and Twentieth Centuries*, Hodder & Stoughton, Sevenoaks, 1978.

Gosden, P., *The education system since 1944*, Martin Robertson, Oxford, 1983.

Green, A., *Education and State formation*, Macmillan, London, 1990.

Halsey, A. (ed.), *British social trends since 1900*, Macmillan, London, 1988.

Halsey, A. H., Heath, A. F. and Ridge, J. M., *Origins and destinations: family, class and education in modern Britain*, Clarendon Press, Oxford, 1980.

Harrison, P., *Inside the inner city: life under the cutting edge*, Pelican, Harmondsworth, 1988.

Henderson, J. and Karn, V., *Race, class and State housing: inequality and the allocation of public housing in Britain*, Gower Press, Aldershot, 1987.

Jackson, B., *Streaming: an education system in miniature*, Routledge & Kegan Paul, London, 1964.

Jackson, B. and Marsden, B., *Education and the working class*, Routledge & Kegan Paul, London, 1964.

Jackson, M. P., *Youth unemployment*, Croom Helm, London, 1985.

Jones, D., *Stewart Mason: the art of education*, Lawrence & Wishart, London, 1988.

Jones, K., *Right turn: the Conservative revolution in education*, Hutchinson, London, 1989.

Katznelson, I., *Black men, white cities*, Oxford University Press, Oxford, 1973.

Kelly, A. (ed.), *The missing half*, Manchester University Press, Manchester, 1981.

Kevles, D. J., *In the name of Eugenics*, Pelican, Harmondsworth, 1986.

Knight, C., *The making of Tory education policy in Post-War Britain, 1950–1986*, Falmer Press, Lewes, 1990.

Kogan, M. with Kogan, D., *The attack on higher education*, Kogan Page, London, 1983.

Krathwohl, D. R., Bloom, B. S. and Masia, B. B., *Taxonomy of educational objectives: handbook two, the affective domain*, Longman, New York, 1964.

Lawrence, R. Z. and Schultz, E. (eds), *Barriers to European growth*, The Brookings Institution, New York, 1987.

Lewis, J., *Women in Britain since 1945*, Blackwell, Oxford, 1992.

Lowe, R. (ed.), *The changing primary school*, Falmer Press, Lewes, 1987.

——, *Education in the Post-War years*, Routledge, London, 1988.

—— (ed.), *The changing secondary school*, Falmer Press, Lewes, 1989.

Marsden, W. E., *Unequal educational provision in England and Wales: the Nineteenth Century*, Woburn Press, London, 1987.

Marwick, A., *Culture in Britain since 1945*, Blackwell, Oxford, 1991.

Massey, D. and Allen, J., *Uneven redevelopment: cities and regions in transition*, Hodder & Stoughton for the Open University Press, London, 1988.

BIBLIOGRAPHY

Mays, J. B., *Education and the urban child*, Liverpool University Press, Liverpool, 1962.

McCulloch, G., *The secondary technical school: a useable past?*, Falmer Press, Lewes, 1989.

——, *Educational reconstruction: the 1944 Education Act and the Twenty-first Century*, Woburn Press, London, 1994.

McCulloch, G., Jenkins, E. and Layton, D. (eds), *Technological revolution? The politics of school science and technology in England and Wales since 1945*, Falmer Press, Lewes, 1985.

Meighan, R., *Flexischooling: education for tomorrow, starting yesterday*, Education Now Books, Ticknall, 1988.

Melling, J. (ed.), *Housing, social policy and the State*, Croom Helm, London, 1980.

Miles, R. and Phizacklea, A., *White man's country: racism in British politics*, Pluto Press, London, 1984.

Millet, K., *Sexual politics*, Avon Books, New York, 1971.

Morris, D. (ed.), *The economic system in the United Kingdom*, 3rd edn, Oxford University Press, Oxford, 1985.

Morris, M. and Griggs, C. (eds), *Education: the wasted years? 1973–1986*, Falmer Press, Lewes, 1988.

Moser, C. A. and Scott, W., *British towns: a statistical study of their social and economic differences*, Oliver & Boyd, London, 1961.

Mullard, C., *Racism in school and society*, University of London Institute of Education Centre for Multicultural Studies, London, 1981.

Newsom, J., *The education of girls*, Faber & Faber, London, 1948.

Novak, T., *Poverty and the State*, Open University Press, Milton Keynes, 1988.

Ollerenshaw, K., *The girls' schools*, Faber & Faber, London, 1967.

Patterson, S., *Immigration and race relations in Britain, 1960–1967*, Longmans, London, 1969.

Pennington, S. and Westover, B., *A hidden workforce: homeworkers in England, 1850–1985*, Macmillan, London, 1989.

Perkin, H., *The rise of professional society: England since 1880*, Routledge, London, 1989.

Plaskow, M. (ed.), *The life and death of the Schools Council*, Falmer Press, Lewes, 1985.

Pumphrey, P. D. and Verma, G. K., *Race relations and urban education*, Falmer Press, Lewes, 1990.

Purvis, J. (ed.), *The education of girls and women*, Proceedings of the 1984 Annual Conference of the History of Education Society of Great Britain, History of Education Society, Leicester, 1985.

Ranger, C., *Ethnic minority school teachers*, Commission for Racial Equality, London, 1988.

Ranson, S., *The politics of reorganising schools*, Unwin Hyman, London, 1990.

——, *Towards the learning society*, Cassell, London, 1994.

Rattansi, A. and Reeder, E. (eds), *Rethinking radical education*, Lawrence & Wishart, London, 1992.

Roberts, K., *School leavers and their prospects*, Open University Press, Milton Keynes, 1984.

Robson, B. T., *Urban analysis: a study of city structure*, Cambridge University Press, Cambridge, 1969.

——, *Urban social areas*, Clarendon Press, Oxford, 1985.

Rogers, R., *Crowther to Warnock: how fourteen reports tried to change children's lives*, Heinemann, London, 1993.

Rubinstein, W. D., *Wealth and inequality in Britain*, Faber and Faber, London, 1986.

————, *Capitalism, culture and decline in Britain*, Routledge, London, 1993.

Sanderson, M., *The missing stratum: technical school education in England, 1900–1990s*, Athlone Press, London, 1994.

Savage, M., Barlow, J., Dickens, P. and Fielding, T., *Property, bureaucracy and culture: middle-class formation in contemporary Britain*, Routledge, London, 1992.

Seaborne, M. and Lowe, R., *The English School: its architecture and organisation, 1870–1970*, Routledge & Kegan Paul, London, 1977.

Seldon, A. (ed.), *The 'New Right' Enlightenment: the spectre that haunts the Left*, Economic and Literary Books, Lancing, 1985.

Seymour-Ure, C., *The British press and broadcasting since 1945*, Blackwell, Oxford, 1991.

Sharp, P. and Dunford, J., *The education system in England and Wales*, Longman, London, 1990.

Silver, H., *Education and the social condition*, Methuen, London, 1980.

————, *Education, change and the policy process*, Falmer Press, Lewes, 1990.

————, *Good schools, effective schools: judgements and their histories*, Cassell, London, 1994.

Simon, B. *Does education matter?*, Lawrence & Wishart, London, 1985.

————, *Bending the rules: the Baker 'reform' of education*, Lawrence & Wishart, London, 1988.

————, *Education and the social order, 1940–1990*, Lawrence & Wishart, London, 1991.

————, *What future for education?*, Lawrence & Wishart, London, 1992.

————, *The State and educational change*, Lawrence & Wishart, London, 1994.

Simon, B. and Chitty, C., *SOS: save our schools*, Lawrence & Wishart, London, 1993.

Simon, B. and Willocks, J., *Research and practice in the primary classroom*, Routledge & Kegan Paul, London, 1981.

Sked, A., *Britain's decline: problems and perspectives*, Basil Blackwell, Oxford, 1987.

Soloway, R. A., *Demography and degeneration: Eugenics and the declining birth rate in Twentieth Century Britain*, University of North Carolina Press, Chapel Hill, 1990.

Stewart, W. A. C., *Higher education in Post-War Britain*, Macmillan, London, 1989.

Street Porter, R., *Race, children and cities*, Open University Press, Milton Keynes, 1978.

Sutcliffe, A. (ed.), *Multi-storey living: the British working class experience*, Croom Helm, London, 1974.

Sutherland, M., *Sex bias in education*, Blackwell, Oxford, 1981.

Swenarton, M., *Homes fit for heroes*, Heinemann, London, 1981.

Taylor, P. H., *Expertise and the primary school teacher*, NFER-Nelson, Windsor, 1986.

Thomas, N., *Primary education from Plowden to the 1990s*, Falmer Press, Lewes, 1990.

Tierney, J. (ed.), *Race, migration and schooling*, Holt, London, 1982.

Thorstendahl, R., *Bureaucratisation in Northwest Europe, 1880–1985*, Routledge, London, 1991.

Troyna, B. and Williams, J., *Racism, education and the State*, Croom Helm, London, 1986.

Ungerson, C. (ed.), *Women and social policy: a reader*, Macmillan, London, 1985.

Vincent, D., *Poor citizens: the State and the poor in Twentieth Century Britain*, Longman, London, 1991.

Walker, S. and Barton, L. (eds), *Gender, class and education*, Falmer Press, London, 1983.

Weeks, A., *Comprehensive schools: past, present and future*, Methuen, London, 1986.

Weiner, M. J., *English culture and the decline of the industrial spirit*, Pelican, Harmondsworth, 1981.

BIBLIOGRAPHY

White, C., *Women's magazines, 1963–68*, Michael Joseph, London, 1970.
Whyte, J., *Girls into science and technology*, Routledge & Kegan Paul, London, 1986.
Woods, A., *Coeducation*, Longman, London, 1903.
——, (ed.), *Advance in education*, Sidgwick & Jackson, London, 1919.
Wright Mills, C., *White collar*, Oxford University Press, Oxford, 1951.
Znaniecki, F., *Modern nationalities*, Longmans, London, 1952.

INDEX